W9-BZG-932

Ned D. Marksheffel, Ed.D., Stanford University, is Professor of Education and Director of Reading at Oregon State University. He has taught at San Jose State College and was Reading Consultant at Central Oregon College and at the University of Southern Mississippi. Dr. Marksheffel has had teaching experience at all grade levels from three to twelve and has served as a reading consultant for elementary and secondary schools and for several school districts. He has lectured and written widely in the field of reading instruction.

BETTER READING IN THE SECONDARY SCHOOL

Principles and Procedures for Teachers

NED D. MARKSHEFFEL
OREGON STATE UNIVERSITY

THE RONALD PRESS COMPANY · NEW YORK

6MP

Library of Congress Catalog Card Number: 66–16850

PRINTED IN THE UNITED STATES OF AMERICA

This book is dedicated to the family who have given me encouragement and inspiration throughout the years.

PREFACE

We have long accepted the fact that one of the most important responsibilities of teachers is to teach children to read. Until recently, few high school teachers have been aware of the need to teach reading. It was previously assumed that when a student reached high school, *he could read.* Research has revealed that a great number of students who are not achieving successfully in the high school are inefficient students primarily because they need help in reading. Available data show that at least 90 per cent of all dropouts have reading problems. Because of such evidence high school teachers are now becoming aware that they have an obligation to use reading techniques when teaching subject matter. Subject matter and reading cannot be divorced.

Most high school teachers recognize that they need help in learning to use reading techniques for improving student learning in subject-matter fields. Because of this need the author has gathered in this volume some pertinent information especially valuable to such teachers and students at the secondary level.

The content of this book has been carefully selected and the areas that are discussed are deemed to be the most important.

The first part of the book deals with the nature of reading, its importance, both in and out of school, and some of its basic principles in secondary reading.

The second section is concerned with procedures and techniques for teaching reading in subject-matter areas. One chapter is devoted to the teaching of spelling, an area that is generally overlooked in most reading texts.

The last two chapters provide information on how to teach study skills, and how to teach students to read and to think critically. The relationships among language, concepts, thinking, purpose, and critical reading are discussed, and suggested procedures for teaching each of these interrelated processes are covered in these chapters.

The writer gratefully acknowledges the encouragement and assistance of those who have worked with him in the reading clinic and the schools where this book began.

Especial thanks are extended to Dr. F. R. Zeran, Oregon State University, for his timely suggestions and comments; Mrs. N. D. Marksheffel, Oregon State University; Mrs. C. R. Rodman, Oregon State University; Mr. Horst Taschow, Central Oregon College; and Dr. E. E. Wallace, Paterson State College.

Corvallis, Oregon
February, 1966

Ned D. Marksheffel

CONTENTS

BETTER READING IN THE SECONDARY SCHOOL

Principles and Procedures for Teachers

1

DEFINITION OF READING

I. WHAT IS READING?

At one time the answer to this question was simply, "Reading is pronouncing words." This statement is no more valid or valuable than another that for years dominated physics textbooks—"Man can never split the atom!"

The question, "What is reading?" must be answered in a number of different ways, but many are still attempting to answer it with the old definition that is now inadequate and false. Furthermore, some very definite but not always sound beliefs about reading are prevalent today. The average person's knowledge of reading and of the teaching of reading is based primarily upon what he has read in popular magazines, newspapers, and occasional best sellers. The bulk of such articles are usually cleverly written, but all too often they are based on little more than false premises and biased opinions.

The student may acquire some insight into the average person's lack of a broad concept of reading by asking ten different people to define reading and by subsequently comparing their definitions. By noting their likenesses and differences, he will begin to have a fair idea of just how few Americans understand the term "reading." If his sample of ten persons is fairly representative of the general population, he will find that practically all of the answers will be similar in certain respects; for example, (1) the majority of them will not be clear or definite; and (2) at best, most of them will be confined to some facet of word recognition and the "getting of meaning from the printed page." These views, the student will soon discover, are exceedingly limited. They were, however, believed adequate by almost everyone in previous times and are so regarded even today by a large number of persons.

On the basis of the minimal amount you have read so far in this book, let us begin to probe for some kind of working definition that we can develop and expand into a meaningful concept of the term "reading." For example *before anyone can read this page, it is necessary that many complex factors be operating simultaneously before reading actually takes place.*

Perceiving, a Prerequisite to Reading

A first step in *all reading* is that of perceiving the differences and likenesses in the size and shape of word symbols. Quick, accurate perception of printed forms is a learned skill. Not only must the beginning reader be capable of perceiving the differences in individual letters and groups of letters, he must learn to see them from the left to the right. Visual perception itself is not reading, but it is certainly one factor that must be considered in the teaching and learning of reading.

Word Recognition and Pronunciation

Before one can read, he must have some means or ability for pronouncing and recognizing individual words. This act is often referred to as *the mechanical* aspect of reading. Unless one can pronounce the words he cannot read them. It can be readily demonstrated that without pronunciation skills, reading is impossible. Note, for example, the following symbols:

Why are these symbols meaningless to you, the reader? The simple fact is that these symbols are unpronounceable to you and are therefore meaningless. You can see the likenesses and differences among these symbols; but as they stand, without any association to sound or meaning, they are just so many marks upon the paper. You, however, experience no difficulty in pronouncing all the words you have encountered in this book. You are a skillful reader. *Because you are a skilled reader,* you may not realize that a tenth-grade boy in your biology class, for example, may be completely confused by such a simple sentence as "An amoeba, one of the aquatic naked rhizopods, is a microscopic nucleated mass of protoplasm." You may be even further shocked to discover that the same student cannot, for example, "read" or pronounce the following sentence: "The little band of Pilgrims set sail for distant shores."

It is fundamental that the teacher understand that he will have such students in his classes. Before one loses patience with these unfortunate pupils, he should recall the meaningless, unpronounceable "hieroglyphics" used in the first paragraph of this section:

The words that are easy for the skilled reader may be just as meaningless or puzzling to the poor reader as were the hieroglyphics.

Now let us put these symbols into pronounceable units and note whether you are reading or not. "Gloph diz el tul." Everyone who is reading this book can pronounce these words, "gloph diz el tul," but is pronouncing words reading? If not, what is lacking? *You can perceive and pronounce these words, but at the moment you have no meaning attached to them.* It is important that you make a clear distinction between pronouncing words and reading.

The difference between *saying words* and reading is a concept that must be kept in mind. We shall discuss it more fully later on. Many persons and pseudoexperts advocate the pronunciation of words as being the sole act of reading. Impossible, you say? Be patient and you will be given evidence that not one, but thousands of Americans believe that "pronouncing words is reading."

Words Must Have Meaning

From our discussion thus far, it can be seen that words or printed symbols must have some meaning attached to them before they can be read. As you perceive the words in these lines, you are reading. You are *perceiving* likenesses and differences in the shapes and forms of these words; you are *recognizing* the words; you are *attaching* meaning to printed symbols. You are, in fact, associating past experiences with these words. You are getting meaning from the printed page. This, then, is one more step in the definition of reading—"getting meaning from the printed page."

Does "getting meaning" constitute the act of reading? No. Much remains before we have a workable definition of our term. The concept of reading that we have discussed so far is necessarily a limited one. One must keep in mind that, among other things, concepts are dependent upon definition, upon one's experience—past, present, and future, upon one's ability to think, upon available facts and evidence, upon the ability to generalize from these facts and to adjust behavior to new situations. Concepts are subject to growth, change, and development. The term "concept," as it is being used here, means one's understanding of what reading is.

We have now reached a point where we can define reading in an extremely limited sense. *For almost 300 years reading was "the act of perceiving, recognizing, and pronouncing words."* Today, such a restricted definition is unacceptable to all but a small minority.

Students who study reading are generally perplexed that such a complex process could be so circumscribed and so accepted until almost the first decade of the twentieth century. There are several explanations that may help the reader to understand better why this naive, incomplete definition was, and is, so strongly entrenched in the minds of many Americans. One of the explanations requires that we digress briefly to look at the first goal of reading.

The First Reading Goal in America

Every schoolboy knows that religion influenced the colonization of America, but few realize the tremendous influence it exerted upon reading and compulsory education. Good (4, p. 157) notes that Martin Luther is credited with being the first modern writer to urge compulsory school attendance as a function of the state. And he had a perfectly logical reason for doing so. His break with "The Church" created *a need for reading,* because he insisted that everyone must learn to read the Bible. You will recall that up to his time there had been no real need for the masses to read. The Bible was practically the only written word with which ordinary people had any contact, and it was read to them by their priest. Their knowledge of history and the world around them was limited. Anything that was not experienced directly reached them only through the auditory senses in the form of folk tales and stories. Even the Bible was read for them, and its messages were given to them through *spoken symbols.* It naturally followed that the "protesters" made *reading—reading of the Bible—a major objective.*

The first reading goal in America, therefore, not only accompanied the Pilgrims as they stepped ashore at Plymouth Rock but actually preceded them. Their goal was simple. To them, *to read meant but one thing: to read the Bible.* Reading the Bible generally implied *reading aloud.* Reading aloud emphasized expressive oral reading because it met the needs of the people at that time; and, in so doing, it dictated the manner of teaching reading.

The concept that reading is pronouncing words was deeply imbedded into our national heritage by the simple agrarian life and customs of the early Americans. Our history is rich with stories expressing the deep regard with which the Pilgrims and pioneers followed certain customs.

We know that, when the evening meal and attendant chores were finished, many a colonial father gathered his family about him and brought the day's activities to a culmination by reading from "The Good Book." This simple, honest act of faith helped to stamp into the listener's minds the idea that *reading was important; reading was pronouncing words.*

Perhaps even the father did not understand the meaning of all of the words he used, but he could pronounce them because he had heard the preachers use the same core of words in sermons. And, like many of the other parishioners, he could tell from the preacher's intonations and gestures the "goodness" or "badness" of a word.

It was a simple and logical transfer to assume that seeing and saying words was reading. The goal of reading was thus wedded to the concept of reading.

The reader should not be misled to believe that all reading in colonial days was meaningless gibberish. There were many efficient, mature readers among America's early settlers, and they read silently and for meaning. The method of teaching reading in the classroom, however, was unfettered by practicality. Countless children were alternately helped and hindered by ill-prepared schoolmasters who talked their way through a prescribed number of textbooks.

Despite much poor teaching of reading in the schools, all educators and laymen did not accept the manner in which reading was taught. There were a few who objected to the prevailing methods. Mann, for example, was one of the early important educators who soundly denounced the overemphasis on pronouncing words and the lack of teaching reading for understanding. In his Second Annual Report to the Board of Education, in 1838, he said, "The result is, that more than eleven-twelfths of all the children in the reading classes, in our schools, do not understand the meaning of the words they read . . ." (11, p. 56).

Huey (9, p. 10), a later educator, argued against the teaching of reading as it was conducted in the public schools. He stated:

> We know that the reading of life is almost exclusively silent reading. Yet in preparing for life we are instructed almost exclusively in reading aloud, and have not troubled ourselves to ask whether habits learned in reading aloud may not be hurtful in reading silently. [9, p. 10.]

Although statements such as those by Mann and Huey were not unprecedented, they were *relatively infrequent.* The feelings of the general public and most educators concerning the teaching of reading are strikingly exemplified by the research that was conducted. Prior to approximately 1910, research studies in reading dealt primarily with the physiological functions of reading. Eye movements and laterality, or dominant handedness and eyedness, were studied extensively. Mechanical devices and machines such as the metronoscope, the forerunner of the tachistoscope, and machines for photographing eye movements were developed and used extensively in an effort to improve the teaching of reading. Interestingly and logically, the study of eye movements led to the discovery that good readers were not merely recognizing words but that they were reading for ideas. This discovery led to yet another step in the sequential development of a definition of reading. The teaching of reading should now include *emphasis on getting meaning from the printed page!*

II. THE NATURE OF READING

Section I hinted that reading may possibly never be defined in a simple, succinct, concise manner. A discussion of the nature of reading, however, is prerequisite to understanding the reading process. It is an aid in interpreting definitions of reading. This viewpoint is expressed also by Causey (3, p. 3), who says that more than semantic analysis and a definitive approach are required for an understanding of the reading process.

The teacher or the student lacking a wide background of experience in reading needs a guide to direct his thinking as he learns. First of all, he must know that *reading is thinking.* Reading, a diamond of the educative process, has many facets, and the way in which the individual sees it will be colored by those facets nearest him. Nevertheless, it must be viewed from every angle in order that the complete process be understood.

Why Bother Defining Reading?

The question has often been asked, "Why bother to define reading?" The question, a good one, deserves better answers than it usually elicits. How would you answer the question?

While it may be true that we shall never get full agreement on any one or several definitions of reading, we should not cease striving for such a goal. For is not one of education's goals to imbue the student with a spirit, a desire, a feeling to do something of value for mankind, and to be not turned back or aside because the task is extremely difficult? Can we do less than we ask our students to do? If for no other reason than this, we should keep at the task of trying to define reading.

There are several other factors pertinent to the need for a definition. *Reading is taught as it is defined.* There is no greater proof of this truth than that of the extremely narrow definition of reading that dictated the manner in which reading was taught in America for almost three centuries. Further evidence floods the market at this moment. Gimmicks to "stretch the eyespan," gadgets to enable the reader to cover 3,000, 5,000, 10,000, 20,000 words per minute, a "brand new" phonetic approach to reading, "the only true phono" approach, machines that resemble TV's (for motivational purposes), programs, wheels, charts, recordings—all are available at a price, and all guarantee to improve the individual's reading. Each professes to have *the* answer. Each strives to teach reading as *one* specific skill or one set of simple skills: *word pronunciation!*

Reading or any other phenomenon must be defined before it can be measured. Teachers often complain that many things that they teach cannot be measured. Granting that some of what is taught may not be measurable in the immediate or near future does not absolve the teacher from teaching certain, definite, necessary measurable skills, facts, knowledge, concepts, and generalizations. We can, for example, measure certain facets of reading such as word-recognition skills, comprehension of various kinds of materials, location of needed materials, ability to skim or scan materials rapidly, versatility in rate of reading according to purpose, reader experience, and difficulty of material. But we can only measure these when they are defined in operational terms.

Agreement on a definition of reading must be reached by those who write about reading and those who teach reading in order that confusion over method, or methods, be decreased. Parents, administrators, teachers, and students are often in sharp disagreement over a method or the method of teaching reading. Such disagreement only adds to confusion and to the lack of adequate or optimum learning by the student.

Tests of reading do not always measure reading because test designers, lacking an acceptable definition of reading, test only minor facets of reading processes. What the tests measure is not a true reflection of the student's actual ability to read printed materials for learning in subject-matter areas. Assigning students to textbooks on the basis of standardized test scores leads to a mismatching of students and materials suitable for optimum reading and learning.

The more one studies reading, the more he becomes aware of the fact that *reading is a complex of activities.* Learned men in various fields view reading in the light of their own interests and experiences—and how else can one interpret reading except in the light of his own experiences? Limited experiences, however, curtail understanding. The psychologist may have a vastly different concept of reading from that of the archeologist, the sociologist, the linguist, the semanticist, or the teacher; yet each one's concept blends into and overlaps the others' concept. Who is to say which definition is acceptable or unacceptable? Staiger says that "each thoughtfully prepared definition is a correct one, as far as it goes" (15, p. 9).

There are, however, *feasible definitions of reading.* As more research is conducted into the area of reading, the entire process of reading is revealed as being much more complicated and puzzling than it originally appeared to be. Many previously held ideas are now found to be baseless. Factors that at one time were not considered as being even remotely connected with the act of reading are now known to influence a person's learning to read and to determine the extent to which he will be able to develop his reading skill. Many authorities feel that reading cannot and should not be limited to the interpretation of printed symbols but must be recognized in a broad sense in which situation, objects, and persons are also materials of reading. This broad view of reading will be discussed more fully in the latter part of this chapter.

All the purposes or definitions attributed to reading cannot be listed in this text. Some of its more popular connotations will be discussed briefly or at least mentioned. Reading has been defined as a means of solving problems, a way of learning, a perception process, a means of relaxation, a tool subject, getting meaning from the printed page, a thinking process, and a stimulator of ideas.

Harris expresses the feelings of numerous persons when he says, "Reading is unique among school activities in being both a subject of instruction and a tool for the mastery of other phases of the curriculum" (7, p. 4). On the other hand, there are those who reject the ideas that reading is a tool subject. They maintain that such a view is too restrictive, that reading has no subject matter of its own. Whatever and whenever one reads printed material of any kind, whether it be the label on a can of beans, directions for assembling a lawnmower, a weather report, a road map, or a scientific report on using the sun's energy for charging batteries, he is reading.

How People Use Reading

Understanding the manner in which people use reading may help the student to understand better the nature of reading. At first, the numerous ways people use reading may perplex the student as he strives for a definition that is relatively concise and all-inclusive. It is possible that he may conclude, as have others who really understand the complexities of the reading act, that a clear-cut, all-inclusive definition is an impossibility. But if he understands some of the complex activities of reading, if he understands *why* the kind of reading one does is determined greatly by one's purposes for reading, if he understands that reading is not a single uniform process that can be used exactly in the same manner for different purposes and different kinds of material, then his professional knowledge will be enhanced greatly.

The student may fail to define reading precisely, but he will learn why a particular definition may be acceptable for a specific situation at a particular time. He will know that definitions often overlap but that none can stand alone, that each is a significant part of the total concept. He can then apply this knowledge to improve his pupil's reading skills for more efficient learning of subject matter.

How America's Youth Use Reading

Surveys show that American youth vary greatly in what they read, where they read, and how they read (8, pp. 8–9). They read newspapers, magazines, books, scholarly journals, and comic books. They read on trains, buses, and street corners. They read in cafes, schools, homes, and libraries. They read for information, further knowledge, entertainment, excitement, and relaxation. Above all, they read for a particular purpose.

Unfortunately, however, some do little or no reading. What little reading they attempt is limited and literal. They read tabloids, sport stories, racing forms, comic books, and other easy-to-understand materials. Why? Because these are the only kinds of materials they *can* read. They have not learned to read easily and efficiently. They are the poor readers for whom reading is hard. Their purposes for reading will differ significantly from those of their more fortunate classmates, the efficient readers. Yet both kinds of readers will be found sitting in the typical classroom, exposed to the same kinds of subject matter, and using the same textbooks.

Reading Is a Personal Thing

Each student views reading according to his own experiences, his efficiency, his purposes, and his available time. His mood, purpose, reading skill, interests, and immediate environment may cause him to look upon the reading assignment in one class as a lot of gibberish or a waste of time. He may actually resent, for example, a teacher-directed lesson in skimming or scanning articles for main ideas and specific details. Yet the same student who abhorred skimming a classroom text may pick up a newspaper and read to find who starred in last night's ball games, who flubbed; he may retain six or seven scores, find out what, where, and when the teams will play next, and be off to his next class all within several minutes.

Another student may tolerate the reading in a particular course because it is a requirement, a chore to be disposed of before he can settle down to enjoying something he wants to read. His leisure-time reading may vary from western yarns to a biography of Albert Schweitzer, from a murder mystery to Tolstoi's *War and Peace.* At one time he may read widely from encyclopedias and at another time shun them.

A brief summary of the nature of reading and definition to this point:

1. For approximately three centuries, a simple, easy-to-understand, but narrow and restrictive definition of reading circumscribed the teaching of reading. The mechanical aspect of reading was stressed in the public schools.
2. The first goal of reading in America influenced the definition and teaching of reading for too many years.
3. Reading, a highly complex process of innumerable facets, is difficult, if not impossible, to define adequately.
4. An acceptable definition of reading is needed to eradicate the confusion about which method or methods of reading should be used for teaching reading in the public schools.
5. Some definitions of reading have been cited but none is complete by itself; each becomes a part of the total concept.
6. The ways in which people use reading influences their views of reading. Individuals differ in their views of reading according to various purposes, circumstances, and time.
7. Above all, reading consists of more than pronouncing words.

III. READING DEFINED

Those who have read sections I and II of this chapter probably recognize that the answer to "What is Reading?" requires concentrated mental participation by the questioner. Although no one succinct definition appears practicable at present, we propose a *limited* but *workable definition.* For our purposes, *reading may be defined as a highly complex, purposeful, thinking process engaged in by the entire organism while acquiring knowledge, evolving new ideas, solving problems, or relaxing and recuperating through the interpretation of printed symbols.*

Four or five decades ago it would have been impossible to define reading as we have done because so little was known about the complexity of the reading process. With few exceptions, people clung to an antiquated and limited concept of reading. The few educators who were critical of the naive, restricted view of reading busied themselves with research to prove or disprove the hypothesis that "reading is more than rolling one's eyeballs across the printed page." Results from their research, coupled with the public's desire for more knowledge and culture, and increased attention to the teaching of reading contributed to events that should be understood by all teachers who use printed materials from which pupils are expected to learn. The importance of these events demands that we take a closer look at them.

Four Significant Events Influence the Teaching of Reading

The period from 1910 to 1920 was a memorable one for education, particularly in the field of reading. The four significant events which radically changed the teaching of reading and enlarged the definition of reading are: (1) "reading for utilitarian purposes"; (2) the discovery that, for most purposes, silent reading is more efficient than oral reading (6, p. 1118); (3) the beginning of the present concept of reading; and (4) Thorndike's contribution that reading is reasoning.

Reading for Utilitarian Purposes

Reading for utilitarian purposes was not an impulsive phenomenon of the twentieth century but was a gradual, ever-growing process. According to Gray and Rogers (5, p. 3), between 1900 and 1925 adults in America showed a surprising and rapid increase in interest in reading. They did more reading for many reasons. Because America was becoming a recognized world power, people were anxious and determined to know more about political happenings at home and abroad. Technological advances, improved transportation, more leisure time, World War I, women's right to vote, prohibition, a general thirst for more knowledge, the growing power of labor unions, improved health conditions, a rise in the percentage of children attending school and continuing in school, and more available reading materials were but a few of the many reasons why adults read more.

The increase in adult reading focused attention on the fact that large numbers of persons lacked the reading skills necessary to understand available reading materials. Tests administered to servicemen during World War I supplied further evidence that large numbers of adults were unable to read satisfactorily. The assumption by the general public that pupils learned to read efficiently and for all time in the elementary school was proven false. The traditional method of teaching reading and the narrow concept of reading which dominated public school instruction were not adequate to meet either school or life situations involving reading. The National Society for the Study of Education, therefore, appointed a National Committee on Reading to study and report the needs and objectives of reading instruction.

The Committee's report, the *Twenty-fourth Yearbook* (13, pp. 1–2), emphasized the need for a planned, systematic program of reading that would continue beyond the classroom and into adult life. The Committee stressed the importance of reading for both pupils and adults. Reading was viewed as being essential for learning in every content area. It was noted also that, for adults, reading was an indispensable means for knowing about current events, social issues, local and national problems, and "American institutions, ideals, and aspirations."

Silent Reading Goes to School

It has been reported that silent reading entered the public schools about 1910 (14, p. 155).* Apparently, silent reading slipped into a few American classrooms at or about that time, but a study of the literature has so far failed to pin down exact dates or places where it made its unobtrusive and surreptitious entry. That it did gain entrance is of utmost importance.

Oral reading, which had reigned for almost three hundred years as the sole method for teaching reading, was finally forced to give up its throne. But its abdication was no sudden act. Theisen (17, pp. 1–8), in 1921, said that the aims, methods, and content of reading instruction were in a period of transition because of the growing dissatisfaction with reading progress. He noted that a movement was afoot to introduce a larger portion of silent reading into all grades because it satisfied individual needs better than oral reading, it improved the rate of reading, and it resulted in greater pupil comprehension.

In 1921, O'Brien (12, p. 54) wrote that research and experimentation by Huey, Dearborn, Schmidt, Judd, and others had demonstrated that silent reading was superior to oral reading for "thought-getting." Judd and Buswell (10) called for a radical change in the method of reading instruction. They said that teachers should recognize the fact that "in the upper grades silent reading is the really useful type of reading." Despite the evidence of research, it was noted that primary teachers

* See also Nila Banton Smith, *American Reading Instruction* (Newark, Del.: International Reading Assn, 1965), pp. 157–86.

had not given up the time-honored method of oral reading because they knew no other way to improve oral reading except by giving more of the same, and that they *knew nothing about teaching silent reading* (17, p. 8). This was the kind of reading instruction to which many present-day adults were subjected.

Summary Statement About Silent Reading

It is difficult for student teachers and young professional teachers to realize that silent reading has been an accepted method for reading in all areas for only a comparatively short period of time—forty years or less. Even today, it is not difficult to find classes where the teaching of reading at the primary level is completely oral. Some teachers actually claim never to have heard of silent-before-oral-reading below the fourth-grade level. These same teachers, however, had reading manuals in their classrooms that gave detailed means of teaching silent reading and stressed *why* silent reading should precede oral reading.

Adequately prepared, professionally educated teachers use both oral and silent reading at all grade levels. The amount of oral rereading will vary according to the purposes for reading and the maturity of the pupils. The writer has found that at the university level rereading orally often helps students to get clearer and deeper meaning from the author's words. This is noticeable particularly when the material is especially difficult, the content controversial, the concepts relatively new to the individual, or the writer is not as explicit as he might be.

Reading Is a Thinking Process

Until recently, the idea that reading is thinking was either overlooked or assumed by those who discussed reading. That reading is a thinking process was first proved by Thorndike (18), in his monumental study, "Reading as Reasoning," published in 1917. For some incomprehensible reason, the consequence of Thorndike's outstanding contribution to reading was rarely recognized by educators prior to about 1950. The statement "Reading is thinking," was used here and there by an occasional writer or speaker, but it created little attention. The late 1950's, however, witnessed a renewed and vital interest in reading as thinking. Recognized educators published books and articles that emphasized how teachers use reading to improve pupils' thinking, and why such teaching is vital to all education. The December, 1961, issue of *The Reading Teacher* (16) was devoted to "Reading Is Thinking."

Some continue to look upon beginning reading as a simple mechanical process of saying words. But even beginning reading is not a mechanical process devoid of thinking. Thinking takes place when an individual recognizes printed symbols, interprets the print and responds by saying the words, and gets meaning from the process. The level of reasoning, however, is not as complex and difficult as it is in critical, mature reading. The mature reader uses reasoning at a highly complex level. He, for example, goes beyond the literal meaning of the words and interprets them in light of the context and his own experiences, selects those ideas that are pertinent to his purpose(s) for reading, evaluates them, compares them with available facts and evidence, and reaches a tentative conclusion or derives new ideas.

The emphasis on reading as thinking is not intended to imply that man thinks only when he reads. It is evident that man thinks in numerous ways and situations. Thinking can and does occur without reading, but *reading without thinking is an impossibility.* When one deals with printed words, the definitions of reading and thinking commingle so completely that experts in both areas generally agree that fusion exists. Burton (2, p. 303) says that reading and thinking are so closely related that when one deals with printed materials one definition covers either or both processes:

> We might add here that *reading* can be defined in such a way as nearly to coincide with critical thinking. When this is done, it is a matter of little importance whether we name the crucial abilities *critical thinking* or *critical reading,* especially when the testing is done by a printed instrument. [2, p. 303.]

To summarize briefly, it is generally known that thinking is done in response to many and varied stimuli. It is not so well known that reading not only involves thinking but that it also stimulates thinking.

WHAT IS MEANT BY READING IN ITS BROADEST SENSE?

Burton says, "*Reading in the broadest sense is the development of meanings in response to stimuli and for the purpose of guiding behavior*" (1, p. 15).

The purpose for presenting the *broad view* of reading is to stress the importance of *the arousal of meaning by stimuli,* words, rather than stressing the stimuli themselves. It was noted previously that many persons continue to place the emphasis in reading on the pronunciation of words rather than upon meaning. Apparently it is assumed that if one can pronounce words he automatically gets meaning from them. Abundant evidence refutes such an assumption. But keep in mind that accurate, clear pronunciation of words is prerequisite to efficient student reading.

The *broad view* of reading points out the fact that words are merely man-made symbols that represent persons, objects, things, and ideas. Words are the stimuli that evoke meaning within the reader, but words themselves have no inherent meaning. They only represent previously agreed upon meanings.

Reading in the *broad sense* includes the reading of much that is not printed or written. Children, adults, artists, critics, skeptics, all read pictures, people, places, and events. Each reads in the light of his own experiences. Each takes from the material a portion that is measured by his own wants, needs, desires, and maturity.

If one visits the picturesque little city of Santa Cruz on Monterey Bay he can see the Italian and Portuguese fishermen "read" the weather. Busily mending nets or straightening lines, they keep one ear trained on their ship's radios for the weather reports. More than once the writer has observed a fisherman listening intently to the weather report from the radio, cast a skeptical, apprehensive eye about him and then shake his head negatively. He knows that in an area where the weather changes quickly he must be alert to *all* the signs of "good" and "bad" weather.

Even if the radiocast notes that predictions for the weather are generally good, the fisherman, detecting the faintest of shifts in the direction of the wind, looks more warily for other signs. He sniffs the sea air. He notes the gulls leaving the open water and heading landward. The rocks in the cove become darker as more and more cormorants land among their huddled, protesting relatives. He "reads" the elements and knows that for his area a storm is approaching and prepares for it.

The artist "reading" the landscape for a prospective canvas is joined by his friend, an engineer. They both "read" the same scene. The subtle, awe-inspiring shifts in the shades of green that evoke aesthetic responses within the artist elicit an entirely different reaction from the dam builder. Both "read" in light of their own experiences and purposes.

Reading, then, must be considered from many angles. Although teachers may appear to be working only with printed words, it is imperative that they recognize that the printed word is only a symbol for an experience—an object—a situation—an idea. Yet all these are, and can be, expressed in words.

Yes, people think with words. Limit the amount of experiences in which one engages, be they direct or vicarious, and that person is limited in his thinking. On the other hand, provide one with an abundance of experiences and limit his words for expression and a similar condition exists with the same net results—*learning and the expression of that learning are limited.* The teacher's job then becomes one of aiding, guiding, helping the student to accept his share of responsibility in profiting from his experiences and in developing his vocabulary in all areas—listening, speaking, reading, and writing.

Concluding Statement

The preceding brief discussion of the "definitions of reading" are not complete but should be sufficient to alert the student to the complexity of the reading process. Authors of numerous books and articles pertaining to reading and the problems of teaching reading have often taken an extremely limited view of reading because of a narrow definition of the term.

It is unfortunate that numerous studies and articles written for the purpose of improving learning in various subject-matter areas ignore the role of reading except as a "skill to be mastered" during the first few years in the elementary school.

Reading is a never-ending, complex thinking process. It cannot be limited to the strictly mechanical interpretation of perceiving and pronouncing words. The words must have meaning for the student. He must learn to interpret the symbols, organize them into logical, sequential units, synthesize these thoughts with his past and present experiences and arrive at reasonable conclusions.

SELECTED REFERENCES

1. Burton, William H. *Reading in Child Development.* Indianapolis: The Bobbs-Merrill Co., Inc., 1956.
2. Burton, William H., *et al.* *Education for Effective Thinking.* New York: Appleton-Century-Crofts, Inc., 1960.
3. Causey, Oscar S. *The Reading Teacher's Reader.* New York: The Ronald Press Co., 1958.
4. Good, H. G. *A History of Western Education* (2d ed.). New York: The Macmillan Co., 1960.
5. Gray, William S., and Rogers, Bernice. *Maturity in Reading.* Chicago: The University of Chicago Press, 1956.
6. Gray, William S. "Reading," *Encyclopedia of Educational Research* (3d ed.), ed. Chester W. Harris. New York: The Macmillan Co., 1960.
7. Harris, Albert J. *How To Increase Reading Ability* (4th ed., rev.). New York: David McKay Co., Inc., 1961.
8. Henry, Nelson B. (ed.). *Reading in the High School and College.* The

Forty-seventh Yearbook, Part II, National Society for the Study of Education. Chicago: The University of Chicago Press, 1948.
9. Huey, Edmund Burke. *The Psychology and Pedagogy of Reading.* New York: The Macmillan Co., 1908.
10. Judd, Charles H., and Buswell, Guy T. *Silent Reading: A Study of the Various Types.* Supplementary Educational Monographs, No. 76. Chicago: The University of Chicago Press, 1922.
11. Mann, Horace. *Second Annual Report Covering the Year 1838 of the Board of Education, Massachusetts* (facsimile ed.). Boston: Dutton & Wentworth, State Printer, 1839.
12. O'Brien, John A. *The Development of Speed in Silent Reading.* The Twentieth Yearbook, Part II, National Society for the Study of Education. Bloomington, Ill.: Public School Publishing Co., 1921.
13. *Report of the National Committee on Reading.* The Twenty-fourth Yearbook, Part I, National Society for the Study of Education. Chicago: The University of Chicago Press, 1925.
14. Smith, Nila Banton. *American Reading Instruction.* Morristown, N.J.: Silver Burdett Co., 1934.
15. Staiger, Ralph C. "What Is Reading?" *The Reading Teacher's Reader,* ed. Oscar S. Causey. New York: The Ronald Press Co., 1958.
16. Stauffer, Russell G. (ed.). "Reading Is Thinking," *The Reading Teacher,* Vol. 15, No. 3 (December, 1961).
17. Theisen, W. W. *Factors Affecting Results in Primary Reading,* The Twentieth Yearbook, Part II, National Society for the Study of Education. (Report of the Society's Committee on Silent Reading.) Bloomington, Ill.: The Public School Publishing Co., 1921.
18. Thorndike, Edward L. "Reading as Reasoning: A Study of Mistakes in Paragraph Reading," *Journal of Educational Research,* Vol. 8 (June, 1917), pp. 323–32.

SUGGESTED ADDITIONAL READING

Anderson, Irvin H., and Dearborn, Walter F. *The Psychology of Teaching Reading.* New York: The Ronald Press Co., 1952.

Betts, Emmett A. "Research on Reading as a Thinking Process," *Journal of Educational Research,* Vol. 50 (September, 1956), pp. 1–15.

Betts, Emmett Albert. *Foundations of Reading Instruction.* Cincinnati: American Book Co., 1957.

Buswell, G. T. "The Relationship Between Rate of Thinking and Rate of Reading," *School Review,* Vol. 59 (September, 1951), pp. 339–46.

Development in and Through Reading. The Sixtieth Yearbook, Part I, National Society for the Study of Education. Chicago: The University of Chicago Press, 1961.

Gray, Lillian. *Teaching Children To Read* (3d ed.). New York: The Ronald Press Co., 1963.

Gray, William S. "Frontiers in Preparing Teachers of Reading," *Frontiers in Teacher Education.* Normal, Ill.: Illinois State Normal University, 1957.

LEARY, BERNICE E. *Information Please.* Monograph No. 28. New York: Harper & Row, Inc., 1941.

PINTNER, RUDOLPH. "Oral Reading of Fourth-Grade Pupils," *Journal of Educational Psychology,* Vol. 4 (June, 1913), pp. 333–37.

RUSSELL, DAVID H. *Children Learn To Read* (2d ed.). Boston: Ginn & Co., 1961.

SCHMIDT, WILLIAM A. *An Experimental Study in the Psychology of Reading.* Supplementary Educational Monographs, Vol. I. Chicago: The University of Chicago Press, 1917. 126 pp.

SMITH, NILA BANTON. *American Reading Instruction.* Newark, Del.: International Reading Assn., 1965. Pp. 157–86.

STRANG, RUTH, MCCULLOUGH, CONSTANCE M., and TRAXLER, ARTHUR E. *The Improvement of Reading.* New York: McGraw-Hill Book Co., Inc., 1961.

TRIGGS, FRANCES ORALIND. *Reading: Its Creative Teaching and Testing—Kindergarten Through College.* Privately printed by the author, New York 1960.

2

READINESS FOR READING SUBJECT MATTER

Is readiness for reading an important factor in reading at the secondary and college levels?

If one answers this question solely on the basis of the attention it receives from writers of books and articles about the teaching of reading, one might conclude that the answer is "No." But such an answer would be hasty and erroneous. Authorities state emphatically, albeit briefly, that readiness for reading is an important factor in reading at all grade levels. Betts (1, p. 103); Karlin (8); Russell (12, pp. 194–96); Smith and Dechant (14); Strang, McCullough, and Traxler (15) are among those who point out that the concept of readiness for reading is *not* limited to beginning reading but is intrinsic to reading no matter what the grade level.

Because the concept of readiness for reading at the secondary and college levels has received insufficient attention and is too little understood, and because it is an important factor in student reading and learning at those levels, this chapter will be concerned with the readiness of the teacher to teach reading in subject matter and the readiness of the student for reading subject matter.

What Is Readiness?

Burton defines readiness as "the stage in a child's development when he can learn easily, effectively and without emotional disturbance" (3, p. 167). Readiness is a condition or state, not a phenomenon that takes place at a fixed age or prearranged time. Smith and Dechant (14) conclude that readiness is not a unitary trait but is the result of numerous interacting factors. Tyler (16, p. 210) emphasizes the necessity for avoiding extreme views of readiness. He suggests that Bruner's (2) views of readiness represent one of the extremes. "For Bruner, readiness is practically an unnecessary concept; children are always ready." Hymes (7, p. 28) and others present the opposite extreme when they maintain that readiness is a product of maturation. They believe, for example, that if a child is unable to read in the first grade, the teacher need not be unduly concerned. When the child is ready, they maintain, he will read, and in the meantime he cannot be hurried.

It is a matter of record that large numbers of teachers and educators have been influenced by the maturation theory of readiness, which implies that if a child upon entrance to school is not ready to read there is little the teacher can do to ready him for reading, and that instruction should therefore be postponed until the child reaches the level of maturation that somehow automatically bestows reading upon him.

However, not all first-grade teachers accept the maturation theory. Most first-grade teachers follow some kind of program of reading readiness or prereading activities that provide experiences and practices that help children to learn to read. These teachers find that *not all* children are capable of learning to read at the same time, the same age, and the same grade.

Many persons in fields outside education see no sense or validity in the reading-readiness concept. Some teachers and educators also express that view. McCracken (9, pp. 271–75) and others (2, p. 33) not only disagree with the maturation theory but disclaim any need for readiness to learn. McCracken believes that with proper instruction any child in the first grade can be taught to read.

Thus far we have touched lightly on two major but opposing views of readiness, and on an eclectic point of view adopted by the majority of elementary teachers. It is appropriate at this point to introduce briefly a neuropsychological theory of learning that is due to receive increased attention among educators.

Pribram (11, pp. 78–110), in a recent thought-provoking and scholarly article, approaches from a neuropsychological viewpoint the problem of learning. He discusses the results of neurological research that show that preparation or *readiness* for the organism to act does exist as a function of the nervous system. He notes also that ascertaining readiness need *not* be left to guessing:

> The neuropsychological laboratory has not only given first glimpses of the mechanisms involved—sufficient to demonstrate their importance as preparation for a learning experience. In addition, this work has also indicated the

method that can be applied in evaluating readiness, viz., the observation of orienting reactions. [11, pp. 78–110.]

The implication here is that the teacher can, as many have done for years, observe the "orienting reactions" of students and then adjust learning activities, including stimulating questions, in order that all students will participate actively.

If you, the reader, have concluded that readiness for reading is a controversial topic, you are in agreement with some of the nation's leading psychologists. Sears and Hilgard (13, p. 207) note that theories of learning are presently in turmoil. Tyler (16, pp. 210–39) expressing a similar opinion about readiness for learning, says there is little disagreement about the notion that pupils learn most effectively and efficiently *when they are ready,* but that disagreement arises over definitions of readiness and means of measuring the pupil's readiness for learning experiences in particular subjects. Because there is disagreement, there is also hope for different and improved research that can help classroom teachers. Psychologists are recognizing that information gained from controlled laboratory experiments with animals is not automatically transferable to and appropriate for classroom practices with children.

A Summary of Readiness

A brief account of some leading but contradictory views about readiness has been presented in order that teachers may broaden their concept of readiness. From the evidence available at this time, it appears that the following conclusions are valid for use by teachers:

1. Readiness is a necessary prerequisite for efficient reading.
2. Readiness for reading is determined not by one but by a number of factors.
3. Readiness is partially but not wholly dependent upon student maturation. For example, no one considers a two- or three-year-old child to be sufficiently mature to enter the mile run. But the two- or three-year-old is developing muscle tone, coordination, and strength for such a future stint by engaging in activities that will ultimately permit him to run the mile. Likewise, the two- or three-year-old child is not capable of reading books but he is acquiring numerous experiences, including an oral vocabulary, that will prepare him for reading.
4. Student readiness for reading can be evaluated by teachers.
5. Readiness for reading is not limited to readiness for beginning to learn to read but applies to all levels of reading.

What Factors Are Important in Readiness To Begin To Learn To Read?

Whenever the writer has discussed readiness for reading in subject matter, whether with students, teachers, or parents, he has been asked invariably for a quick overview of factors considered as important indicators of a pupil's readiness to begin to learn to read.

Factors considered important to a child's readiness to learn to read can be categorized as being *mental, physical, social, emotional,* and *experiential.*

Mental Readiness for Reading. Some authorities consider general intelligence the most important single factor in readiness to read (14, p. 89). Expressing intelligence in terms of mental age (M.A.), they believe a minimum M.A. of six and one-half years is necessary for success in learning to read. But there is much dispute over this figure. Many teachers believe a mental age of six years is adequate for successfully beginning to read.

Children can and do learn to read before they enter school, a fact long known. Recently there has been much interest, and some overenthusiasm about teaching two- and three-year-old toddlers to read. Some children with high intelligence and with physical, emotional, and social maturity in keeping with that intelligence have been taught to read at that early age under experimental conditions. However, the children were exceptional children and received the highest quality of individualized attention from specially prepared teachers with materials and time that no school district could afford.

Durkin (4, p. 164) recently studied 49 children who read before entering school. She says, "In some instances this reading began at the age of two," a statement that has been overgeneralized and misunderstood by some writers in popular magazines. One must remember, in the first place, that the 49 children in Durkin's study were a selected group representing slightly less than 1 per cent of the children in her sample; they were not 49 average first-grade children. Next, one must ask, how many children among the select 49 are represented in the phrase, "in some instances"? Writers of popular articles have given the impression that *all children* in Durkin's study were reading at age two. There is a world of difference between "reading began" and "they were reading."

Calling attention to the overgeneralizations and misinterpretations of Durkin's study is not a criticism of her study but is merely a reminder to the reader that while a small percentage of children may read at an early age, not *all* children are ready to learn to read at two, three, four, five, or even six years of age. Many educators, psychologists, teachers, and medical doctors seriously question the practice of trying to teach children to read at very early ages.

Physical Readiness for Reading. Physical readiness for reading depends upon the child's physical growth and general health. The child who is often ill, undernourished, or continually tired is not in optimal condition for learning to read, and teachers of beginning reading are concerned about the child's general health. They are equally concerned about the development of his hearing, speech, and vision.

It is a matter of record that young children are naturally farsighted. Many are unable to focus their eyes for close-up reading without strain. In fact, some vision specialists believe strongly that the problems of vision in many children can be traced to their premature exposure to reading.

Emotional Readiness for Reading. The child who is extremely shy or overly belligerent is exhibiting symptoms of emotional difficulties. The child who is overly dependent upon his mother, or who is frightened, insecure, or anxious is not ready to begin to learn to read. Trying to teach him to read before he has made his adjustments may increase his emotional tensions so much that they affect his reading. They can make him a reading problem.

Social Readiness for Reading. Some children are much slower than others to make friends among their peers. Some shy ones cry at the slightest provocation; others run and hide. A few become social outcasts, isolates who are in the group but not part of it. They are overlooked or ignored by their classmates. Seclusive behaviors are indications of undue disturbances. The child who lacks social skills, who is ignored by his peers, or who is uncooperative is not likely to be an apt pupil when he tries to learn to read.

Experiential Readiness for Reading. A child's background of experiences is one of the most important factors in his learning to read. The child who comes from a home, as many do, where there is little conversation, where there are few or no books, where the house is merely a center for bickering or a place to grab a bite to eat, usually has little of the experiential background necessary for learning to read.

The background of experience necessary for learning to read includes:

1. The child should have the ability to use and understand language. He should have command of approximately 2,500 words, according to the older vocabulary count, that he understands and can use in simple sentences in order that he can express his ideas and make known his needs and desires.
2. The child should have sufficient preschool experiences with the world around him so that he understands such terms as a "supermarket," "highway," "animal," "beautiful," "dinner," and "train."
3. The child should have had the privilege of having had someone read and share stories with him. He needs to know that the words he speaks are the same as those that people read in magazines, newspapers, and books.
4. If he is to be a successful beginning reader, he must be able to hear the likenesses in the endings of words such as "man" and "can." He needs also to hear the differences between words such as "tip," "top," and "tap."
5. The child should have a speaking vocabulary enabling him to call objects and things by specific names rather than by such indefinite terms as "this," "that," or "that thing." He needs to learn early that a *pencil* is called a "pencil" and not a *pen* or *that.*

The preceding discussion of reading readiness samples but a few of the many factors that most first-grade teachers, educators, and psychologists believe to be necessary for successfully attempting to begin to learn to read. They represent factors within major areas of reading readiness. For a more detailed discussion of these and other factors, including pupil attitude, interest, motivation, sex, poor attendance, large classes, improperly prepared teachers, etc., the reader is referred to the bibliography at the end of this chapter.

TEACHER READINESS FOR READING

Readiness for reading subject matter in high school and college is a fairly new concept to most teachers. However, for years, some teachers have been using principles of readiness for reading and learning without calling the activity readiness. These teachers have sensed that for numerous reasons all students are not ready to read and learn the same materials at the same rate and at the same levels of efficiency. These are the teachers who are ready to improve student learning through reading.

What is meant by the term "readiness for reading subject matter"? As used in this book, readiness for reading means that the individual who is to read has reached a particular level of learning and has learned certain basic reading skills that include using word-recognition clues, reading for main ideas, getting understanding from reading, referring to the dictionary when necessary, and seeking further help from the teacher when needed. In addition, he has acquired a reasonable background of experiences, learned how to set purposes for reading, and has a desire for further learning. Such statements imply that the student is physically and mentally capable of engaging in reading and learning, and that he is socially and emotionally adjusted to the reading-learning task. This view of readiness includes the idea that each succeeding level of learning is influenced by and is dependent upon previous learning experiences. For example, neither a master bridge player nor an outstanding athlete becomes a champion the first time he plays the game. He must be prepared or readied to learn. After he learns certain basic rules he is capable of learning more about bridge or his chosen athletic activity, but the acquisition of a number of rules and patterns of playing does not make him a champion. To be a champion, he must be physically and mentally capable of sustaining rigorous practice. The practice may be that of engaging in minor tournaments, of teaching others less skilled than he, of practicing by himself, or of devising new ways to throw his opponent off balance while maintaining his own emotional stability.

Likewise, readiness for learning subject matter through reading is a state or condition that promotes further learning. A tenth-grader in an American history class, for instance, who is to be a successful learner must have acquired some knowledge of the colonists who settled this country, their hardships, their joys and sorrows, and their reasons for coming to a strange, new land. He also must have developed the necessary basic reading skills that enable him to read more difficult materials containing new vocabulary, new concepts, and new relationships. But all students in American history do not have the same or even similar experiential backgrounds in history nor do they have the same kinds and levels of reading skills. Some will be so self-motivated and eager to learn that they brighten a teacher's dullest day, but others will only be as interested as a sleepy, well-fed cat. Some will be challenged by new and difficult terms and concepts while others will be frustrated and lost by the strange, new words. Yet, each must learn a minimum amount of history in an efficient manner, in a minimum of time. As a teacher of the inspired and the uninspired, the capable and the incapable, it is your obligation to teach so that each student gains from the instruction. If you are to meet your responsibility, *you* must be ready to teach reading in order that *your* students learn subject matter. Let us, therefore, look at the steps or stages of readiness that you should consider because an understanding of such steps will improve your teaching.

Steps in Teacher Readiness for Reading

Step I. Realization That Students Differ Greatly in Reading Ability. Few high school and college teachers are ready to teach reading in their subject matter because they *assume* that students are ready to learn. Students and teachers can ill afford such fallacious assumptions. It is only human for an enthusiastic teacher, well prepared in his own choice of subject field, to forget that many students may have little interest in the particular subject matter but are taking the course only because it is a requirement, a hurdle, that must be cleared. Such students are not ready to read material that may be entirely new to them and for which they have little background, meager vocabulary, and few, if any, concepts.

Inasmuch as the major portion of advanced learning in any subject-matter area is based primarily upon the efficient use of written materials, teachers must know how to teach students to use the materials most effectively.

There are many valid reasons *why* subject-matter teachers must help students to read materials that are assigned. The most logical reason being that not all students read equally well, although they are in the same class. Betts (1, p. 583) has shown that at the fifth-grade level a few pupils may be reading at first-, second-, and third-grade levels while at the other extreme, some pupils may be reading twelfth-grade materials. And the higher the grade level, the greater the difference in reading achievement between the achieving and the non-achieving readers.

In a tenth-grade English class, for example, some students may be unable to read materials above the third- or fourth-grade level; a number will be capable of reading at the eighth-, ninth-, tenth-, or eleventh-grade level; and several will be capable of reading at much higher levels. Therefore, the tenth-grade teacher must be prepared to meet the reading needs of ten or twelve grade levels. The average high school teacher, however, will find that most of his students will be reading from the fifth to thirteenth grades. The range between bottom and top reading levels will average from six to nine grades. There is no escaping such a fact or pretending that it does not exist. Look to your own classes to check on the accuracy of the statement.

Does the wide difference in the ability to read among students indicate that some students will need relatively little help while others will need much help? It does most definitely. Therefore the first step toward improving student learning of subject matter is to get teachers to accept the idea that all students do not read at the same level. But regardless of differences of student reading levels, teachers can help all students to improve their reading.

Step II. Recognition That Many Inefficient Readers Are of Average or Superior Intelligence. Parents and teachers who have little preparation to teach people how to read generally look upon inefficient reading as a sure sign of mental retardation. Research refutes such assumptions. Studies by Betts (1) show that 80 per cent of the retarded readers in the elementary schools have *average or better than average intelligence.* At the high school level, Durrell (5, pp. 201–8) found that at least 25 per cent of the poor readers have *average or superior intelligence.* The tragedy of such findings is not only that they are unknown to teachers, parents, students, and the general public, but that intelligent students with poor reading skills are wrongly treated as mentally incompetent. How would you, the present reader of these words, feel if you were treated as mentally inferior simply because you had never learned to read? Remember, research evidence shows that a large number of non-readers and inefficient readers have average or superior intelligence.

For example, the writer has recently been working with Clyde, who came to the Oregon State Reading Clinic accompanied by his distraught mother. Statements from his elementary school cumulative folder said that he was "mentally retarded" and "academically retarded." He was a small lad for his eleven years. He was shy, yet inquisitive, and never sure of anything. A standardized test of reading placed him at a "high" first-grade reading level. A word-recognition check showed that he had sufficient sight vocabulary for preprimer reading only. An informal reading inventory placed his instructional level at the primer level. *However, when materials at the ninth-grade reading level were read to him by the examiner, he answered questions about fact, vocabulary, and inference, and he made a score of 85 per cent in comprehension.* This youngster had been classified as mentally retarded. Not only had he been catalogued as mentally unfit for classroom instruction, but during his entire school life he had been treated as a subnormal child.

Step III. Recognition That Teaching Reading and Teaching Subject Matter Are Not Two Separable Processes. The competent subject-matter teacher must teach his students how to read the written materials he assigns. He has no choice in the matter. When he chose teaching as a profession, he assumed an obligation to encourage and to help students learn regardless of the degree and kind of aid needed. He should accept his obligations as unhesitatingly as he accepts his salary. Naturally this allows for some legitimate grumbling, but acceptance is paramount. Any time a teacher uses or assigns written materials for learning in his content area, he is using reading as a teaching and learning aid. When he uses reading as an aid to learning, he must accept the responsibility that goes with it—to use it at its maximum. If reading is used at maximum, then the content-area teacher must help his students read the materials *in the fullest sense.*

Teaching reading in subject-matter areas is not a divisive activity; it is a complementary learning process, inseparable from the subject matter. Teachers at secondary and college levels usually fail to see the inseparability of teaching reading and teaching subject matter because they are prone to think that *the teaching of reading* means *teaching beginning reading.* Teaching reading in subject matter and teaching beginning reading are not synonymous.

To clarify any misunderstanding about the meaning of *teaching reading in subject matter,* let us look at an outline of the steps followed by a successful teacher of subject matter who uses reading to increase the students' learning of content. We need to keep in mind that teaching reading and teaching subject matter are so intertwined that we cannot separate them except for purposes of discussion. In this section we consider procedures for teaching reading for the learning of subject matter.

1. A successful teacher is first of all an expert in his subject-matter field. He has proved that he has a broad knowledge of content in a particular area of learning. He has a clearly stated, but not inflexible, written outline of proposed procedures for teaching. His objectives for students are specific measurable and attainable goals. His objectives act as guidelines for the structure of proposed student activities that provide learning experiences for each student.
2. The teacher has available sufficient and adequate materials for each student. In most subject-matter fields this means that various textbooks and reference materials are used extensively by students. The teacher recognizes that the students who use these written materials from which to learn subject matter vary among themselves in reading ability from six to nine grade levels. It is, therefore, necessary that he provide books, pamphlets, and other materials written at different levels of reading difficulty. Some students will find sixth-grade-level materials sufficiently challeng-

ing for their reading skills, while others will be capable of reading and learning from materials anywhere from one to seven or eight grade levels higher. Whatever the reading level of a student, he must have materials at his own reading level from which to learn facts, information, vocabulary, and concepts.

3. The successful teacher introduces each lesson with an assignment. Before he presents that assignment to the class, he has considered carefully the following questions:
   a) Is this assignment one that leads specifically to students' learning?
   b) Is it clear and direct?
   c) Will it challenge students sufficiently, or is it perhaps too directive, too rigid?
   d) Is there sufficient allowance for the students' ingenuity and creativity in solving the proposed problems?
   e) Does the assignment provide for differences in students' abilities or is it too difficult for some and too easy for others?
4. After the lesson has been assigned, students should read the assigned materials silently for the purpose of learning subject matter. In most secondary schools some class time is given for silent reading in order that the teacher may help students by clarifying ambiguous or puzzling information, by helping students set purposes for reading, by checking on students' understanding of reading, by helping with pronunciation of difficult terms, and by attending to any unusual problems that may arise during the silent reading.
5. After students have completed the silent reading, the teacher should evaluate by various means students' learning. He may raise questions for class discussion, or he may ask for written answers and reactions to the reading. In some instances, he may have certain students reread orally portions from the reading material to clarify or prove a disputed point. At other times he may assign additional reading or reports on specific aspects of the lesson. In some instances, the silent reading may be a necessary prelude to a demonstration or an experiment. In other situations, silent reading may accompany or follow demonstrations, experiments, and discussions.
6. During the silent reading and the discussion, experimental or demonstration periods, the successful teacher has been making notes of particular students' needs and strengths. These notes provide clues for further individual and class experiences that are vital to students' continued learning.

Step IV. Preparation of Students for Reading and Learning During the Assignment Period. Few high school and college teachers utilize the tremendous potential of the assignment period for launching students' energies into immediate, purposeful learning activities. Students who are prepared adequately for engaging in the learning experiences developed by a skilled teacher begin to learn immediately. They waste little time and effort in bumbling trial-and-error activities. Their energy is directed by and toward recognizable, attainable goals.

The assignment period is the readiness period for students' learning of subject matter. It is more than a hurried admonition by the teacher to "read the next chapter and be prepared to answer questions." It is a carefully prepared part of the teacher's plan to capture students' interest and motivate students' learning.

How Can Teachers Assign Lessons in Order That Students Learn Most Effectively?

There are six factors that teachers must consider when assigning a lesson (10, pp. 269–72). These six factors need not necessarily be handled in the exact order given here. Each teacher may vary the presentation to fit his particular classroom situation.

We shall discuss each of these factors separately, but the reader will realize that this classification is for the purpose of discussion only. Like other factors in reading and learning, there is much overlap and intertwining of the various factors.

Arousing the Students' Interest. During the assignment or readiness period, the teachers should use psychological motives for initiating learning. One of these motives is that of the students' interest. Student interest in the lesson may be aroused through student-teacher discussion; the teacher's questions; introduction of a new word; the student's or teacher's demonstrations; reaction to assigned television viewing or radio listening; newspaper accounts of local, national, or world events; magazine articles; a moving picture, slides, or other visual aids.

Developing Motivation. Aroused interest motivates action. During the assignment period, the successful teacher interests and motivates students to read by presenting some part of the proposed lesson in such a way that it will meet student needs. Upon reading the preceding sentence, some teachers will throw up their hands in disgust and say, "Here we go again. Meet their needs and they'll learn. How do I know what their needs are?" Nevertheless, students do have many needs that can be used to get most of them interested and motivated in becoming active in the proposed learning situation. Let us look briefly at some of them.

Students have numerous needs that can be fulfilled by reading whether the reading is done in literature, science, history, home economics, or industrial education. When the teacher recognizes the specific needs of individual students and the general needs of all students, he can use the assignment period to meet some of these needs and to initiate the fulfillment of others. Studies in psychology show that all students need *success, reward, recognition,* and *social approval.* The competent classroom teacher knows the specific needs of individual students. Some students need to learn to solve problems, to acquire information, to develop their meager experiential background, to build concepts, to acquire a larger vocabulary, to associate language with experience, to learn better word-recognition techniques.

The student, for example, who has met continual failure in learning subject matter from reading because he skipped over many of the multisyllabic words that were unpronounceable to him, and therefore meaningless, is not succeeding in learning, is not being rewarded, is not developing self-esteem. When such a student is helped to look critically at words such as "unprepossessing," "desegregationist," and "contractibility," to note the individual prefixes and suffixes in these words, thereby discovering the root word, he is often able to pronounce many other words that he previously was unable to pronounce. Once the student has associated the written word with the spoken word, the word often has meaning for him. However, mere pronunciation of words does not guarantee that meaning is associated with the words, but a student who cannot pronounce words accurately seldom can attach meaning to them.

Imagine the positive reaction within a student who suddenly discovers that what were once long, difficult, unpronounceable words are no longer impossible barriers to him. Will such a student achieve more *success* in learning subject matter? Will he be *rewarded* extrinsically by teacher and classmate *approval?* Will he be *rewarded intrinsically* by knowing that he has achieved? Will he develop more *self-esteem?* Will he be *motivated* to read more? If you can accept the word of a former "retarded reader," he most certainly will.

We have given but one brief example of how a student's single need may be met and become a motive for reading. The next several pages include additional techniques and approaches that teachers should use to improve students' reading and learning of subject matter.

We know from research evidence and classroom experience that most students, despite oftentimes expressed disavowal of learning, actually want to learn. As members of the human family, they appear to have an inborn *desire* or *drive* to be active, to want to know. Present students with problems that are within their understanding, give them materials that are at their instructional reading levels and that contain information necessary for solving the problems, and they will read to learn.

Other techniques that teachers can use to interest and motivate students to read and to learn are: (1) introducing some of the unusual *vocabulary* contained in the lesson; (2) setting purposes for the reading; and (3) clarifying and developing *concepts*. You are reminded to note in the following discussion how each of these factors of readiness can be related to motivating and interesting students during the assignment period.

Introducing New Vocabulary

Each new area of learning in subject matter includes a number of words that are strange or unknown to most of the students. The wise teacher knows that telling students to look up the words they do not understand is a waste of time. A few of the better students will use their dictionaries without being reminded to do so to find the meaning of some words. The remainder of the students will do one or both of the following: (1) They will attempt to derive the meaning of unusual words from context, or (2) they will skip completely the difficult words, rationalizing their failure. In either case, they derive little or no meaning from their reading.

What can a teacher do to motivate students to learn new words? He can and should introduce some, but not all unknown words during the assignment period. He should *pronounce* each new word accurately and distinctly as he *writes* it on the chalkboard. He *pronounces* the word as he writes it in order that students can associate the proper sounds with the printed symbol. In some instances students should pronounce the new vocabulary under the teacher's direction. Research shows that when students mispronounce or cannot pronounce written words, they either associate the wrong meaning with the written symbol or associate no meaning with it. A study conducted by Edwards (6) shows that university freshmen are helped to learn new words by hearing the pronunciation of these new words, especially when the students themselves pronounce the words.

After the new vocabulary word has been written and pronounced for the students, the teacher should use it in a sentence to help students to get the meaning associated with the word. He may give a definition of the word or have a knowledgeable student define the word for the class. In some instances, he may work briefly with students in using dictionaries to derive meaning for a new word. In any event, the teacher should introduce some of the new vocabulary and should make sure that students hear the words accurately, that they relate them to the proper written symbols, and that they associate the preferred meanings of the words with the spoken and written forms.

Can the introduction of some new words by the teacher be related to the students' needs? It certainly can. Sufficient evidence indicates that, as a group, secondary students are especially interested in new words. Most of them feel a need for improving their knowledge of words. The alert teacher not only introduces some of the new words to students but also uses all the means he can devise to develop their interest in learning words independently. Few teachers, however, have initiated their students into the fascinating study of the etymology of words. A discussion of word origins and their value in vocabulary development is given in Chapter 11.

Purpose for Reading

Few students at the high school and college levels know how to read for definite and positive purposes. Most of them read to cover a certain number of assigned pages and somehow hope that this practice will provide them with a sufficient number of facts to pass some teacher's examination. What a waste of student energy!

Part of a teacher's job is to teach students *how* to set purposes for reading, and to know *why* it is necessary to set purposes *before* reading. The assignment period provides him with a perfect opportunity for presenting this learning experience. In the beginning, he asks several pertinent questions that direct students' reading. Instead of students reading material only because it has been assigned, they read for a definite purpose. They have *goals* to reach. When they find answers to purposive questions, they *know* they have accomplished a defined task.

After the teacher has set purposes for the reading by asking questions about content, he should encourage students to discuss how his questions have given them a purpose for reading. Experience shows that students are quick to recognize the value of questions for making reading a purposeful process. Thus students may be led to discover that chapter titles and bold-faced headings can be turned into questions that become *student* purposes for reading. For example, a student may note the heading *Purpose for Reading* and ask himself, What does *Purpose for Reading* mean? Who sets Purposes? Why set Purposes? When a student reaches this stage of learning, in which he manifests the ability to set his own purposes for reading *before* he reads, he has moved a step closer to being a mature, independent reader.

A Note About Questions

Teachers at all levels too often ask questions involving only *facts,* a poor practice because students learn to look for and remember only *facts.* Facts are of utmost importance in learning, but a student's acquisition of facts is only a small portion of his learning. Facts are too often memorized but never used purposefully by students. If facts are to be of value for learning, they are best used as the raw material for arriving at decisions, creating new ideas, guiding future studying, and comparing and evaluating previously held convictions. When a teacher's questions are almost exclusively those demanding only fact-type answers, students learn to look for and to memorize facts that often are no more than worthless, memorized gibberish without meaning.

In order that students learn to form judgments from known facts, it is necessary that they have guided practice in doing so. The teacher's task is to ask questions that require students to be able to draw inferences. We shall call them *inference-type questions.*

Teachers should ask students questions that require them to learn new words and should help them to develop skill for acquiring larger vocabularies. Students can many times get a hazy idea of the meaning of a key word from the context in which it is found, but a hazy idea of a key word is not sufficient for effective learning. The alert teacher, therefore, during and after the assignment period will always include some *questions about vocabulary,* a technique that helps to make students aware of the importance of learning specific meanings of words.

Teachers might find it helpful to remember to use continually *fact, inferential,* and *vocabulary* types of questions, but there is no definite rule for using a particular number of them. A rule-of-thumb might be, try to use about one-third of each type during any questioning of students whether the questions are for setting purposes for reading or for the evaluating of learning. Such judicious use of the proposed three types of questions will promote students' thinking rather than mere memorization.

Concepts Are Developed and Clarified

During the assignment period, the productive teacher uses student-teacher discussion to develop new concepts, to broaden other concepts and to clarify hazy or faulty concepts. Concept development is not done apart from the introduction of new vocabulary and the setting of purposes for reading, but is interwoven into the whole of the assignment period.

Following the silent reading of subject matter, teachers need to check on student understanding of concepts and vocabulary that were introduced during the assignment period. Again, fact-, inference-, and vocabulary-type questions should be used.

Time and the Assignment Period

How much time is required to properly assign a lesson? The answer to this question varies greatly with the kind of lesson being presented, the number of new concepts and vocabulary involved, the specific purpose of the teacher, and the kinds of students involved in the lesson. In some instances the readiness period may require no more than two, three, or four minutes. In other instances, thirty or forty minutes may be necessary to prepare students for the proposed reading-learning experience.

Teachers sometimes object when they first hear that an assignment period may require as much as thirty or forty minutes. "How will I ever teach if it takes that long to assign the lesson?" they ask.

Such a question implies that an assignment period is an act apart from teaching but such an implication is unrealistic. Many competent teachers agree that the assignment period *is* a most important part of teaching. An assignment is not a side dish, an afterthought that is plunked "willy-nilly" into the main course of learning. It is a carefully considered plan for preparing students for reading and learning. No matter how effectively one may teach, his teaching is like tossing seed on dry ground if students have not been prepared to receive it. The assignment period is an integral part of teaching.

Developing student interest, motivating students, introducing some new vocabulary, developing and clarifying concepts, and setting purposes for learning subject matter may be done in a matter of several minutes. But if the new assignment is difficult, and if forty or fifty minutes are required to go through these steps before students know what is expected of them and before they are ready to read the material by themselves, how much will students learn from the assignment if adequate time is not spent in preparing them? No one preparing for an automobile trip would hesitate to spend forty or fifty minutes in readying the car for the trip. He would prefer to take care of any minor adjustments in order that the vehicle would not break down and leave him stranded in an isolated area. Is not the preparation for a learning experience that involves a student's complex reading and thinking process to make possible the communication of ideas and knowledge as important as that of preparing for transportation? Would you prefer to minimize students' preparation for learning simply because a clock ticks a given number of times? Or would you, if you felt it were necessary, spend forty or fifty minutes to insure that students' learning of subject matter did not bog down in a quagmire of uncertainty or become lost in a fog of meaningless words. When you teach, you must make the choice. The decision is yours.

When the teacher has finished assigning a lesson, each student should know the objectives of the assignment and should be capable of setting his own additional purposes for reading as he learns during the reading. He should know what he is expected to do, how he should proceed, when he should have completed the assignment, and why he has been given this particular task (10, pp. 269–72).

It is suggested (10, pp. 269–72) that teachers assign lessons at the beginning of class period rather than at the end. Assignments given at the beginning of class allow time for students to become mentally and physically ready to learn. Furthermore, teachers then have sufficient time to properly assign the new lesson. Too often students and teachers become so engrossed in classroom activities that the period ends before any realize the time has passed. On such occasions, students may be beyond hearing distance of the teacher's words as he frantically calls after them "Don't forget to read the next chapter for Monday." Nor can he blame those who turn a deaf ear to such a hazy, haphazard assignment.

SUMMARY

In this chapter we have discussed some of the important but oftentimes contradictory views about readiness for learning and reading. *Readiness for learning to read* and *readiness for reading subject matter* are not identical or synonymous terms, although many of the same factors are involved in and contribute to both kinds of readiness. Readiness for reading applies to reading at all levels. Readiness for reading applies to both teachers and students.

The assignment period is an important part of every lesson. It is the preparatory or readiness-for-learning period. How much time will be given to this aspect of learning depends upon the teacher's knowledge of his students and the difficulty of the new material. He must decide the kinds and amount of help that his students need for optimal learning.

SELECTED REFERENCES

1. Betts, Emmett Albert. *Foundations of Reading Instruction.* Cincinnati: American Book Co., Inc., 1957.
2. Bruner, Jerome S. *The Process of Education.* Cambridge: Harvard University Press, 1963.
3. Burton, William H. *Reading in Child Development.* Indianapolis: The Bobbs-Merrill Co., Inc., 1956.
4. Durkin, Dolores. "Children Who Read Before Grade One," *The Reading Teacher,* Vol. 14 (January, 1961), pp. 163–66.
5. Durrell, Donald D. "Learning Difficulties Among Children of Normal Intelligence," *Elementary School Journal,* Vol. 55 (December, 1954), pp. 201–8.
6. Edwards, Thomas J. "Oral Reading in the Total Reading Process," *Elementary School Journal,* Vol. 58 (October, 1957), pp. 36–41.
7. Hymes, James L., Jr. *Before the Child Reads.* New York: Harper & Row, Inc., 1958.
8. Karlin, Robert. *Teaching Reading in High School.* Indianapolis: The Bobbs-Merrill Company, Inc., 1964.
9. McCracken, Glenn. "Have We Over-emphasized the Readiness Factor?" *Elementary English,* Vol. 29 (May, 1952), pp. 271–75.
10. Marksheffel, Ned D. "Reading Readiness at the High School and College Levels," *Education,* Vol. 81 (January, 1961), pp. 269–72.
11. Pribram, Karl H. "Neurological Notes on the Art of Educating," *Theories of Learning and Instruction.* The Sixty-third Yearbook, Part I, National Society for the Study of Education. Chicago: The University of Chicago Press, 1964.
12. Russell, David H. *Children Learn To Read* (2d ed.). Boston: Ginn & Co., 1961.
13. Sears, Pauline S., and Hilgard, Ernest R. "The Teacher's Role in the Motivation of the Learner," *Theories of Learning and Instruction.* The Sixty-third Yearbook, Part I, National Society for the Study of Education. Chicago: The University of Chicago Press, 1964.
14. Smith, Henry P., and Dechant, Emerald V. *Psychology in Teaching Reading.* Englewood Cliffs, N.J.: Prentice-Hall, Inc., 1961.
15. Strang, Ruth, McCullough, Constance M., and Traxler, Arthur E. *The Improvement of Reading.* New York: McGraw-Hill Book Co., Inc., 1961.
16. Tyler, Fred T. "Issues Related to Readiness to Learn," *Theories of Learning and Instruction.* The Sixty-third Yearbook, Part I, National Society for the Study of Education. Chicago: The University of Chicago Press, 1964.

SUGGESTED ADDITIONAL READING

BLAIR, GLENN MYERS, JONES, STUART R., and SIMPSON, RAY H. *Educational Psychology.* New York: The Macmillan Co., 1955.

Edwards, Thomas J. "The Language–Experience Attack on Cultural Deprivation," *The Reading Teacher,* Vol. 18 (April, 1965), pp. 546–51, 556

Harris, Albert J. *How to Increase Reading Ability* (4th ed., rev.). New York: David McKay Co., Inc., 1961.

Henderson, Kenneth B. "Interpreting Materials in Arithmetic and Mathematics in Grades Seven to Fourteen," *Reading in the Secondary Schools,* ed. M. Jerry Weiss. New York: The Odyssey Press, Inc., 1961.

Hildreth, Gertrude. "Reading Methods for the English Language," *The Reading Teacher,* Vol. 15 (November, 1961), pp. 75–80.

Smith, Mary Katherine. "Measurement of the Size of the General English Vocabulary Through the Elementary Grades and High School," *Genetic Psychology Monographs.* Provincetown, Mass.: The Journal Press, 1941. Vol. 24, pp. 311–45.

3

PRINCIPLES OF READING

READING BROUGHT MAN FROM THE CAVE TO THE SATELLITE

Man's slow climb from savagery to barbarism to civilization has been achieved through education.

Even the most primitive type of society assumes responsibility for educating its youth. If the obligation for educating the young is not assumed or accepted, the group or society perishes. There is no alternative.

In the more primitive types of society, the obligation for perpetuating the culture is assumed primarily by the parents. As the society progresses from its primitive state to a more civilized one, the parents, unable to meet individually the growing educational needs of their young, consign or relegate portions of their educational responsibilities to other individuals or agencies.

In a democratic society one of the agencies for educating youth is the public school. As a part of society, each community assumes its share of the responsibility for perpetuating the culture by establishing a public school system. An integral and fundamental part of the educational system is the classroom.

The classroom is a place where pupils meet to learn. It is the place where each child is supposed to have the opportunity to acquire those skills, attitudes, responsibilities, and knowledge necessary to realize his worth. In order that learning take place according to the dictates of the society and according to each child's needs, interests, and potential, a teacher is provided for necessary guidance and direction of the learning process.

Today the teacher in the secondary classroom assumes a tremendous responsibility. He is responsible to the community, the culture, and students. He is charged with improving each pupil's skills, attitudes, and knowledge. He is supposed to motivate, interest, and provide educational experiences that result in pupil learning. Among other things, he is expected to produce more scientists, more mathematicians, more technicians, more capable thinkers, more creative students, more efficient readers. This is no simple task.

Does the secondary classroom produce the kinds of pupils for which it is created? Does the secondary teacher fulfill his obligations and responsibilities as a director of learning in the classroom? Honest answers to these questions must be qualified. Critics of education, including some teachers and professors, answer with a resounding, unqualified "No!" Others disagree partially or wholly with the critics. Let's look briefly at some pertinent facts.

If the achievement records of all graduates from the secondary schools are examined, one may conclude that a large portion of youth receive an education in keeping with the aims of society. For them, the classroom has served its intended purpose. The teacher has satisfactorily met his obligations. These youths have profited from the educational system provided by society and are capable of maintaining and improving the culture that nurtures them. Many of them become scientists, mathematicians, technicians, capable thinkers, and efficient readers. A high proportion of them continue their education by attending institutions of higher learning or some other formal approach to learning such as special night schools, company, trade, or labor schools. Many seek self-improvement in learning by enrolling in correspondence courses, attending lectures, discussions, and by reading widely and wisely. These are the students about whom we hear little. These are the products of the school whom the critics overlook.

On the other hand, many potentially capable but poorly educated students graduate from high school. An alarming number read and write no better than average elementary pupils. Another large number of youth, unable to compete academically, quit high school before graduation. *Penty's study (7) of dropouts reveals that 90 per cent of those who leave school early have reading problems!* What chance have these youth to compete in the modern labor market? How can they possibly learn on their own when they lack the basic reading and related language skills?

In short, available evidence indicates that a large majority of youth are receiving a commendable education in American secondary schools. But commendable education for a large majority of youth is not sufficient. Many, many youth are being short-changed by the schools.

The schools, however, are not totally to blame. *Every teacher, every parent, every pupil* has a responsibility to see that *each pupil, in light of his own interests, needs, and potential,* receives the best education possible. Unless each child learns to read efficiently according to his own abilities, we shall continue to have pupils who are not being educated as they should. When this happens, neither the teacher nor the classroom is meeting society's needs or demands. And they must be met.

Much available evidence, including the expressed opinions of secondary and college teachers, points to one of the major instructional problems of content-area teachers—large numbers of students fail to learn subject matter because they cannot read the assigned materials.

If a student's learning in content area is obviously limited by his inefficient reading, it should be obvious that the student *needs* to improve his reading skills. The obvious in this instance, however, is not obvious. Teachers, for example, generally agree that student reading is poor and needs to be shored up, but they disagree greatly on *how* to cope with the poor reader.

In order that the reader better understand how teachers view poor readers, let's look briefly at some teacher statements.

Teacher A, for example, is representative of many teachers. He says, "Lets face it. If a student is too stupid to read my texts, he's too stupid to be in my class, or any other class. The sooner we realize this and kick the stupid ones out of school, the better off we'll be. The only solution is to get rid of the poor readers."

Teacher B is also representative of a large number of teachers. He says, "I recognize that many of my students don't learn the subjects I teach because they can't read. I'm sure they are not all ignorant; its just that they are poor readers. I wish I knew what to do with them. I sometimes send a poor reader to the counselor but it doesn't do any good. The counselor tells me what I already know, the pupil can't read. So what am I supposed to do? I just don't know. I wish I did."

Teacher C speaks for another group of teachers. He says, "There isn't much anyone can do about poor readers at the high school level. I put up with the poor readers and just hope that they somehow learn something. I pass them. What else can I do? Maybe some other teacher will be able to motivate them to read."

Teacher D is representative of a growing group of teachers. "In my classes," he says, "I have an SRA reading kit (6) and some Smith Books (11), *Be a Better Reader*. These materials are pretty good and help some students, but it doesn't do much for helping them in my subject. I know that some of my students learn to read better but it's not because I helped them. I've been reading a couple of texts on reading and I might even take a summer-school course in reading. I have to do something for my students."

The reader of this text has no doubt heard many teacher comments similar to the above, and a few that are not printable. Teacher comments help to focus our attention on some of the problems associated with improving reading in the secondary schools and colleges.

Generally speaking, most secondary teachers want to help students improve their reading skills, but they do not know *where* or *how* to begin. In addition, a number of them confess that just the idea of teaching reading gives them feelings of apprehension. Actually, a number of good secondary teachers are teaching reading, but they are unaware that they are doing so.

Most teachers agree that when they use various aids and materials to provide learning experiences in content areas, they assume the responsibility for seeing that the most efficient use is made of them in light of student needs. If this is an acceptable viewpoint, then teachers who use printed materials for learning experiences must assume the responsibility for helping students to obtain and read such assigned materials according to student needs.

Secondary and college teachers usually agree with the above premise but say, "This is the same old dilemma: How can I teach reading and subject matter? I can teach reading or I can teach subject matter, but I can't teach both."

Such statements are indicative of the general lack of knowledge of what reading really is. There is no dilemma. Reading and subject matter cannot be divorced. When one learns from printed materials, such as textbooks, notices, brochures, letters, he is reading in the true sense of the word. The teacher who uses principles of reading to help his students get more knowledge and understanding about content from the printed page *is* teaching reading *and* subject matter.

The principles of reading that are introduced and discussed in this chapter are based upon results from research in the fields of anthropology, child growth and development, education, guidance, psychology, and sociology. They are not all-inclusive but are limited purposely to a few basic principles that can be used by the classroom teacher to improve his teaching of subject matter.

Principles of reading, like principles in any other field or discipline, are subject to change in light of new evidence. And this change is to be expected. Progress and improvement occur when research reveals new facts and the facts are put into practice. In view of present knowledge, and available evidence, the following principles of reading are proposed:

Basic Principles

1. *Reading is a highly complex thinking process in which the entire organism participates. It is composed of innumerable skills, abilities, processes, and conditions so interwoven and integrated that much of what occurs during the reading act is purely hypothetical.*

Because reading is so complex, an entire chapter has been devoted to defining reading. In the meantime, a brief discussion of only one of the many facets of reading, the perception of words is presented now.

An alarming number of Americans believe that reading is basically seeing and saying words. It is irrefutable that the average reader must see and pronounce words, but this is only a minor, albeit, an important part of the process called *reading.* People *read* with their eyes to about the same degree that they *write* with their fingers and a pen. Reading and writing consist of much more than running one's eyes across a line of print or moving a writing instrument across a sheet of paper. An enlightening but inadequate idea of the complexity of the reading process can be obtained by looking briefly at some of the different skills and learning involved in the comparatively simple act of seeing words.

Efficient reading demands quick, accurate perception of words. Yet a number of inhibiting factors enter into the act. Man's eyes, authorities say, were never intended for the concentrated, close vision required by reading (1, pp. 172–202). In addition, poor health, emotional distress, neurological defects, and eye injuries are but a few of the many other factors that impede singleness and clearness of vision so vital to perceiving words.

Not only must the reader's eyes be functioning satisfactorily, but the learned part of vision must be working in absolute harmony. Precise, accurate visual discrimination depends upon the reader's learning to focus his eyes on words, and the letters within the words in proper sequence. Words must be perceived from a left to right direction. The words must be seen a line at a time, without the reader skipping lines or losing his place.

The quick, accurate perception of words is not a simple task. Mastery of this skill requires many hours of practice, and it is prerequisite to efficient reading. Nevertheless, it is one of the least difficult of all the reading skills that comprise the highly complex reading process.

2. *The reading achievement of secondary and college students varies greatly. One cannot assume that all students are efficient readers.*

The secondary or college teacher must be prepared to expect a wide range in the reading achievement of students enrolled in his classes. One of the shocking realities of teaching at the secondary level is the fact that all students are not efficient or mature readers. Several authorities state that most pupils at the secondary level are immature readers (4, p. 67). Numerous investigations show that differences in reading achievement exist at all grade levels. Contrary to popular belief, the better the teaching, the greater will be the spread of achievement between good and poor readers. Russell says that "this is perfectly usual and normal" (9, p. 23).

Beginning teachers often find a statement such as Russell's hard to believe. They feel, and many state, that they will be able to bring the reading achievement of all pupils up to grade level. Such statements are, in a sense, commendable because they reflect the speaker's honest desire to help pupils who need help. On the other hand, the teacher's inexperience and limited concept of reading is doing the talking. *All pupils can never be brought up to grade level.* Pupils vary greatly in intelligence, physical well-being, emotional adjustment, social environment, experiential background, attitude, level of aspiration, needs, etc. No matter how much we may want them to achieve at the same rate and same level, they will not.

Teachers should understand that grade levels are merely one approach to grouping pupils for more efficient instruction. At one time all elementary schools in America were one-room schools. Teachers grouped and taught pupils at their own instructional levels. In the early one-room schools it was not unusual to see grown men, gangling youth, and youngsters all working in the same primer but on different pages according to each individual's needs.

Grade levels are not inflexible standards, but they are usually accepted as such by teachers and laymen. The important points to understand about grade levels are that they are arbitrary approaches to meeting large numbers of pupils' needs, that they are far from satisfactory, that they are not inviolate, that they are not intended to produce students who achieve at the same rate, at the same time, in the same manner.

If, for example, it were possible to have a tenth-grade class all reading at the same level at the beginning of the school year, the pupils would not be reading at the same grade level at the end of the year. Youth just do not grow and develop uniformly, although they follow the same general pattern. And *the more efficient the teacher, the greater will be the spread between the bottom and top readers.*

Pupil differences in reading achievement begin at the first-grade level, where some pupils are already reading when they enter school. Other pupils are ready to perceive reading instruction, while some are not, and will not be ready to read after a full year of attendance.

By the time pupils reach the second grade, it is found that there is a difference of about four grade levels between the top and bottom readers. At the fifth-grade level, Betts (1, p. 583) says that the teacher may expect in some cases the reading achievement of pupils will range from the first to twelfth grades.

Not all studies of differences in reading achievement agree on the range of differences at specific grade levels, but they do agree that the range varies greatly. This may be due to the types of tests given, the samples of pupils tested, or a combination of many factors. The point is that differences do exist, and that they are usually greater than most people, including teachers, expect them to be.

Until recently, the American public, including secondary teachers, has considered that students attending high school are capable of reading effectively. This general misconception is probably a carry-over in thinking from earlier years when only a small percentage of the school population, the academic elite, attended secondary schools.

Today's teacher in an average tenth-grade classroom will have some students who are reading from six to nine grade levels above the poorest readers. In many instances the range of differences in students' reading achievement will be even greater. Some students may be capable of reading only second- or third-grade materials while the most efficient readers will be reading as well as high school seniors and graduates (2, p. 323), and it is this range of reading differences that creates numerous educational problems for subject-matter teachers.

One might assume that college professors at least would not be plagued by inefficient readers. Such an assumption is contrary to facts. For example, Halfter and Douglas (5, pp. 42–53), after eight years of careful testing found only one-third of the entering college freshmen had sufficient reading skills necessary for academic success.

Carter studied 1,029 freshmen who were completing their first year of college and found that many were lacking vital reading skills. Eighty-two per cent of these students felt that a high school course in reading would have helped them. Sixty-eight per cent of them "reported that they had never been taught to concentrate upon a reading activity, 64 per cent had not been shown how to develop an awareness of problems, and 70 per cent had not been taught how to critically evaluate a writer's bias and use of preconceived ideas" (3, p. 156).

Preston and Tufts (8, pp. 196–202) studied the reading skills of forty juniors who were eligible for the Phi Beta Kappa Fraternity and found that not all were efficient readers. They attributed their high scholastic achievement to superior ability and many hours of study.

For the past six years the writer has tested the reading achievement of all juniors, seniors, and graduate students enrolled in his classes, Methods of Reading for Secondary Teachers. Each student is administered a Triggs Diagnostic Reading Test (12), and an informal reading test on material taken from one of the assigned texts.

According to student scores on the Trigg's test, many students are good-to-excellent readers judged by the norms for high school seniors and college freshmen. On the other hand, a large number do not read as well as the average high school senior or college freshman. Results from the informal tests used tend to confirm the findings from the Trigg's test. In addition, the informal tests invariably pick out some students who have reading problems that were not indicated by the standardized test.

Judging from student questions, comments, and reactions to both tests and their accompanying scores, approximately half the poor readers admitted that they knew they were not reading efficiently but didn't know what to do about the problem. The remainder of the inefficient readers reacted more aggressively. There were those who "knew" they were at least average when compared with their present college class (junior, senior, or graduate); some admitted they might have a reading problem; others insisted that they were either good or superior readers.

George, for example, received a score on the standardized test that is representative of scores at the fourth percentile. He asked if he might take another standardized test because he knew the test rated him too low. His score on an alternate form of the test placed him at the eighth percentile on the college freshman norms.

Subsequent informal reading tests showed that George was a frustrated reader on general reading materials at the ninth-grade level. But science materials at a ninth-grade reading level were best for his instructional needs. This is the level at which he began receiving reading help. After approximately thirty hours of individualized help he reported that his study time had been cut in half and his semester-grade point average increased one full point.

George's specific problems were too numerous to mention here, but three major inhibiting factors were: (1) his inability to use correctly consonant blends such as *str, bl,* and *br;* (2) his total lack of ability to set purposes for reading; and (3) his stubborn insistence on clinging to previously learned inaccurate ideas and inadequate concepts.

An interesting sidelight in his case is that he learned to read with a minimum of help from his parents. According to him and his parents, he was, "reading newspapers at four years of age."

Much available evidence indicates that many college and university students are reading well below their capabilities and needs. Many of them attain academic and professional success despite their inefficient reading, but only because they have superior ability, an intense desire to achieve, and the determination to spend many extra hours in study.

3. *Improvement in reading and learning in content areas is best achieved when reading is taught by subject-matter teachers.*

Secondary teachers are beginning to accept responsibility for helping students improve their reading in subject-matter areas. Although there has been no general acceptance to teach reading, more and more secondary teachers are discovering that when pupils are given help with reading the text, greater learning in both reading and subject matter takes place.

By now, it should be apparent that every teacher will have some students in his classes who are unable to read the assigned texts. It should be equally clear that if a student cannot read efficiently his learning will be definitely limited. This alone should be sufficient justification for secondary teachers to teach reading in their subject areas. If we view the student reading problem from the teacher's role as a director of learning, the reader may conclude that there are other valid reasons why improvement in learning and reading are inseparable.

With few exceptions, the subject-matter teacher is the best-qualified person in the school for teaching reading in his subject, although he may deny it, or may fail to realize his potential.

What are the secondary or college teacher's competencies for teaching subject matter and reading? First of all, through his interest, preparation, and education, he is an expert or specialist in his field. He has acquired a large, meaningful vocabulary necessary for intelligent communication when receiving or relating facts vital to adequate concept development. He has engaged in numerous direct and vicarious experiences basic to general and specific knowledge in his subject-matter field.

If the above, admittedly brief, statements about the teacher's capability are acceptable, who is most capable of helping a student learn to pronounce new words accurately, and associate meanings with new symbols? Who can best detect student strength and weaknesses in concept development? Who is better prepared to motivate and create student interest in the subject? Who else knows the important parts of the text that require slow, deliberate, thoughtful reading and which areas need only to be read quickly for main ideas? Who has the background and understanding for helping the student obtain and read materials that provide the vicarious experiences essential to mastery of the content in this area? Who is most qualified to help students set specific, attainable goals necessary for learning the subject?

There is no dodging the fact that the subject-matter teacher is unquestionably the most adept. His Achilles' heel is that he has had no experience in how to relate reading and subject matter. He is usually unaware that helping students with pronunciation and meaning of words, building concepts, setting goals, creating interest are aspects of reading. Helping him understand *why* and *how* he can improve student learning in subject matter through reading is the purpose of this text.

4. *Optimum learning in subject matter is dependent upon teaching the student at his instructional level in reading.*

Experienced teachers generally agree unanimously with this principle. In addition they can cite research evidence to substantiate their stand. Students preparing to become secondary teachers are equally adept in subscribing to this principle. But what teachers say and what teachers do about using reading materials at the student's instructional level are rarely consistent.

It is possible that their statements are only empty words that they verbalized as students in return for grades from some professor; it is possible that some understand the import of the words but are unable to put them into practice. In either case, the facts are that large numbers of secondary students are forced to try to learn subject matter from written materials that are far above their instructional levels.

There is hardly a secondary teacher in America who does not have students who are unable to read the assigned text. In many classes, for example, only forty to sixty per cent of the students can read the prescribed text, yet every pupil is given the same book. Why? And in those same classrooms there are students who are bored by having to read materials that they know and that are not challenging to them. In both cases, *pupils are not being given reading materials at their instructional reading levels.* Such practices damage student learning.

In the first instance, pupils can become so emotionally and socially upset from meeting constant failure in the classroom that they will do almost anything to avoid attending school. Their reactions are expressed in various ways. Some students, forced to attend school, withdrew mentally from the situation. They refuse to answer known questions or to participate in any classroom discussions. They sit in an almost zombi-like trance, impervious to all directed learning experiences. Others seek relief by becoming such disciplinary problems that they are expelled from school.

A smaller, but important group of students may suffer just as much as the previously discussed groups, not because the text is difficult, but because it is too simple for them. They may exhibit the same or similar symptoms of frustration as the less-efficient readers. The solution for these kinds of problems must begin with knowing and treating the problem rather than treating symptoms.

5. *Improvement of reading instruction must begin with an evaluation of student reading.*

Before a teacher can adequately promote learning in content areas, he must have at least the following information about each student: (1) Can he read this textbook at this time without any teacher help? (2) Is the book sufficiently challenging, or is it too simple? (3) Is the text too difficult for him to read even when he is given help? (4) If he cannot read the text, at what grade level can he read successfully? (5) Is he reading up to his own capacity?

The teacher can get a rough idea of the reading ability of each student from his past records. Such information will also give an indication of the range of reading achievement within the group.

Almost all larger high schools and many smaller ones have cumulative records of each student. Standardized reading test scores and the dates of the tests are recorded. By themselves, the scores are not too informative, but they are at least indicators of approximate reading achievement. In a large number of schools the records are inadequately kept; in other schools, well kept; and, in some, so well kept that teachers are rarely able to see them because those in charge feel that the material is confidential, that teachers might be biased by the information, and that each teacher should discover what the pupils can or cannot do.

The teacher who finds himself in any of the above predicaments should be capable of administering his own reading tests, both standardized and informal. Intelligent interpretation of the test data and competent use of the information thus gained is crucial to improved student learning.

Every teacher will have some students who are reading at grade level, some above grade level, and some below grade level. He should know *why* this situation exists. Is the student who is reading at grade level reading up to his own ability? Is the student who is reading below grade level doing the best he can? Is the student who reads above grade level capable of doing better? Information that will answer these questions is vital to the mental health of both teacher and student; it is information necessary for efficient student learning.

Because only a comparative handful of secondary teachers have any preparation for teaching reading, a brief look at several examples of students with different kinds of reading problems may prove beneficial to both experienced and beginning teachers. The following four illustrations are not isolated cases. They are representative samples of the kinds of problems with which the writer works. Similar problems can be found in practically every classroom in America.

CASE REPORTS ON READING

Meet Bob—Case 1

Bob, eighteen years old, physically well developed, good looking, and pleasant, was referred to the writer by a fellow teacher. The teacher said, "Will you see if you can find out what we can do for Bob? I know something is wrong, but I am not sure what it is. He just cannot do anything in history. Look at this examination. You would think he never read the book. Maybe he is lazy, or stupid—maybe both. Anyway, see what you can find out."

Available information from Bob's cumulative folder indicated an I.Q. of 69. Further checking verified that the score was as nearly valid as a score can be. He had been checked at intervals over a period of twelve years by competent psychologists from one of the finest universities in California.

Bob was rarely absent from school. He was cooperative, he caused no trouble in the classroom, and he was well liked by students and teachers, but he had problems with history.

Bob was tested on his ability to read his history text. With help, he struggled painfully through the following sentence in two minutes flat. "The rigors of the New England winter took a heavy toll of the pioneer women." When asked to explain what the sentence meant, he said, "Well, them Indians (rigors) came down an' captured the pioneers' women an' tol' 'em what to do. When they wouldn't do what they were tol', they beat 'em with clubs an' sticks an' things."

"What gave you the idea the women were beaten, Bob?"

"Anybody knows that when Indians captured women they made slaves of 'em. An' when they tol' the slaves what to do an' they didn't do it, they beat 'em with clubs. They always used clubs."

Bob was one of those unfortunate lads who cannot compete successfully in the classroom. He could read third- and some fourth-grade materials with meaning, but *that was his limit.* To force him to "read" eleventh-grade texts was inexcusable, unjust, and inhumane.

What would *you* have done for Bob? Do you feel that after being tested he was given materials he could read and understand? It is too late to help Bob, but there are many other boys in school who have similar problems with reading. How will *you* treat them?

Sally—Case 2

Sally was an enigma to all her high school teachers. As an entering sophomore her grades were among the top 15 per cent of the student body, but at the end of one semester they were among the bottom 10 per cent. Several of Sally's teachers had questioned her ability to read, but after hearing her read orally they were convinced that her reading was fluent. They said, "She can read anything, but she has trouble in remembering what she reads. We feel that she might be lacking in ability to concentrate. Please tell us what to do for her."

According to the records in Sally's file, she was of "high average intelligence." Scores from five different standardized reading tests taken during her elementary and junior high school years consistently placed her reading achievement at or slightly above grade level.

Sally was given an informal reading test. Her word-pronunciation skills were exceptional. She zipped through college texts with almost flawless pronunciation. Her understanding of the material, however, was negligible. She replied to all questions with, "That's my trouble, I just can't remember what I read."

She had lived all her life in a seaside resort famous for its beaches. After reading a selection about her own city, she was "unable to remember" much about the story. When asked a question based on the word *kelp,* she could not remember because *kelp* had no more meaning for her than *prolix* has for the average reader. She said that the whistling *buoys* referred to in the story were sailors on leave who were whistling at the girls.

Fortunately, Sally had sufficient intelligence to recognize her reading inadequacies when they were brought to her attention. With the help of classroom teachers, she learned how to set purposes for meaningful reading, and *how, when,* and *why* she needed to use a dictionary and context clues to attach meaning to unfamiliar words. By the end of the school year she was making consistent and remarkable progress in all her schoolwork. Two years later she was graduated from high school with an academic standing equal to that with which she had entered. She was among the top 15 per cent of her class.

There are "Sallies" in every school. Reading experts call them "verbalizers." Verbalizers, usually girls, generally fool themselves and teachers into believing that they are reading because they can pronounce words.

Joe, the "Low I.Q."—Case 3

Joe represents another kind of reading problem. His teachers said: "He doesn't try." "He has no interest in school." "He's a good boy at heart but more interested in looking out the window than at his book." "I'm afraid he doesn't have the intelligence to do any better."

Joe's records were unimpressive. According to group tests of intelligence, his scores fluctuated between 72 and 84. Standardized reading test scores administered in grades seven, eight, and nine ranged from 4.2 to 6.0.

When Joe was asked to read orally from his tenth-grade text, he was hopelessly lost. He mispronounced at least half of the words. Obviously, his understanding of the material was no better than Sally's. *But when the same or similar material was read to him, he answered at least 90 per cent of the questions asked him.* His ability to get meaning from materials read to him was ample evidence that *he possessed sufficient intelligence and experiences to comprehend tenth-grade materials.* His problem was to learn how to pronounce words.

Joe was diagnosed as a *remedial reader.* A *remedial reader,* as the term is used in this text, means that the individual has such a severe reading problem that he must have the help of a reading specialist. The classroom teacher does not have the time or preparation for teaching remedial readers. He should, however, be capable of identifying the severely retarded reader and doing everything possible to see that the pupil receives adequate help. Too often, teachers without any experience or preparation in reading unintentionally do great damage to a *remedial reader* by erroneously labeling him as a mentally retarded student. The writer and others (13, pp. 20–21) have found that severely retarded readers have I.Q.'s that range from 70 to better than 150.

Subsequent tests and diagnoses revealed that Joe's intelligence was at least "high-average" and that his instructional level for reading was the third grade.

Oscar, "Plain Lazy"—Case 4

Oscar attended a junior high school where pupils were grouped according to the scores they received on standardized achievement tests. His scores on these tests placed him with the average group where he managed to get a straight "C" grade.

His teachers, with one exception, considered him "fairly intelligent." His spelling was atrocious. He "didn't try," "wasn't interested in school," and was "just plain lazy."

Available test data indicated that he had an I.Q. of 124. A Stanford Binet test of intelligence administered by the University psychology staff showed a score of *150!* Informal tests of reading indicated that his instructional level for reading was at sixth grade, while his spelling achievement was that of the average third-grade pupil.

A retarded reader, with rare exceptions, is not an inefficient reader because he so desires. His problem is usually due to multiple and, oftentimes, devious causal factors. Oscar was no exception. His attitude toward school, teachers, and himself was conflicting, and uncertain.

During several interviews he volunteered comments similar to the following. "Sometimes I'm real stupid in school, and at home, too. Sometimes I know more than anybody in our class. I even know more than our teacher sometimes, but I quit telling her because she said I just tried to show off."

Testing revealed that Oscar had an exceptional knowledge of words when they were presented in isolation, but he rarely applied his vocabulary knowledge to reading school books. He "read" assigned seventh-grade texts with difficulty and boredom. He read for broad general ideas that were incorrect many times because he skipped necessary supporting details. When this weakness was pointed out to him, he brushed it aside with, "All that little junk is for kids and teachers. Anybody can read that little stuff."

After a thorough evaluation and diagnosis, he was transferred to a more understanding and sympathetic teacher who understood reading problems. He was given *reading instruction* with sixth-grade materials and taught to read for *specific purposes,* including supporting details. He was allowed to choose supplementary reading materials according to his own interests and at a more difficult reading level. In addition, he volunteered to participate in a six-week corrective reading program.

One year after he was tested, Oscar brought his latest report card to the writer and said, "You probably won't believe your eyes but look at this—all 'B's.' Next year I'll get all 'A's'!"

6. *The continuous, cooperative evaluation of reading is the keystone to student growth and development in learning.*

An ever-growing number of high school personnel are recognizing that the giving of standardized achievement tests is only a part of an evaluation program. Administrators and teachers are discovering the need for, and the value of, a continuous program of evaluation. The evaluation of student growth in reading, for example, is dependent upon *qualitative* as well as *quantitative* information about student progress. Objective test scores have merit in an evaluative program but these data must be supplemented with qualitative information from teachers and counselors. No one person or group has the time, opportunity, or insight to evaluate adequately the overall growth and development of each student. An efficient, worthwhile evaluative program must be a *cooperative* and *continuous process.*

Continuous evaluation of reading is one of the classroom teacher's most useful techniques for improving student learning in content areas. Some students who are presently reading in keeping with their overall growth and development may *not* be reading efficiently a year or two hence unless evaluation is continuous. Ample evidence, and experience reveals that some students who have difficulty in learning subject matter actually regress in both learning and reading after attending classes for a full year. In these instances, continuous evaluation by the teacher might have prevented a serious reading problem and the loss of valuable student time.

Continuous classroom evaluation helps the teacher to determine the effectiveness of the learning experiences that he has provided for the students. Any weaknesses or extreme difficulties can be remedied immediately without undue loss of pupil-teacher time. Guided practice, reteaching, review, reinforcement—call it what you will—necessary for student retention of learning can be initiated when it is needed. Granted, some learning takes place with but one exposure to a stimulus, or stimuli. The amount of learning occurring from one exposure to a teaching experience is determined largely by: (1) the extent of the learner's need; (2) the receptiveness of the individual at the time; and (3) the strength of the stimuli. Few teacher-provided experiences meet the criteria necessary for learning to occur from a single presentation.

A master teacher is constantly making on-the-spot appraisals of observed student behavior. He may note, for example, that Ralph tries hard to study his assigned reading; but he scowls, twists his ear or scratches his head, he looks out the window, he sharpens his pencil, or he gets a drink of water. In addition, the teacher notes that he *vocalizes* or says some words aloud. He often uses his finger or a pencil to point out each word.

What should be the teacher's reaction to Ralph's behavior? Should he request Ralph to cease scratching, twisting, and moving about? Or should he seek the causes of the undue activity and inability to concentrate on reading? In this instance, the teacher recognized Ralph's actions as symptoms of nervous tension. His actions were signals that the material he was trying to read was too difficult for him. When the teacher provided him with easier reading material, the cause of his behavior was removed and the symptoms disappeared.

In another instance the teacher may note Mary's puzzled expression as she rereads a particular section, checks her dictionary, and then refers to an encyclopedia. Mary's look of puzzlement changes to bewilderment, and he knows that she needs help now. He may only need to ask her a single question to help bring meaning to the perplexing material, or it may be necessary for Mary to reread the material again in order that she understand the nuances of several of the author's words. Whatever the cause, he is there to give help at the time it is needed.

Sole responsibility for continuous evaluation should not be delegated to or limited to the teacher, however. After, and during each major learning experience, each student should be given guidance in how to think through his difficult or worrisome spots. He should learn to evaluate his own weaknesses and strengths. He should know *what* he knows, and *why* he knows it. He should know also *when* he needs additional help and information and *where* to search for further information and help for a full understanding of the learning experience.

Many teachers have reacted to the preceding statements about continuous evaluation by saying, "What you call *continuous evaluation* is just good teaching." Continuous evaluation *is* a part of good teaching. It is more than on-the-spot help; it is more than a test or several tests; it is more than teacher judgment. It is a combination of all these techniques. It is the weighing of one set of measurements against another, judging them in relation to the total learning experience, diagnosing pupil needs, and structuring new learning experiences according to each student's needs at that time. It is a never-ending process composed of objective data, observed student behavior, anecdotal records, checklists, informal inventories, expressed attitudes. It is *never final nor is it exact,* but it is a sound, systematic procedure for improving teaching and student learning.

7. *The reading of subject matter must be a satisfying experience.*

When the student has finished reading an assignment in history, literature, or science, he should feel that he has spent his time well. He should feel that he has learned something of value. He should have a feeling of satisfaction, a justifiable pride in a job well done.

The satisfied reader is one who has solved some problem, acquired new facts, unearthed additional information, or gained new knowledge. He *knows* that he has learned. He has achieved definite, clearly defined goals. He is ready and eager to achieve further goals of learning. Classes are not a bore or situations to be dreaded; they are opportunities for further learning.

On the other hand, far too many students leave a classroom or finish a reading assignment with emotionally unhealthy feelings. The reading and the teacher's discussion of the material leaves them with a feeling of anxiousness, hopelessness, and frustration. These students know that they have either done poorly nor failed in their attempts to learn. Release from the classroom and/or the textbook is not an escape but only a temporary reprieve. The emotionally upsetting experiences of today must be met tomorrow, and tomorrow, and tomorrow.

The student in this kind of situation will rarely, if ever, feel the pride of accomplishment. For him, there is no positive achievement. He probably will never reach his potential or expectations. For him, reading is a bitter experience. He probably will never learn the facts, the vocabulary, the concepts involved in the particular subject areas.

The student who is assigned reading materials *at his own level of reading*, and who has definite purposes for reading, will acquire some facts, some vocabulary, and some concepts of subject matter. He will be one of those who achieve satisfaction from reading. The satisfaction he receives can become a powerful motivator for further reading and learning.

8. *Efficient reading is a prerequisite for successful student learning of subject matter.*

There is no dodging the issue, today's schools are reading schools. The student who is a poor reader is seriously handicapped. Generally speaking, the inefficient reader faces an almost insurmountable task in attempting to learn successfully in any subject-matter area. Even the most cursory glance at any secondary curriculum will support the estimates that from 80 to 90 per cent of school subjects demand efficient student reading.

An accepted psychological and educational principle is that learning comes through experiencing. The student must, and can, only learn through self-participation. The teacher can no more give a student the vocabulary and concepts of his course than he can digest his food for him. Vocabulary and concepts must be developed by each student through his own direct and vicarious experiences.

Fortunately, the poor reader may participate in many meaningful, though limited, learning experiences in some subject-matter areas. In biology, for example, the poor reader may, with a minimum of help, learn much during a laboratory period. In addition, he may acquire additional learning through vicarious experiences such as listening to pupil-teacher discussion, viewing film strips, watching moving pictures, looking at pictures, and observing demonstrations.

Unfortunately, no one can possibly engage in all the direct experiences required for learning. Although numerous direct experiences are basic to all learning, vicarious experiences may be equally, or more, meaningful than direct experiences, *if* the student has a vital foundation of direct experiences. Even when an intelligent, but inefficient, reader is provided with many of the previously mentioned vicarious experiences, he is handicapped in learning. Because he cannot read successfully, his overall vocabulary will be inadequate or limited. His concepts will often lack depth because of a general lack of adequate language development. The poor reader's concept development and inspiration for new ideas are restricted *by* and *to* the kinds and depth of experiences in which he engaged. If he is unable to read the discussions and share in the written thoughts of great thinkers, his thinking is definitely circumscribed.

Teachers can provide students with a number of experiences that are helpful in learning subject matter, but there is no adequate substitute for reading. The efficient reader has the experience, skills, and understanding that enable him to seek and to use the kinds of materials he needs and wants. His time and learning are not determined by the rate of a group, class, lecture, or program; how rapidly or how slowly he reads is governed by his needs, his purposes, and the difficulty of the material.

SUMMARY

Lack of knowledge of what reading really is, has generated in the minds of secondary school and college teachers a disharmony between teaching reading and teaching subject-matter area. There is no dilemma, there is no contradiction; for *reading and subject matter cannot be divorced.* Recognizing, knowing, and understanding the complexity of the reading process, however, will undoubtedly place in the teacher's hand the tools necessary to lead his students to the maximum performance ability. In addition to the mechanical part of the reading process, teachers and students must realize that the greater part of the reading process is embedded in and grows out of the psychological components of the individual. Research further evidenced that there exists a wide range of reading ability within any class or group of secondary-school students and college freshmen, and that successful teaching can only be accomplished if the teacher knows the what, how, and why to cope with this problem.

These then are the principles to be noted:

1. Reading is a highly complex thinking process in which the entire organism participates.

2. The reading achievement of secondary and college students varies greatly and all students are not efficient readers.
3. Improvement in reading and learning in content areas is best achieved when reading is taught by subject-matter teachers.
4. To achieve maximum learning, teaching must begin at the student's instructional reading level.

SELECTED REFERENCES

1. Betts, Emmett Albert. *Foundations of Reading Instruction.* Cincinnati: American Book Co., 1957.
2. Bond, Guy L., and Kegler, Stanley B. *Reading Instruction in the Senior High School.* Sixtieth Yearbook, Part I, National Society for the Study of Education. Chicago: The University of Chicago Press, 1961.
3. Carter, Homer L. J. *Effective Use of Textbooks in the Reading Program.* The Eighth Yearbook of the National Reading Conference for Colleges and Adults. Fort Worth: Texas Christian University Press, 1959.
4. De Boer, John J., and Whipple, Gertrude. *Reading Development in Other Curriculum Areas.* The Sixtieth Yearbook, Part I, National Society for the Study of Education. Chicago: The University of Chicago Press, 1961.
5. Halfter, Irma T., and Douglas, Frances M. "Inadequate College Readers," *Journal of Developmental Reading,* Vol. 1 (Summer, 1958).
6. Parker, Don H., *et al. SRA Reading Laboratory.* Chicago: Science Research Associates, 1960.
7. Penty, Ruth. *Reading Ability and High School Drop-Outs.* New York: Bureau of Publications, Teachers College, Columbia University, 1956.
8. Preston, Ralph C., and Tufts, Edwin N. "The Reading Habits of Superior College Students," *Journal of Experimental Education,* Vol. 16 (March, 1948), pp. 196–202.
9. Russell, David H. *Children Learn To Read* (2d ed.). Boston: Ginn & Co., 1961.
10. Shaw, Phillip. *Reading in College.* The Sixtieth Yearbook, Part I, National Society for the Study of Education. Chicago: The University of Chicago Press, 1961.
11. Smith, Nila Banton. *Be a Better Reader.* Vols. I–VI. Englewood Cliffs, N.J.: Prentice-Hall, Inc., 1959.
12. Triggs, Frances Oralind, *et al. Diagnostic Reading Tests.* New York: The Committee on Diagnostic Reading Tests, Inc., 1947–1963.
13. Woolf, Maurice D., and Woolf, Jeanne A. *Remedial Reading.* New York: McGraw-Hill Book Co., Inc., 1957.

SUGGESTED ADDITIONAL READING

Carter, Homer L., and McGinnis, Dorothy J. *Learning to Read: A Handbook for Teachers.* New York: McGraw-Hill Book Co., Inc., 1953.

Gray, William S. *Principles of Methods in Teaching Reading*. The Eighteenth Yearbook, Part II, National Society for the Study of Education. Chicago: The University of Chicago Press, 1919.

Hook, J. N. *The Teaching of High School English* (3d ed.). New York: The Ronald Press Co., 1965.

Sheldon, William D. *Reading Instruction in Junior High School.* The Sixtieth Yearbook, Part I, National Society for the Study of Education. Chicago: University of Chicago Press, 1961.

Townsend, Agatha. "An Investigation of Certain Relationships of Spelling with Reading and Academic Aptitude," *Journal of Educational Research,* Vol. 40 (February, 1947), pp. 465–71.

4

MOTIVATING READING FOR LEARNING

Why do some children learn to read and become efficient readers by the time they enter high school while others remain inefficient? Reasons why students do or do not become efficient readers are too numerous to be included in one chapter or even in one book. But motivation is one of the most important of these reasons. Inasmuch as it plays a leading role in reading and learning, this chapter will concern itself with students' motives for reading and with the teacher's role in motivating students to read.

Most of the reading done by high school and college students is assigned. Since teachers assign materials, they expect and usually assume that each student will read the assignments. They plan classwork on the assumption that each student has read as directed. Is the teacher's assigning of material a sufficient motive for the student's reading? That many students do not read and do not learn what is expected of them or what is assigned to them is not a secret. Teachers and students know that reading achievement varies and that some students never read all that is required for a course, while other students read not only everything that is assigned but numerous additional materials.

Students who do not do the required reading in high school and college frequently complain that they do not have time to read all of the assigned materials. In many cases, their statements are true. Some students read so slowly that they can never complete all of their assignments that require reading. In other cases the "lack of time" statement is a camouflage for the real reasons. What are some factors that lead certain students to read widely and intensively while others do little or no reading, assigned or unassigned? What kinds of reading materials encourage student reading? What kinds discourage reading? Can teachers do anything to *motivate* students to read?

When we seek to find out *why* students act as they do, we look to the field of psychology for some of the answers. In this instance we shall investigate the role of motivation and its effect on student reading. The reader must be prepared for dissenting points of view. Not all psychologists are in agreement in all areas of learning theory. Travers (8, p. 165) likens the various theories of motivation to the parts of a jigsaw puzzle: some of the pieces seem to fit together but the total picture remains a blank. Although we shall be unable to place all the pieces of the jigsaw puzzle into the total picture, we should be able to help the teacher to gain a better understanding of how to motivate reading in the classroom. For this purpose, it is necessary to review simply and rapidly some reasons *why* students act as they do.

Physiological Motives

Most students and teachers have taken courses in psychology in which motivation is described as being rooted in the *physiological needs* of the organism. This theory of motivation is based upon the concept of homeostasis. Homeostasis, stripped of esoteric terminology, means that an organism continually attempts to maintain a physiological balance or equilibrium. If the organism becomes too warm, it *acts* to cool itself. It may cease physical activity, perspire, seek a cooler spot, swim, or drink water until it again feels comfortable.

Some of the better-known terms that have been used to describe and account for motivation are "basic motives," "basic systems of drives," and "basic needs." The motives or drives include hunger, thirst, pain, and sex, but at the present there is no single agreed-upon list of basic drives (8, p. 147). Nevertheless, psychologists believe that the motivated person is one who has certain basic drives or needs that must be satisfied. McDonald (2, pp. 182–209) says that drives such as hunger and thirst have fairly obvious physiological bases. "A *drive is an initiating neuro-physiological condition, that is a change in the neuro-physiological structure of the person which is the organic basis for the energy change we call 'motivation'* " (2, p. 83). But not all motivation is initiated by internal stimuli. External stimuli, especially painful ones, can also cause the organism to act.

Sears and Hilgard (6, pp. 182-209) suggest that the theory of basic drives has recently undergone some serious questioning, and in certain cases it has been subject to criticism. However, they note that, although the precise relationship between motivation and learning may be uncertain, the general importance of student motivation in learning can scarcely be denied. Gates and Jennings say that regardless of the manner in which motivation is conceived, "it is recognized as an important concept of nearly all current systems of psychology" (1, p. 110).

Psychological Motives

Although some psychologists suggest that all motives can be explained by organic needs (6, p. 207–9), teachers need information about motivation that they can use in the classroom. Withholding food and water from a student until he completes certain learning experiences or inflicting pain unless he reacts positively to a particular lesson is hardly an accepted educational practice. Fortunately students respond to other than *physiological stimuli;* they act on *psychological* motives. Psychological motives are especially powerful because they are difficult (7, p. 270), sometimes impossible, to satisfy. Some of the psychological motives that teachers recognize and can use to improve student learning are: curiosity, success, achievement, activity, self-esteem, and belonging.

Man's Desires as Motivators

Simply because man is the kind of a creature that he is, he has a number of desires and wants. Some of his desires are based upon physiological needs; others are initiated externally. Maslow (3, pp. 370–96) discusses man's wants and his desires as giving rise to powerful drives or needs that form hierarchies of prepotency. He lists the major needs in order of prepotency as: (1) The physiological needs, (2) The love needs, (3) The esteem needs, (4) The need for self-actualization, and (5) The need to know.

According to Maslow's theory, man's basic needs are physiological and must be met before further needs can make their appearance. Hence his use of the term "prepotency." In Maslow's hierarchy of needs, the need to know is at the top of the list. If his theory is acceptable, it has a definite message for teachers. It means that a student needs to be reasonably well nourished, be relatively free from fatigue and pain, be an accepted member of the class, be accepted and respected for what he is, and be making reasonable progress in the class. When he reaches the stage of a need to know, he is curious about all that is in his environment. He, for example, both satisfies and stimulates some of his curiosity through listening. He is fascinated by the roar of an automobile engine as it is accelerated and decelerated. He is moved by the rhythm of the poet's words and wonders why and how words can awaken such feeling within him. He notes the traveling V of wild geese honking a pathway south and asks himself, "How do they know where to go? Will they return by the same path? Do they ever get lost? What causes one goose to come from far back and take over the lead?"

When he reaches the stage of being curious about what is happening around him, of being interested in why particular events occur and others do not, of being ready to learn for the sake of knowing, he is propelled into learning by the most powerful of all incentives—self motivation.

Desire for Success as a Motivator

Built-in motivators for student reading and learning are the desires for *success* and *achievement*. Most children attending school want to achieve. No child wants to be a failure. Students rarely fail because they want to, although at times a harassed secondary teacher may feel that because Willie takes no interest in reading and tries little to learn his lessons, Willie *desires* to be nothing more than a failure. To conclude that Willie wants to fail is usually to do Willie an injustice.

Teacher's must use caution, insight, and much common sense when interpreting observed behavior. Willie's actions may be his way of saying, "Look teacher. I want to learn but I just can't. You say, 'Read your book.' Day after day after day I sit and I look at your old book. I know the answers you want are in there, but them words don't make sense. Maybe if you had an easier book I could read that. Please help me read."

It is pertinent that teachers seek the causes of student behavior rather than inferring that students prefer to fail rather than try to succeed. There is a world of difference between causes of student behavior and inferences drawn from observed behavior.

Socioeconomic Class as a Motivator

Students differ in the kinds of needs they have and in the way in which they meet their needs. The social class in which a student is reared, the kind of home life he experiences, and the kinds of friends he keeps affect his needs and the manner in which he seeks to satisfy them. Knowledge of a student's total environmental background is a prerequisite for teacher understanding of *why* a student reacts to a learning situation as he does. For example, a number of studies have shown that, as a group, children from middle-class families show a greater desire to be successful in school than do children from lower-class families.

The secondary teacher who attempts to help a particular student to improve his reading may become frustrated because the student has no apparent desire or need to improve his reading. The student may have the potential to become a highly efficient reader and an excellent student, but until he himself feels the need to become such a reader he will not make the necessary effort. He will not be motivated. He may, for example, be working after school as an apprentice and be doing well. As a part-time worker, he may at this time have little need for reading and writing. All he can see is that he is kept from earning more money because he must attend school. For him, schooling is a servitude that must be endured until he reaches a prescribed age or grade. Motivating this kind of student to become an effective reader is most difficult, especially if his feelings about school are reinforced at home and work.

When parents hold reading in low esteem, their views may affect their children's attitudes toward reading (1, p. 113). A secondary student from this kind of home may see little reason for reading. Recognition of these facts does not imply passive acceptance of them. It means that teachers must use every bit of their knowledge and understanding to make use of psychological motives for furthering each student's learning.

Social Acceptance as a Motivator

The desire to learn to read is prevalent among most children who enter school. They want to learn to read because learning to read is the socially accepted expectation. Children's parents, relatives, and friends expect youngsters to read, and when children demonstrate that they can pronounce written words and get meaning from them, they are *rewarded* for their achievement. The reward may vary from a pat on the head or an approving smile to loving praise from mother or a dime from Uncle John. Regardless of the kind of reward, the important factor is that a reward has been given. The reader has achieved *success.* His achievement has been noted. His self-esteem has been elevated.

Do you feel that the child who learns to read, even in the restricted sense of reading noted in the preceding paragraph, will be interested in improving his reading? Did he get off to a good beginning? Will he develop self-esteem if he continues to have successful reading experiences? Will he become a self-motivated reader who finds reading satisfying? The answers to these questions are obvious.

Not all children respond to the same incentives, nor are all children rewarded for learning to read. Some children experience great difficulty in learning to read. Instead of finding reading to be a *rewarding, successful,* pleasurable experience, they find it a difficult, distasteful, sometimes impossible task leading to reproof. In extreme cases, children can become so frustrated by their inability to learn to read that they become reading problems. Some of these children respond to the efforts of reading specialists, some need additional therapy, some never learn to read efficiently, and some never learn to read.

At the secondary and college levels students are sometimes inefficient readers because they are not interested in reading. Some are not interested because they have never learned to read effectively. They managed to pick up sufficient facts and information, through listening, to pass required courses without reading. Others are uninterested in reading because they have never had the opportunity to read books that they wanted to read. Teachers and parents combined to force them to read so many assigned books that they never had time to read something of their own choosing. Such practice often contributes to a student's lack of desire to read.

High school and college students can be motivated to want to read when they have real and recognizable purposes for reading. As students read more, especially when they set their own purposes for reading, they improve their reading skills and they satisfy certain needs. When students realize that they read more effectively and reach many goals through reading, they become highly interested in reading.

Student Curiosity as a Motive for Reading

Teachers in any subject-matter area can capitalize upon the student's curiosity as a means to increasing his motivation for reading and learning. How can a teacher of subject matter arouse a student's curiosity about that subject matter in order to stimulate his reading in it? The teacher can discuss an interesting incident or topic; or he may ask questions about a picture or about a demonstration that has been performed, after which he can refer students to reading materials that will answer their questions. Too often, a teacher does an injustice to students by answering all their questions. If he wants them to become independent readers and learners, he must provide opportunities for them to learn through reading.

One technique that teachers use to arouse student curiosity in reading is that of having interesting, well-written books available for reading. Sometimes teachers display book jackets in an eye-catching arrangement and place the books on a table beneath them. At other times the teacher may read to the class short selections from several books. Books about animals and strange lands and peoples, joke books, humorous books, and books about sports and adventure appeal generally to junior high school boys, but many of these kinds of books should also be available to high school students because, although high school students are usually most interested in magazines and newspapers, they retain an interest in books about adventure, science, and romance. Girls are not so fussy as boys about the kinds of books they read. They will read and enjoy books that are preferred by boys, but as a group girls express preference for romantic tales, and for stories about family life, mystery, and humor. Regardless of grade level or intelligence, most students enjoy reading comic books. And there are many reasons why students enjoy them. All comic books are not trash, but all can be read by even the inefficient readers. The better comic books are interesting, action-packed stories whose characters use a language that the reader can understand.

The teacher of subject matter can arouse student curiosity for reading and learning in multitudinous ways if he so desires. He may present a new learning experience or open up a new area of learning by demonstrations, using film strips or slides, showing moving pictures, and asking questions. For example, the teacher of science who wishes to introduce a unit on pressure may have a picture of a deep-sea diver and ask why the diver must guard against *bends.* Some students will have a knowledge of *bends* and can help to give the word meaning for the other students. Or it may be necessary for students to clarify their idea of *bends* by using the dictionary and other books. The cause of *bends* can lead the pupils into the unit on pressure.

In another instance the teacher of science might arouse student curiosity by telling about the can of soft drink that "blew up" when he left it in the "deep freeze." Some students will insist that freezing does not cause cans to burst, because they have frozen soft drinks without bursting the can. Others may have had an experience similar to that of the teacher. The students then need to learn why one can explodes while another does not.

Any subject-matter teacher may sometimes simply write a new and unusual word on the chalkboard. Since most students are conditioned to note what the teacher writes on the chalkboard, someone is sure to ask, "What's that for? What does it mean?"

The shop teacher has myriad opportunities for arousing the student's curiosity. He may display a new tool, an example for scroll work, or a mold for casting. Students want to know what these objects are and how they are used.

What Is the Teacher's Task After He Has Aroused Student's Curiosity?

After arousing the students' curiosity, the teacher should *avoid giving them the answers.* Teachers too often destroy students' incentives for learning by their willingness to supply the answers for the students. The teacher's job is to have materials available or know where to direct students in order that they may read to find the answers. Finding answers is a first step toward problem-solving. And problem-solving is an excellent means for developing critical reading and critical thinking.

The preceding paragraph is an oversimplification of the process of going from student curiosity to critical reading and thinking through problem-solving, but space does not permit a more thorough discussion of the process in this chapter. Critical reading is discussed more fully in Chapter 11.

The motivation of students does not consist of tricks, gimmicks, and devices. Student motivation is the product of goals and purposes. Students must learn to set purposes for reading and learning, but, like teachers, they need to be shown *how* to set purposes and *why* purposes are necessary. Purposes must be real and must make sense to students. Purposes lead to the achievement of recognized goals.

Habit as a Motive for Reading

One of the strongest, and probably one of the most overlooked, motives for reading is that of habit. Can reading become a habit, and, as such, can it be its own energizer for further reading? There is ample evidence in every schoolroom in America that reading often becomes a satisfying habit. The student who is an efficient reader finds reading to be a pleasurable experience. He finds answers to perplexing questions, satisfies his curiosity about strange lands, roams through outer space, or stalks deer in primitive forests. By means of a book he becomes an explorer, scientist, missionary, or a buccaneer. He communicates with the founders of America. He witnesses the fall of Rome.

The good reader almost instinctively reaches for something to read when he has completed assigned school tasks or when he is not engaged in other activities. The good reader reads anything and everything. The observant teacher will note students reading in buses, in automobiles, on trains, in libraries, in the halls, and even on the playgrounds. Children at breakfast become engrossed in reading the messages on cereal boxes. In restaurants, some customers read the entire menu, front, back, and in between. Such activity is in keeping with what psychologists tell us—that reading may become its own motivating force (7, p. 272).

The student who develops the habit of reading is a thrifty person. He rarely wastes time because he has nothing to do. If his friends are elsewhere, if the television is not working or unappealing, or if no pressing tasks are demanding his attention, he turns to reading.

The student who reads widely is rewarded by the acquisition of additional information, facts, vocabulary, and concepts that make him a more interesting person and permit him to participate intelligently in discussions on diverse subjects with many people. He is abreast of new developments and problems. He is aware of the rich heritage of his country and his ancestors. And, because he has acquired a wide background of vicarious experiences through reading, he is more apt to be tolerant of, if not sympathetic to, the views of others who may disagree with him.

Success as a Motivator

Success is one of the most powerful motivators in any human endeavor. A popular saying among businessmen is, "Nothing succeeds like success." Teachers also recognize that students must achieve some degree of success if they are to continue to learn. But in the majority of secondary classrooms in America there are some students who regularly meet failure face-to-face because they are inefficient readers.

They have difficulty with reading for various reasons, and lack of self-motivation may be a contributor to their poor reading. But no matter how motivated a student may be, he cannot do the impossible. If he is unable to pronounce the written words in the textbook, they may as well be written in a foreign language. It is impossible for him to associate meaning with symbols that evoke no response, except frustration. For him, reading connotes failure instead of success.

If students could become achieving readers simply by being highly motivated, there would be few problem readers in high school and college. Important as it is, motivation alone will not solve reading problems.

Some secondary teachers become almost as frustrated as their inefficient readers because they fail in their attempt to teach subject matter to students who cannot read the assigned textbooks. Many of these teachers have assumed that all students who enter high school can read textbooks written for secondary subjects. Other teachers have assumed that the student who is having difficulty with reading is a hopeless case. These kinds of assumptions may appear to be plausible to teachers who have never had even a single course in reading. The assumptions, however, are erroneous.

Is it just, however, to blame secondary teachers for making the kinds of assumptions we noted? It must be recognized that the teaching of reading in high school and college is a comparatively new concept of the total reading program. Few secondary teachers, including English teachers, have had a course on how to teach reading. And many students who are now preparing to become teachers have not had, nor will they have any background for teaching reading. If blame must be placed for the secondary teacher's lack of understanding of the reading problem, it must be distributed widely.

Attempting to place blame for the lack of better teaching of reading in high school does not alleviate the "poor" reader's problem. Such a student needs help to improve his reading. Many students who enter high school as underachieving readers do receive help from their teachers and become more effective readers.

If secondary teachers would do no more than provide each student with reading materials that he could understand, many reading problems would solve themselves. Teachers who have given students reading assignments in materials below the level of the regular textbook are rewarded and, oftentimes, amazed at the change that occurs within the student. The difference between success and failure is great. And no one realizes how great that difference is until he experiences it.

Coincidentally, a high school science teacher who was a student in the writer's class during the 1963 summer session dropped into the office as this page was being written. He had seriously questioned that his tenth-grade students would even attempt to read materials other than the assigned textbook. But he was willing to try the experiment. What were the results? His words are: "You won't believe it, but this is the first time in my ten years of teaching that I know I really taught a lot of guys that I thought could never learn. I had to rewrite a lot of the lessons because there weren't any textbooks that I could get for the poor readers, but they read what I wrote. I can't tell you how much the boys learned but even their parents came to see me about it. Why didn't I do that before?" Later he said, "You know, this year I had only a couple of disciplinary problems. Last year I had to send lots of boys to the office."

The preceding example, only one of many, demonstrates the potency of success as a motivator for learning. The teacher's students learned science because he provided materials that they could read. They were able to concentrate on content instead of becoming confused by great numbers of unpronounceable words. They realized, perhaps for the first time in years, that they were not failures, that they were not stupid. They were learning. They were like the other students! Is there any question about why there were fewer disciplinary problems among them than in previous years?

Success as a motivator of reading and learning is not limited to students with reading problems. The average readers and the more efficient readers need the stimulation of having done well. At higher levels of reading, students who read critically and who gain new insights into problems recognize their achievements. They are spurred to further learning. And it is important that the student recognize and be aware of his successful achievement.

Student Interests as Motivators

Student interests are wide and varied and are influenced by many factors. The student's physical condition and makeup and his intelligence are primary determiners of his interests. For example, the small, somewhat frail, nearsighted, intelligent boy is more apt to be interested in reading than in playing baseball. The well-developed, physically rugged, intelligent boy is better equipped to excel in sports and will usually spend more time on athletics.

Numerous secondary and college students who seek help in reading at the Oregon State Reading Clinic say that they never had much interest in reading. With very few exceptions, these students are above the average in intelligence. Most of them experienced some difficulty with reading at the first- and second-grade levels. Only a few recall that their reading problems began in the intermediate grades. Most of these students had trouble in learning to read. They could recall particularly embarrassing episodes that occurred when they were called upon to read orally and failed miserably.

Mel is representative of the group. He said, "I always had trouble trying to say the words. All the other kids laugh when you make a mistake, so I just lost interest in trying to read. I found out I was pretty good in athletics so I spent all my time in the gym or on the field. I found out that when you're good, say in football, they quit laughing at you an' even try to help you get the answers to the tests. But I got good grades. I had a three-point* average when I graduated from high school. I didn't even know I wasn't good. I had offers of seven athletic scholarships but I went to ——— university my first year on an academic scholarship. I was first string on the frosh squad and could have been on the varsity my second year but I got hurt and the doctor says I can't play ball anymore so I transferred here. Now, how am I

* A three-point average is equivalent to a "B."

going to read right? I'm interested in reading now because I have to pass these courses."

What Are Interests? Almost everyone has a general idea of what is meant by the phrase "student interests." But, no one has yet captured an "interest" to put it on a slide, to study it under a microscope, or to draw clear, unchallengeable conclusions about it. Nevertheless, let us discuss some of the prevailing information about interests.

Interests have been classified as traits or attitudes (5, pp. 289–331), dispositions or tendencies (9, p. 129); they have been discussed as manifest interests, expressed interests, and inventoried interests (8, p. 178).

Although it is assumed that interests represent motives (8, p. 178), there is no research available that proves they are motives. However, most authorities agree that even though *interest* is a vague term (8, p. 177) for an elusive factor in human behavior (9, p. 128), *interest* is that *something* that impels or motivates the learner to strive for a particular goal.

It is generally agreed that interests are learned, acquired, and developed (7, p. 272). For example, the boy who has never gone fishing or whose friends do not go fishing knows nothing about fishing and will have no interest in it. Likewise, a boy will develop little interest in fishing if all of his experiences with fishing are miserable ones. Similarly, developing and acquiring an interest in reading and learning is not fostered by a lack of knowledge about reading, by inefficient reading, or by frustrating experiences with reading. The inefficient reader is rarely interested in reading. His interests are in those areas in which he can be *successful,* in which he can promote his *self-esteem,* and in which he can be *rewarded.*

Morse and Wingo (4, p. 119) see interests as modes of life that are closely associated with the student's emotional and social health. Students who develop interests that they can pursue successfully tend to acquire self-concepts that are in line with reality. And acquired interests apparently initiate behavior and continue to motivate that behavior until a particular goal is attained.

Summarizing our discussion of interests thus far indicates that: (1) interests are not inborn but are learned, acquired, and developed; (2) interests are related to meaning; (3) interests are closely associated with a person's social and emotional health; and (4) interests are, in some manner, capable of initiating and directing human behavior.

Goals, Interest, and Motivation

Teachers should realize that adult goals usually differ from student goals. The goals that adults set are not the goals students set, although students may be induced to strive for adult goals. A student, for example, may learn a particular lesson or skill, not for the purpose the teacher had in mind but for the grade he will receive for doing the lesson or learning the skill.

Because students, with varying degrees of success, reach goals set by teachers, many teachers argue that, if the grade calls forth student effort, the grade has justified itself. Has it really? Is it possible that the grade indicates that the student has learned to answer questions the way the teacher wants them to be answered? Is it possible that the student's goal becomes one of working for a grade rather than for knowledge? Is it possible that because teachers have not understood how to help students set their own goals for learning that they have unintentionally forced students to strive for a false goal—getting grades—rather than learning?

When teachers assume the responsibility for setting the goals of learning, the student is relieved of most of the responsibility for reaching those goals. When parents and teachers place great emphasis on grades, they force their goals upon the student. The student's goal may then become that of doing just enough work to acquire a passing grade. Even at the university level the primary goal of many students appears to be satisfied when the student receives an average grade. The student will do just enough work to keep him in school and eligible for certain student activities. His goals are not those of his parents or the institution. If he does not do well in a course he is often satisfied by saying, "The course is uninteresting." or "The professor doesn't motivate me."

Teachers can help the student by discussing his interests and goals with him, and by showing him that responsibility for learning is his own and not theirs.

Students often need teacher guidance in clarifying their goals and interests. Students develop interests in activities that give them an opportunity to succeed and to develop self-esteem. Many an intelligent student lacks interest in subject matter because he is handicapped by his inefficient reading skills. Because he is an inefficient reader he does poorly, or has failed in subject matter so often that he begins to believe that he is incapable of doing better. This kind of student must be given reading material that is at his *instructional level.* This means that if he is going to get meaning from reading, he must first be able to pronounce 95 per cent of the words. The student who is reading at his *instructional level* knows the vocabulary words and sufficient concepts with which to develop further concepts. He is not hampered by having to spend most of his time in working out the pronunciation of words but can concentrate on getting meaning from his reading. He learns the subject matter. No one needs to tell him that he has achieved success. He knows it. And the wise teacher will let the student know that he is also aware of the student's achievement.

If you, the teacher, can recognize when a student is hopelessly frustrated because he is forced into trying to read material beyond his reading skills, you can help him a thousandfold by giving him materials he can read. Oftentimes the difference between student failure and success is only a matter of one grade level in the difficulty of material!

Teachers can take advantage of student interest and student motives by asking pertinent questions about the reading material *before* the student begins to read. And, instead of being an answering service for student questions, *the teacher should ask the questions* that will place the responsibility upon the students for reading to learn and find the answers to the questions.

SUMMARY

The problem of motivating students to read to learn is an amazingly complex one. We have noted that although there is some disagreement and uncertainty about the exact relationship between reading-for-learning and motivation, there is an important general relationship between the two.

We know that there are certain motives that teachers can use to arouse student interest in reading and learning. We know that disagreement over technical terms does not detract from the fact that students act and react when they achieve success and self-esteem, and when they are interested. We know that student purposes or student goals are the real reasons for student activity; that the teacher's job is to initiate activities that will foster student motivation for learning; that the interested student will read and learn if he is given materials that he can read.

The following list of generalizations about motives and interests is based upon information presented in this chapter. While not extensive, the list should be of value in helping the teacher of subject matter to understand better why students act as they do. It should help him in planning activities that will encourage student learning.

1. Motives may be derived from both physiological and psychological needs.
2. Little learning occurs unless the student wants to learn.

3. Psychological motives for student learning can be induced by the teacher who is capable of arranging activities that assure each student some measure of success.
4. Interest is a powerful incentive for learning. Interests are learned. Students who have limited interests can develop new interests.
5. Student goals are more important to students than are teacher goals. But students, if they must, will work toward the teacher's goals. It is highly probable that students substitute goals of their own that are compatible with teacher goals.
6. A student who is working to achieve his own goals is self-motivated and assumes responsibility for his own learning.
7. Teachers should strive to provide learning activities that encourage student goals.
8. If a student is to be motivated to read to learn, he must have materials which he can read.
9. The student who is an inefficient reader is rarely interested in learning through reading.
10. The efficient reader is a successful reader and is therefore motivated to read extensively.
11. Reading may become its own motivator for learning.

SELECTED REFERENCES

1. Gates, Arthur I., and Jennings, Frank G. *The Role of Motivation.* The Sixtieth Yearbook, Part I, National Society for the Study of Education, Chicago: University of Chicago Press, 1961. Pp. 109–26.
2. McDonald, Frederick J. *Educational Psychology.* Belmont, Calif.: Wadsworth Publishing Co., Inc., 1959.
3. Maslow, A. H. "A Theory of Human Motivation," *Psychological Review,* Vol. 50 (July, 1943), pp. 370–96.
4. Morse, William C., and Wingo, G. Max. *Psychology and Teaching,* 2d ed. Chicago: Scott, Foresman & Co., 1962.
5. Ryans, David G. "Motivation in Learning," *Psychology of Learning.* The Forty-first Yearbook, Part II, National Society for the Study of Education. Chicago: The University of Chicago Press, 1942.
6. Sears, Pauline S., and Hilgard, Ernest R. "The Teacher's Role in the Motivation of the Learner," *Theories of Learning and Instruction.* The Sixty-third Yearbook, Part I, National Society for the Study of Education. Chicago: The University of Chicago Press, 1964.
7. Smith, Henry P., and Dechant, Emerald V. *Psychology in Teaching Reading.* Englewood Cliffs, N.J.: Prentice-Hall, Inc., 1961.
8. Travers, Robert M. W. *Essentials of Learning: An Overview for Students of Education.* New York: The Macmillan Co., 1963.
9. Witty, Paul A. "The Role of Interest," *Development In and Through Reading.* The Sixtieth Yearbook, Part I, National Society for the Study of Education. Chicago: The University of Chicago Press, 1961.

SUGGESTED ADDITIONAL READING

Development In and Through Reading. The Sixtieth Yearbook, Part I, National Society for the Study of Education. Chicago: The University of Chicago Press, 1961.

GETZELS, JACOB W. "The Nature of Reading Interests: Psychological Aspects," *Developing Permanent Interest in Reading.* Supplementary Educational Monographs, No. 84. Chicago: The University of Chicago Press, 1956.

HOLLINGSHEAD, A. B. *Elmtown's Youth; The Impact of Social Classes on Adolescents.* New York: John Wiley & Sons, Inc., 1949.

WARNER, W. LLOYD, HAVIGHURST, R. J., and LOEB, MARTIN B. *Who Shall Be Educated?* New York: Harper & Row, Inc., 1944.

WARNER, WILLIAM LLOYD, MEEKER, MARCHIA, and EELLS, KENNETH. *Social Class in American.* Chicago: Science Research Associates, 1949.

WITTY, PAUL. "Interest, Effort, and Success—Bases for Effective Reading," *Education,* Vol. 79 (April, 1959), pp. 48–87.

5

EVALUATION OF READING IN SUBJECT MATTER

One of the most baffling problems confronting the secondary teacher is that of trying to teach subject matter to pupils who are unable to read the assigned text. But if the teacher is baffled, and sometimes exasperated, what are the feelings of his students? Until the teacher knows which students can read the assigned text, and until he makes necessary adjustments for those who cannot read it, effective learning in subject matter in his classroom will be limited. This critical problem must be solved because it affects the mental health not only of the student but of the teacher.

Improving teacher education and preparation in the evaluation of student reading achievement is the first step toward solution. According to informal surveys conducted by the writer, great discrepancy exists beween teacher judgment of student ability to read assigned textbooks and actual pupil reading achievement. Some professors and high school teachers say that from 95 to 100 per cent of their students can read the assigned text, while other teachers and professors in the same school and subject area feel that only 10 to 25 per cent of the students can read assigned materials. These statements are evidence that teachers are often totally unprepared to understand and cope with students' reading problems in content areas.

Evaluation Defined

"Evaluation" is an illusive, loosely used term. Teachers and administrators tend to think of testing and evaluation as being synonymous. Testing skills and facts is but one important phase of the evaluative process. "Evaluation," as it is used in this text, recognizes that, although testing is an important part of evaluation, it is not the total process. *"Evaluation" may be defined as an educated, honest, orderly attempt to judge the approximate achievement of a student in light of clearly defined goals.*

The reader will note that the definition stresses *an orderly attempt to judge the approximate achievement of a student in light of defined goals.* The words "approximate achievement" are used advisedly because scores and judgments are too often taken at face value. Test scores and judgments are necessary for evaluating, but they must be viewed as *indicators* and *not as determiners* of student progress or potential. Ebel, an authority on tests, cautions teachers against overemphasizing test scores when he says, "No test score is as precise as the numbers with which it is reported" (5, pp. 20–24). All other facets of evaluation such as teacher observation, ancecdotal records, autobiographies, and cumulative records, which are also subject to some error or misinterpretation, must be considered in the evaluation of students.

Another point contained in the definition of evaluation is that of *defined goals.* Every teacher has certain broad, general goals that he hopes will be attained by the students in his class. Sometimes these goals are clearly stated, but many times they remain only vague generalizations. Until goals are *specifically defined,* we are never sure that they have been reached because we have no way of assessing them. Students and teachers must be aware of, and must define, specific goals in any area of learning. In English, for example, a broad goal may be to "develop an appreciation of good literature." Frankly, this is a long-term goal that cannot be measured in a short period of time. That is not to imply that the goal is valueless or unattainable, but it does imply that, by themselves, long-range goals are insufficient for guiding classroom learning. Students need the challenge, the motivation, and the satisfaction of achieving specific, measurable, attainable goals. The English teacher who states specifically that all students in English must master the spelling of the most common 2,000 words in English has set a goal that the pupil understands. Further, he can measure his objective and, with minor exceptions, pupils can achieve the goal.

Students Are More Than "Good" or "Poor" Readers

The terms "good reader" and "poor reader" are used continually to describe the reading achievement of students. Although these terms enjoy wide use and have broad connotations, they contribute little to the understanding of the "poor reader's" problems or to the techniques to be used for improving his reading. Conversely, to say, "Bill is a good reader," may be not only erroneous but detrimental to him. The following example illustrates the fallacy of such inadequate terms when discussing reading.

Miss X, a secondary teacher, well prepared in subject matter but totally lacking experience in the teaching of reading, was determined to help her students read better. She called upon a reading consultant for advice and said, "I want to see what we can do to help Dave. He is a poor reader, but I'm at a loss to help him."

Dave was given standardized and informal tests of reading and the results were diagnosed. Data from the informal inventory indicated that he was *not* a poor reader but that he was reading as well as could be expected. A check of his ability to understand material read to him showed that he was reading up to his probable capacity. The examiner explained that according to the test results, Dave was probably a slow learner but *not* a retarded reader. However, the examiner noted that his conclusions were tentative and stressed the need for a more thorough evaluation of Dave's competencies and reading potential. Accordingly a competent psychologist tested Dave and concluded that on the basis of Dave's performance on two different individualized tests of intelligence, he was a slow learner. Further checking of Dave's past records showed that he had consistently received scores on various types of intelligence and achievement tests that were indicative of a slow learner.

Does the fact that Dave was a slow learner and not a retarded reader have any implication for the secondary teacher? Emphatically yes! When Miss X understood that Dave was working to the best of his ability, she stopped trying to force him to do more than he was capable of doing. Her action led to a better student-teacher relationship and, more importantly, it helped to dissipate all the built-up tensions in both of them.

While discussing Dave's problem with the examiner, Miss X pointed to Alex and said, "Now, there is a *good* reader. His problem is that he's too good. He has too much free time." When it was suggested that Alex might also like to be tested for reading achievement, he and Miss X were pleased. Both, however, were greatly displeased when the results of the tests showed that Alex was a *retarded* reader. "But that isn't possible!" Miss X protested. "Alex is one of my best students. He can read eleventh-grade texts as easily as he can these tenth-grade texts!" She punctuated each sentence with the snap of spike heels against the floors.

She was correct about one thing. Alex could read eleventh-grade materials. According to the informal tests, his instructional level of reading was at the eleventh grade. But had he been reading in keeping with his ability, he would have been reading college-level materials. Because he had rarely been assigned materials that were challenging reading for him, he lacked vocabulary and many of the higher-level reading skills necessary for college reading. *Alex was a retarded reader* because he was reading much below his potential. He was not a good reader. A "good reader" is one who is making optimal use of his mental equipment. To use less makes of him a *retarded reader.*

In this instance, calling Alex a "good reader" was neither prudent nor helpful. Fortunately both Alex and Miss X recovered quickly from their first shocked moment of truth. Both were sufficiently intelligent to recognize and to understand that the examiner was dealing with facts and was as eager to help Alex as was Miss X. The teacher, the examiner, and Alex discussed Alex's needs, and together they developed a program of reading for him. A year later Alex said, "That was the best thing that ever happened to me. I found out that I had been kidding myself and my teachers for a long time."

The preceding illustrations are not unique. Similar examples can be found in most secondary classes. They have been used to point out: (1) that students may suffer from being forced to read constantly above or below their own capabilities; (2) that teachers must know more about reading and reading levels; (3) that teachers need to use specific vocabulary when discussing reading retardation; and (4) that teachers should know what is meant by the terms "developmental reader," "corrective" or "retarded reader," and "remedial reader."

Clarification of Reading Terminology

Teachers, and students preparing to be teachers, are confused often by the indiscriminately synonymous use of the terms "remedial reader," "retarded reader," "corrective reader," and "disabled reader." These terms are not synonymous; they are distinct, definite, and precise in their differentiation of specific kinds of reading problems. For example, the term "remedial reader" denotes a specific kind of reading retardation, indicates the approximate severity of the problem, and implies the kind of instruction necessary for improvement. It should *not* be used as a label for any student with a reading problem. Similarly, each of the other terms has a professional, precise meaning that teachers must understand if they intend helping students to read better.

Definition of Terms

The terms "developmental reader," "corrective reader," and "remedial reader" are herein defined as they are used in this text:

Developmental reader. *A developmental reader is one who is reading up to his own ability or potential.* He is achieving success in reading and developing in a normal and acceptable manner in keeping with his intelligence, maturity, and experiences. He will continue to progress in reading with regular classroom instruction.

Corrective Reader. A *corrective reader* is commonly referred to as a retarded reader, *one who is not reading up to his own ability or capacity.* He has problems of various kinds that keep him from reaching his reading potential. He may, for example, lack certain phonetic skills, such as the ability to pronounce words with consonant blends. He may be able to pronounce such a basic word as "cover," but is unable to pronounce related words, such as "discover," "uncovered," or "recovering." He may not read for main ideas, relevant details, or specific purposes. He may be unable to use context, or meaning clues, to aid in the pronunciation of words. His dictionary skills may be almost non-existent. A number of factors may be operating that keep him from becoming a developmental reader. His problems, however, are not so severe that he needs the help of a specialist. His classroom teacher can help him to overcome his deficiencies through regular classroom instruction. His problems, while multiple, are corrective in nature.

Remedial Reader. *A remedial reader is one who is severely deficient in reading skills. In addition to having reading problems that plague the corrective or retarded reader, he has psychological and/or neurological problems* (7, p. 542). For these reasons, he must have the help of a reading expert. He must be taught individually. In some instances he may benefit from working in a small group of no more than four or five students. The classroom teacher rarely has the education, experience, or time to help him learn to read.

No one can say exactly how many remedial readers will be found in a particular classroom. Authorities estimate that from 1 to 10 per cent of the school population is in the remedial category. The exact number of remedial readers in the regular classroom, however, is not the crux of the discussion. What is important is that teachers recognize students who have reading problems and those who do not. It is important also that they know which kinds of reading problems they can help in their classrooms and which kinds will require the help of a reading specialist.

PROCEDURES FOR EVALUATING STUDENT READING ACHIEVEMENT

Evaluation of student reading in high school is often a hit-or-miss affair. The larger high schools generally have a testing program that includes reading-achievement tests. In some of these schools, adequately prepared counselors interpret test data, send reports of student reading achievement to classroom teachers, and help teachers interpret test results. In most instances, however, the secondary teacher receives little or no information from any source about his students' reading achievement. Occasionally, he may be given a sheet of standardized test scores of general achievement, but otherwise he is strictly on his own.

Whenever and wherever teachers discuss evaluation, the question invariably arises, "Doesn't evaluation of reading take time and effort?" The answer is, "Yes, evaluation does require time and effort. Doesn't all worthwhile teaching demand effort and time? Education is not merely a question of expending time and energy. Education is, or should be, a never-ending process in which the *most prudent use* of time and energy is paramount. And the teacher, working with the most complex of all 'thinking machines,' can ill afford to waste time and effort by attempting to teach subject matter without knowing everything possible about his student's reading strengths, weaknesses, needs, and progress. Evaluation of reading reveals this information to the teacher."

Evaluation of reading is not outside the scope of the subject-matter teacher, nor is it too time-consuming, too difficult, or too involved. Following is a plan of evaluation that can be used by the subject-matter teacher. The general procedures apply to all subject-matter fields, whether they be science, history, English, industrial arts, or home economics.

Outline of Procedure for Evaluation

1. Determine *what* you want to measure.
2. Decide *how* you will measure it.
3. Indicate some necessary *observations.*
4. *Record* all data.
5. *Interpret* data, evaluate, diagnose.
6. *Use* the information for improving student learning experience.

Determine What You Want To Measure

Knowing what to measure is one of the keys to sound evaluation. Anderson (1, chaps. 9, 17) says that deciding what is to be evaluated is the most important question to be asked. Deciding whether we will measure skills, interests, attitudes, vocabulary, concepts, or some other aspect of reading determines the kinds of measures we will use in evaluating student reading.

The way one uses reading determines how he views reading, how he measures it, and how he evaluates it. For example, the school administrator may look at reading as a means for dividing students into instructional groups; an overall reading-achievement-test score will be sufficient for his purpose. The biology teacher or the English teacher, however, needs far more information about the student's reading ability than is revealed by a single-test score.

Determining what one wants to measure cannot be done hastily. Much thought and effort should be expended before one arrives at a decision. And such a decision should be tentative; it needs to be tested in the classroom in the light of previously established goals. One of the primary goals of all teachers should be to help each student become an independent reader, a reader who knows *how* to read, *what to* read, and *why* he reads.

If we accept the proposed goal that each student should be helped to become an independent reader, we need to know what specific reading skills are so basic that the student must acquire them *before* he can read subject matter successfully. Furthermore, we must know if the student has acquired these skills, if he can use them efficiently, and if he has mastered all or only some of them. We must know the specific skills, if any, that he needs to review or to relearn before he is ready to read content material.

Basic Reading Skills

The following is a minimal list of basic reading skills that are necessary for the reading of subject matter. The secondary student should have mastered these skills. If he is weak in one or more of these basic skills, he will have difficulty in reading and learning subject matter. He should have:

1. An adequate sight-vocabulary of the most common words in English
2. Word recognition and pronunciation skills
3. The ability to use a dictionary independently and successfully

4. The ability to follow written and oral directions
5. An understanding of the meaning of a large number of vocabulary words
6. The ability to get meaning from what is read
7. The ability to organize mentally and to outline material read so that he can recall and use it when needed
8. Some knowledge of how to establish purposes for his reading
9. The ability to adjust speed of reading according to his own experience, and to determine the reasons for his difficulty in the material he is reading, and his purposes for reading it
10. The ability to use the index, table of contents, glossary, and author's clues found in a textbook
11. A knowledge of when to use additional reference materials
12. The ability to use the library and its reference materials

In addition to the basic reading skills, there are numerous higher-level reading skills that the student must master before he becomes an efficient, independent reader. These skills include being able (1) to read critically; (2) to read maps, charts, and graphs; (3) to evaluate what is read; (4) to use reading for solving problems; (5) to read between the lines, or to draw inferences from the material; and (6) to question the author's purpose for writing. All of these skills are discussed in subsequent chapters concerned with reading in content areas.

The classroom teacher who understands that the student must master these *basic reading skills* before he can read content materials at the secondary level knows the specific reading skills we must measure. However, secondary teachers are oftentimes impatient with such suggestions and say, "I agree that we need to know more about our student's reading abilities but what I want is a test that will tell me if the student can read my text."

The truth is that no single test is marketed that can give a teacher such comprehensive information. He can get information but only by digging it out for himself. Most secondary teachers will do their own digging if they receive guidance and encouragement and some information in how to dig. The purpose of this chapter is to give teachers some guidance and encouragement and the information necessary for discovering which students can read the assigned textbook. If a teacher is to help students improve their reading and learning of content materials, he must have much specific information about each student's reading achievement and progress.

At the beginning of the school year, teachers should know (1) which students can read the assigned text independently; (2) which students can read it with a minimum of help; (3) which students cannot read the text under any conditions; and (5) which students will benefit from more advanced materials.

Decide How You Will Measure Reading

The preceding discussion should warn the reader that attempting to measure reading accurately with a single test is akin to trying to assess the Mississippi by measuring one of its tributaries. If one could take enough samples from every tributary over a period of time, he could perhaps make a limited number of judgments about the Mississippi which would be reasonably accurate although never absolute. So it is with the measurement of an individual's ability to read. The highly complex reading process has many facets or tributaries. It cannot be accurately assessed by any one test, or even by several tests which at best measure only a limited number of reading skills and achievements. To get a fairly accurate estimate of a student's reading ability, the teacher needs information from a number of samples of that ability as shown by standardized reading test scores, informal reading tests, teachers' observations, ancedotal records, and the student's own evaluation of himself. Reading is such a complex process that the limited sampling of it represented by a test score or two is no more valid for making generalizations about it than is the measurement of one tributary valid for generalizing about the river.

Standardized Tests of Reading Achievement

Many kinds of standardized tests of achievement are used widely in American schools. For the past fifty years standardized tests have played an important role in education. Their use has been both acclaimed and condemned. Their results, likewise, have been both used and abused. A large number of standardized reading tests are available to classroom teachers. Two commonly used types are *survey tests* and *diagnostic tests.*

Survey tests of reading are probably the most widely distributed reading tests used in public schools because they are relatively easy to administer and to score, they can be given in one class period, and they furnish objective information about a student's general reading achievement.

Standardized reading tests, if used judiciously, are good measures of certain aspects of reading. They have been constructed by test experts and have statistical reliability and validity. Their alternate forms make them useful instruments for measuring a student's reading progress at intervals during a year. Because they have norms, they may be used to compare a class, a group, or an entire school with national averages. They become means to measure the reading growth of students over a period of time.

Standardized test results, however, are not always used wisely. Oftentimes teachers and administrators tend to place undue emphasis on average class achievement and to overlook the wide range of students' differences within the class. In other instances, teachers tend to overemphasize the validity and importance of a student's test score. Knowing something about how and why the student received the score he did is always more important than the score. Test scores with their unyielding, precise exactness may label a student incorrectly. They were never so intended by the test makers, nor should they be so interpreted.

Betts (3, p. 441) has repeatedly warned teachers that scores from standardized tests tend to categorize a student at frustration level rather than at instructional level of reading. For example, if Willie in a tenth-grade history class receives a score that indicates that he is reading at the tenth-grade level, a tenth-grade text will be too difficult for him approximately nine out of ten times.

Records of students receiving help in reading at the Oregon State University Reading Clinic during the past eight years are in agreement with Betts's findings, which showed that *standardized tests of reading tend to place a student from one to four grade levels above his actual instructional reading level.*

A teacher does not attain overnight the skill required to interpret test results. It requires much practice and experienced understanding. It is not developed fully in an education course nor in a single year's teaching. It is the product of the experience, the intelligence, and the sensitivity of a willing, capable teacher.

At this point, let us summarize briefly the foregoing principles and procedures for evaluation:

1. Evaluation of reading is a responsibility of the classroom teacher.
2. The classroom teacher must determine the specific aspects of reading he wants to measure, be they skills, achievements, growth, or attitudes.
3. After the teacher has decided what he wants to measure, he is in a position to know the particular tests to select to meet his needs.
4. Standardized tests of reading are valuable measures of some aspects of reading *if* the teacher interprets them cautiously and wisely.

5. Standardized reading test scores tend to place a student at his frustration level in reading rather than his instructional level.

Informal Reading Tests

In the preceding pages of this chapter, we have discussed some of the values, limitations and uses of standardized reading tests. We shall consider now the relevancy of teacher-made tests and of the teacher's observation for evaluating student reading skills.

Although some teachers rely entirely upon standardized test data for diagnosing student reading problems and achievement, informal reading tests differentiate a student's reading achievement more specifically than can any standardized test yet available. After a capable teacher has administered an informal reading test to a student, *that teacher will find himself in possession of more accurate information about the student's independent, instructional, and frustration levels of reading than he can obtain from any other kind of test.*

Informal or teacher-made tests are of inestimable value for detecting a student's specific reading strengths and weaknesses. Their worth has been proved in reading clinics. As their value becomes known to teachers who learn to administer them, their use increases widely at all grade levels.

A number of informal tests or quick-screening techniques for determining whether a student can or cannot read the assigned textbook have been advocated by various reading authorities. Dolch (4, pp. 273–74) suggests having each pupil read orally, without previous preparation, one sentence from a new text. Pupils who have difficulty in reading a sentence, or who refuse to read, are usually inefficient readers. As Harris (6, p. 155) has pointed out, such a procedure provides a "very brief and unreliable" sample for appraising pupil reading; but it is, as Harris also notes, useful for quick-screening purposes. It is much preferred to assuming that all pupils can read the assigned text.

A quick-screening technique, which the writer often uses with secondary or college students, is that of having the student read orally a paragraph or two from one of the student's regular textbooks. The examiner notes the student's mispronunciation, omissions, and additions of words. A rough estimation of his understanding of the material is reached by asking him to answer several questions about it. Using this technique, one can get a quick idea as to whether the material is at about the right level of reading difficulty for the student or if it is too difficult for him. Such a procedure also provides clues for further testing.

Sight-Vocabulary Tests

Students and their teachers often complain about students' inability to read fast. In far too many instances they resort to the use of gadgets "guaranteed" to improve one's speed of reading. *Speed of reading is dependent upon a number of factors. Some of these factors are the reader's word-recognition skills, his sight vocabulary, the kind of material he is reading, his purpose for reading, his experiences with reading, and his experience with the concepts and vocabulary of the material.*

One, but only one, factor, often causal, to slow reading is the student's lack of an adequate *sight vocabulary.* The term "sight vocabulary" is usually associated with elementary or beginning readers and rarely has meaning for the secondary or college teacher. Nevertheless, every efficient reader has a large sight vocabulary, words that he recognizes immediately at sight. For example, how rapidly could you read this page if you had an extremely limited sight vocabulary and had to take note of each letter in each word before you could recognize it?

Students who read at a very slow rate may be doing so because they have never gotten over the habit of looking at each letter in each word. A sight-vocabulary test will help the teacher *to make a quick estimate of the approximate extent of a student's sight vocabulary, to note the kinds of letter combinations in words that cause the student difficulty, to provide a clue to faulty pronunciations, and to estimate the starting level for giving an informal reading test.*

The teacher who suspects that a student's slow rate of reading may be due, at least partially to the lack of an adequate sight vocabulary, should investigate this possibility. It will be necessary for the teacher to develop his own sight-vocabulary test from his own textbook and reading materials. He can develop such a test by taking a sample of 25 or 50 words from several representative pages of the textbook he uses regularly in his classroom. Because he wants to sample generally the words necessary to understanding of the textbook, he should avoid selecting only the most difficult words. For example, he might select every ninth, fifteenth, or twentieth word. If the fifteenth word happens to be one of the most common words in English, such as "town," "life," "about," or "begun," the following word should be used.

We offer herewith a sample of words taken from two pages of a high school textbook in history. Every twenty-fifth word was used. In eleven instances, it was necessary to use the twenty-sixth word because the preceding word was among the most common two or three thousand words in English.

monarch	republican
imprisoned	achieve
massacred	condemned
convention	coalition
abolished	national
sentenced	ruthlessness
extravagant	guillotine
opinion	reign
audacity	tragic
flushed	aristocrats
determination	escapades
consequence	unnecessarily
included	

Using the Sight-Vocabulary Test

The sight-vocabulary test must be given individually. The teacher needs two copies of the test. One of these he will use as a tally sheet for recording the student's responses, the other is the test placed before the student. The teacher should present the words in a flashing or tachistoscopic manner that will expose the word for approximately one-tenth of a second.

Learning the technique for flashing the words in a word-recognition test is not difficult. The procedure for administering the test follows:

1. Obtain two 3 × 5-inch filing cards. Fold each card in the center so that the size of each card is reduced to 3 × 2½ inches. Do not cut the cards in half. Place a small x on the folded edge of each card.
2. Take one card in the left hand. Hold onto the card and place the folded edge of the card parallel to and directly above the word that is to be flashed to the student. The folded edge with the x mark is almost touching the top of the word.
3. Take the remaining card in the right hand and place the card directly above the card in the left hand so that the two folded edges of the cards meet. The two x's should now be like this $\frac{X}{X}$.
4. Pull the card in the left hand down so that the first word in the list of test words is exposed. This leaves the word with one card above it and card below it.
5. Next, bring the right-hand card down against the left-hand card, which again covers the word. The word should be exposed approximately one-tenth of a second.
6. A word may be reexposed by moving the right-hand card upward.

If the student fails to respond to the flash stimulus of the word, or if he mispronounces it, the word is presented again and the student is allowed as much time as he needs to try to pronounce it. The teacher should record *all* responses and should note also the occasions when the student fails to respond to a word. These data form the basis for a diagnosis of the student's pattern of errors.

The student who recognizes at least 95 per cent of the words at flash presentation has sufficient sight vocabulary for rapid reading. His reasons for slow reading may be due to other factors previously mentioned. Some students, however, cannot recognize more than 10 to 20 per cent of the flashed words, but they can pronounce every word on the list when given unlimited time. These students must develop adequate sight vocabularies before they can increase their speed of reading.

The sight-vocabulary test is *limited* to testing a student's *word-recognition* and *pronunciation skills only*. It does not indicate whether the student knows the meaning of the word or not. Some students are excellent word-pronouncers but lack any knowledge of the meanings of the words. Teachers should not be deceived into believing that all students understand all the words that they can pronounce accurately. The teacher can be reasonably sure, however, that, *if the student cannot pronounce the word, he cannot get meaning from it.*

The sight-vocabulary test is also a good indicator for selecting the grade level at which to begin giving an *informal reading* test. Teachers should develop sight-vocabulary tests at several grade levels. For example, suppose that the student is having difficulty reading a tenth-grade textbook and the teacher decides to give him an *informal* reading test. He might start with a sight-vocabulary test at the eighth-grade level. At this level, if the student can score 95 per cent on the flash presentation of the words and 100 per cent on the untimed words, the teacher can be fairly certain that the student has the necessary sight-vocabulary for reading at this level. He should then give the student another sight-vocabulary test at the ninth-grade level. If the student can score 90 per cent on the flashed words and 95 or 100 per cent on the untimed words, the teacher knows that this would be the level at which to begin the *informal reading test.*

A Group Informal Reading Test

Secondary and college teachers who use informal group screening tests find them useful for determining which students can or cannot read the assigned materials. An informal group test is not extremely difficult to develop. It can be made from any reading materials used for instructional purposes. In this instance we shall discuss the preparation of the test, using a regularly assigned textbook. The following directions are reasonably detailed because few students or teachers have experience in making or using this useful measuring device.

Preparation of the Test. First, select a representative page or two from the regularly assigned textbook. Care must be taken to choose a selection that is not the easiest or the most difficult. Second, prepare ten or twelve questions that can be answered from the reading. The questions should be written so that they can be answered with one or two words or a simple sentence. The questions should be of three kinds; fact, inference, and vocabulary. Third, duplicate the questions so that a copy is available for each student.

Administration of the Test.

1. During one of the first class meetings, prepare students for taking the test by explaining briefly the purpose of the test. It is wise to inform students that the test is not for the purpose of grading them but rather for determining how much they can learn from reading the particular textbook.
2. Have the students locate the previously selected pages in their textbooks and then turn the opened books face downward on their desks. Students should be cautioned to refrain from reading until they are given the signal to do so. When all students have found the correct pages and turned their books downward, advise them about how much they should read. When they have completed reading the selection, they should close their books and wait for a question-answer sheet. Having students close their books when they have finished reading gives a rough estimate of which students are fast or slow readers.
3. After all students have finished reading, a question-answer sheet should be given each student. Allow a reasonable length of time for students to answer the questions.

Scoring the Test and Interpreting the Results. The teacher may mark the tests or have each student mark his own test as the answers are read aloud.

The teacher can be reasonably sure that all students who answer at least 70 per cent of the questions correctly can read the text. Those who score 50 per cent or less will be frustrated by the difficulty of the reading and their learning of subject matter from reading this particular textbook will be negligible.

This short test, however, *does not locate the specific level* at which each student should be reading for his optimum learning; it merely separates the class into two groups, those who can read the textbook and those who cannot. And it does differentiate those students who can learn subject matter by reading this particular textbook from those who cannot learn that subject matter from the assigned text because of lack of necessary reading skills. Those students who cannot read the assigned text are in need of further testing to determine the level at which each *can read and learn content material.*

The Informal Reading Inventory

The informal reading inventory originally developed by Betts (3) is one of the most valuable diagnostic measuring instruments yet devised. It first gained acceptance from reading specialists and clinicians who recognized its value for diagnosing specific reading disabilities and needs of retarded readers. A survey of reading texts and articles shows that during the past decade an ever-increasing number of classroom teachers are recognizing and using the informal reading inventory.

The informal reading inventory tests a student's oral and silent reading, his comprehension, his word-recognition skills. The teacher can also get a reasonably accurate indication of the student's potential reading ability by reading selections of the test to him.

Betts (3, pp. 438–87) discusses four levels of reading that may be identified by the use of the informal inventory:

1. *The basal reading level*—the level at which the student has no word-recognition problems and at which he reads independently with complete understanding.
2. *The instructional level*—the level at which the student is challenged but not frustrated by the material. He comprehends a minimum of 75 per cent of what he reads and pronounces at least 95 per cent of the words without the teacher's help.
3. *The frustration reading level*—the level at which the student understands less than half of the material and is upset emotionally by having to read material that is incomprehensible.
4. *The probable capacity level*—the highest level at which the student can understand materials that are read to him.

Criteria for High School and College Reading Levels

Although no one has tabulated exactly how many students are being forced to try to learn subject matter from the textbooks that they cannot read, the number is known to be shockingly great. One can get a rough idea of the extent of such educational malpractice if he consults research evidence and if he is alert to his own observations in his own classroom.

Survey after survey shows that in most every classroom there is a spread of at least six to nine grade levels of reading ability between the poor readers and the efficient readers. Observation will show that approximately 95 out of every 100 teachers at the secondary and college levels require *all* students to read the *same level textbook.* There is no doubt in the writer's mind that at least 40 to 50 per cent of the secondary students in America's public schools are being forced to try to learn subject matter from books that are beyond their instructional reading level.

How can a high school or college teacher determine whether the assigned textbook is at the proper reading level for a student?

Before a teacher can determine whether the assigned textbook is most appropriate for a particular student, it is mandatory that the teacher know the criteria for determining reading levels. The following discussion is concerned with the four levels of reading: (1) the independent level, (2) the instructional level, (3) the frustration level, and (4) the potential reading level.

The Independent Reading Level. This is the level at which the student reads with almost complete freedom from mechanical or word difficulties. His comprehension or understanding of the material at this level is very good. It is at this level that he will do most of his leisure-time reading. If any attempt is made to improve his speed of reading, materials at this level should be used.

The student can acquire much information from reading materials at the *independent reading level.* Few vocabulary words that he encounters will be new or difficult for him. It is possible that concepts may be broadened and developed through wide reading at this level. The textbook he uses, however, should be more challenging to him than is material at his independent reading level. The student can improve his reading skills only when he reads materials that challenge but do not frustrate him.

Criteria for this level are a minimum of 99 per cent word recognition, 90 per cent or better comprehension, and freedom from all symptoms of nervous tension.

The Instructional Reading Level. The instructional level is the level at which the student is sufficiently challenged by the material to continue to improve his reading skills and to learn content materials with some teacher guidance, but the material is not so difficult that it frustrates and defeats him. He will need help occasionally with the pronunciation and with meanings of new words. New concepts and new vocabulary may be introduced and developed, and known concepts may need to be expanded or refined. Some teacher guidance will be necessary also for student improvement in critical reading skills. His reading of textbooks in subject matter should be at this level.

At the instructional level a student should be able to pronounce 95 per cent of the words. Only in rare instances should he read instructional materials in which his pronunciation drops below 95 per cent. In addition, the student should be able to understand a minimum of 70 per cent of the material without teacher help. He should show no evidence of such nervous tensions as finger-pointing, vocalizing, or undue shuffling and twisting of the feet or body.

The Frustration Level. When the student's word recognition drops to 90 per cent or less, and his comprehension drops to 50 per cent or lower, he is in extreme difficulty. This is his *frustration level,* and it is the level at which many secondary and college students are struggling vainly to learn subject matter. It is almost impossible for them to learn subject matter when their assigned text is at this level; they may as well be given texts printed in a foreign language.

There are a number of observable classroom actions that are symptomatic of student reading problems. A bored indifference, lack of attention, extreme shuffling of feet or other body movements, finger-pointing, vocalizing, or complete withdrawal from the "learning" situation, are danger signals that the reading level of the assigned material is too far above the student's present reading ability. Time after time, teachers *do* observe these symptoms but unknowingly *treat the symptoms* rather than the cause. Admonishing the *frustrated reader* to "read your book" or to "get to work" is not the answer to the problem. Students who are capable of reading rarely have to be driven to do so. Students who must continually be forced to read are usually unable to do so. Their feigned compliance or outright refusal to read the textbook should be sufficient evidence for the teacher to check on the student's capability for reading the material.

The Potential Reading Level. A student's potential reading level is the highest level at which he can understand material read to him. It is an indication of his ability to use and understand written material that someone reads to him but that he is unable to read for himself.

It is the level at which he could be reading and learning if he had the necessary reading skills.

These simple statements appear to be easy to understand, but experience indicates that secondary teachers have a difficult time understanding them because teachers are confused about the role of intelligence in reading. Such confusion is understandable because the exact mental processes contributing to reading achievement have not been identified or experimentally appraised.

Most secondary teachers accept a record of a student's intelligence-test scores as being valid. If the student is an efficient or achieving reader, the standardized test of intelligence is recognized as being a good indicator of his intelligence. On the other hand, if the student is an inefficient reader, he needs an individualized test of intelligence. Scores from group intelligence tests based upon the ability to read will not be valid for him.

A common practice at the secondary level, and one which can be tolerated no longer, is that of giving an inefficient reader a standardized group test of intelligence and falsely judging his ability to learn from such invalid evidence. All that has actually happened in giving such a test is that the student has taken two tests of reading and has failed both. Because the student failed the tests is no justification for the teacher's failing in his obligation to the student by assuming that the student lacks the intelligence to learn.

If as so often happens, the teacher finds it impossible to procure an individualized test of intelligence for the student, he can get a fairly accurate indication of the student's *reading potential* by reading to the student several pages from the assigned text. He then asks the student previously prepared questions about the material. If the student comprehends at least 75 per cent of the material thus read to him, the teacher can be reasonably certain that this is the student's potential reading level.

Constructing the Informal Reading Inventory

Construction of an informal reading inventory is not difficult, but it requires practice and understanding. An informal inventory is a specially designed instrument for helping a teacher to determine student reading levels and to select reading materials at the *learner's instructional level.* The informal test is ideally suited for this purpose because it can be devised from the various kinds of reading material which the teacher assigns for student learning in his specific subject matter. Procedures for constructing an informal reading test are as follows:

First, the teacher needs several textbooks covering the same area of learning, but at different levels of reading difficulty. From each text he selects two interesting, representative samples of material of about 400 to 450 words each. The introductory chapter is usually too general to be representative of the remainder of the text and should not be used for testing. On the other hand, an understanding of the material selected for testing should not be dependent upon information presented previously.

Second, ten questions should be developed for each selection. The questions should follow the sequence of the material as the author developed it rather than being chosen on a random, hit or miss basis. The purpose of the questioning is to ascertain if the student is capable of understanding the material. *A good reader in content areas must be able to outline and organize mentally what he reads so that he can understand and apply what is read to the purpose for which he is reading.* Questioning, therefore, should be organized to reinforce learning.

Third, at least three different kinds of questions should be used. About one-third of them should test knowledge of facts found in the reading while one-third should check on vocabulary understanding, and the remainder should be based upon generalizations or inferences that can be deduced by making use of factual knowledge contained in the selection.

Fourth, teachers should avoid using trick questions. "Yes" and "No" types of questions should not be used because of the 50-50 chance of guessing. If it is felt that either a "Yes" or "No" answer is necessary, the student should give a correct answer as to *why* he chose the particular answer. If he cannot give an answer to the "Why" part of the questions, he receives no credit for his previous correct guess.

It is better to ask vocabulary-, fact-, and inference-type questions as they would naturally appear in order of the reading rather than grouping all fact, all inference, and all vocabulary questions into separate bundles. Like good seasoning, the various types of questions should be dispersed throughout the entire selection.

It is further suggested that teachers label each question as to whether it is a fact (F), vocabulary (V), or inference (I) question and write down acceptable answers for each question. The writing of acceptable answers will help the teacher understand the variety of answers students may give to each question. It is good to keep in mind that students often give answers to questions that are superior to those selected by the teacher.

Procedure for Using the Informal Reading Test

The informal reading test may be used as a group test if presented in the manner previously described for informal group testing if the answers are written. The real value of the informal reading test, however, is revealed when it is used as an *individualized test.* It is then that the teacher has an opportunity to observe students closely during both oral and silent reading. Following are steps to be followed in giving tests to a student on an individual basis.

Step I. A Brief Readiness Period Is Necessary. At this time the teacher acquaints the student with some of the procedures he is going to use and why he will use them. If the teacher has an informal vocabulary word list like the one discussed on page 90, he should use it to get an approximate starting level for the informal test. If he has not previously made a word list, he should do so for further testing purposes. He can, however, get a quick approximation of where to begin the informal test by having the student read a short paragraph or two from the lowest-level book he has. He can work upward through the levels until the student begins to mispronounce a word or two. For purposes of illustration, suppose the student reads several paragraphs from materials at the fifth- and sixth-grade levels without any pronunciation errors, but misses several words at the seventh-grade level. For best results, the teacher should begin testing at the last level where there were no errors, or in this case, the sixth-grade level.

The first sample of the inventory must always be read orally at sight. This is a testing situation and the teacher needs to know what words, if any, are difficult for the student to pronounce. He needs to know the student's reaction to difficult words. Does he ask immediately for help or does he try to apply previously learned word-recognition skills? Does he have sufficient phonetic skills for correct pronunciation? Does he use context or meaning clues as an aid to pronunciation or does he guess wildly at words? Does he skip over difficult words, or does he insert words? How long will he attempt to pronounce a word before asking for help? All these should be noted on the teacher's duplicated copy.

Step II. Oral Reading at Sight. The teacher, using a sixth-grade text gives the student, Mary, a brief account of something about the material to be read. He avoids using any vocabulary words contained in the selection lest such use give Mary a pronunciation clue she might otherwise miss. The teacher sets a limited purpose for the reading, such as, "Mary, the part of the story we are going to read discusses why a certain group of people came to the United States. When you finish reading *aloud,* I shall ask you some questions about these people. Why did they come here? Where were they from? And, what did they bring with them?"

Mary reads the material orally at sight. If she mispronounces a word(s), the teacher writes the mispronunciation on his copy of the informal reading test. Any word that Mary cannot pronounce is pronounced by the teacher and noted also on the informal test.

When Mary finishes reading the material, she is asked questions from the informal test. Her answers are marked "Right" or "Wrong," and when possible they should be written down for later diagnosis.

For the moment, let us suppose that Mary asked for help in pronouncing one word and mispronounced four other words that gave her a *word-recognition score of 98 per cent on the oral reading at sight.* She answered correctly *85 per cent of the questions,* and was not unduly nervous or tense.

The teacher now goes to Step III.

Step III. Silent Reading. Mary is given a sample of material at the same level (sixth grade) and given the same preparation for reading it as was given for the oral-reading-at-sight test. She is again advised to ask for help with the pronunciation of any words about which she is unsure.

After Mary completes the silent reading, she is asked questions about it. The teacher keeps a record of all her answers.

Again, let us suppose that she made the following scores on the silent-reading portion of the test: She asked for no help with any word, and we assume her *word recognition is 100 per cent,* but this will be rechecked shortly; she answered all questions correctly for a score of *100 per cent in comprehension.*

Before we total her scores on oral reading at sight and on silent reading, we should check her *oral rereading.* We *assumed* momentarily that she had no word-pronunciation problems during the silent reading because she did not ask for help, but we cannot diagnose reading achievement via assumption. We now check her word recognition by giving her a new purpose for *rereading orally.* We might, for example, say, "find the part of the story that tells us how the sailors felt about the Pilgrims and read that paragraph aloud."

Mary locates the paragraph and rereads it perfectly. We observe that this oral reading is better than her oral reading at sight. This is noted on the test. Also, her word-recognition score of 100 per cent is verified by this sample of the total silent reading. We can now total her scores. We note the following:

Oral Reading at Sight	*Word Recognition*	*Comprehension*
(No signs of nervous tension)	98 per cent	85 per cent
Silent reading (No signs of nervous tension)	100 per cent	100 per cent
Total reading score	99 per cent	92.5 or 93 per cent

According to the criteria for reading levels, this is Mary's *independent reading level.* We do not know, however, whether she will do as well, better, or worse with seventh-grade materials. Our next step is to test her in the same manner but using seventh-grade materials.

Step IV. For purpose of illustration, let's assume that Mary reads seventh-grade material and receives the following total score:

Total pronunciation of words, or word recognition (oral reading at sight plus silent reading)	95 per cent
Total comprehension	75 per cent

No visible signs of nervous tension except the vocalizing of one word

This is the level where Mary can learn, and improve her reading skills. She is not frustrated by the content of the material or the pronunciation of words. This is her *instructional reading level.*

Step V. Mary is given reading material at the eighth-grade level and receives the following scores:

Total word recognition	90 per cent
Comprehension	55 per cent

It was also noted that she used her finger to point out many of the words, she vocalized a great many of them during silent reading, she twisted about, she ran her hand through her hair several times, she began to perspire around her nose and upper lip. These are all symptoms of nervous tension. The material at this level presents too many problems for her. She is at her *frustration level.* She cannot learn subject matter efficiently or improve her reading skills on this level at this time. To insist that she read material at this level is unjustified and is nothing less than mental cruelty.

At this point, let us recapitulate what the informal reading test has revealed about Mary's reading:

1. Mary can read sixth-grade materials *independently* or without a teacher's help.
2. Her *instructional level* for this kind of material is at the seventh-grade level.
3. She *frustrates* on eighth-grade material.
4. She has a number of the basic word-recognition skills, but is weak in certain areas. A close examination of the informal test will reveal the specific areas in which she needs help.
5. We have evidence of her ability to read orally at sight, reread orally, and read silently.
6. We have some knowledge about her vocabulary at the sixth-, seventh-, and eighth-grade levels.
7. We know some of her strengths and weaknesses in recalling fact, using the facts to make judgments or inferences.
8. We know that she can improve her oral rereading at the sixth- and seventh-grade levels.
9. She has demonstrated her skimming skills by locating paragraphs for oral reading.
10. Because we do not have a valid test of her intelligence, we do not know if she is reading at her potential or not. We may, however, get a reasonably accurate estimate of her reading potential by continuing to use the informal reading test (2, p. 120–22).

Determining a Student's Reading Potential

All teachers are interested in knowing how intelligence affects the reading process. Some have very definite views about the intelligence of inefficient secondary readers; others are less certain. For purposes of clarification, the experts themselves are not so certain as they once were about the way in which intelligence affects reading.

Teachers are interested also in knowing how they can determine if a student is reading as well as he should according to his intelligence or if he is reading below his intellectual level.

No one can say exactly how much intelligence affects a student's reading, but some generalizations can be made that will serve as guidelines. Educators, psychologists, medical doctors, and reading specialists generally agree that *a valid test of intelligence is one of the best indicators of one's reading capability.* The fact that a student has a high I.Q., however, does *not* guarantee that he will be an efficient reader. A great number of factors, in addition to intelligence, influence this quality and the extent of a student's reading achievement. The student with a high I.Q. has the potential to become an efficient reader, but the student who is limited in intelligence can never read beyond a certain point. For example, Oscar, a sixth-grader with a valid I.Q. of 140 may be reading slightly better than his friend Jerry, in the same grade with an I.Q. of 90. However, Oscar has the potential to become a highly efficient reader on a level that Jerry can never hope to approximate. Smith says that "intelligence is a major factor in reading success at any level" (8, p. 29).

Teachers should be cautious in accepting scores of intelligence as being valid measures of an individual's intelligence, or as being the sole indicator of reading success or failure. Most I.Q. scores of students are based upon survey-type intelligence tests. These kinds of tests require that the student *read* them *before* he can answer the questions. The student who has a reading problem cannot help receiving a spuriously low I.Q. from such a test. The secondary student who is having difficulty with reading should be given an individualized test of intelligence. In many schools it is impossible for the teacher to get an individualized test score of a student's intelligence because no one on the staff is prepared to administer one.

Teachers who for various reasons are unable to get an individualized test of intelligence for a student with a reading problem need not give up in despair. There is a measure that will provide them with excellent information about a student's probably reading capacity. Many teachers and reading clinics use a *reading-potential test* to help them determine the highest level at which a student might read if he fully developed his reading skills. When used properly, the reading-potential test is an excellent instrument for indicating a student's mental capacity for reading. Recent research indicates that the *reading-potential test* is a valid measure for determining one's capability for reading. Some authorities believe that it may prove to be a more adequate measure of a student's capability for reading than is a valid test of intelligence. However, additional research is needed in this area before definite conclusions can be reached. Nevertheless, the *reading-potential test* has great value for the teacher. Besides being a valid instrument, it is a functional one. It can be developed by a teacher from any kind of classroom reading material that is graded. Many times it is the only available valid measure of a student's capability for reading.

The *reading-potential test* does not invalidate nor make obsolete the need for a good test of intelligence. It should be used for determining reading capability in conjunction with tests of intelligence or in the absence of valid tests of intelligence. Although there is growing evidence that the *reading-potential test* gives a more accurate estimate of a student's reading capability than does a test of his intelligence (2, p. 120). Such evidence should not raise argument among professional educators about the merits of one test over the other. Teachers need every shred of available valid evidence for helping them to determine a student's specific reading levels. When valid tests of intelligence are available, full use of them is imperative. When such information is not available, the teacher need not remain ignorant of the level of material a student can understand when it is discussed with him simply because the teacher has no measure of intelligence. He himself can get this information by giving the student a *reading-potential test.* This test is fairly easy to make and to administer. Patience, skill, and understanding are necessary for properly interpreting the results.

How To Administer a Reading-Potential Test

Using a graded selection from an informal reading test, the teacher reads the selection aloud to the student, who is then asked questions about the material in the same manner as if he had read the selection himself. The student's responses are recorded and scored by the teacher. In addition, the student's use of vocabulary and his ability to contribute to the material from his own experiences are important.

When the student answers correctly 70 per cent of the questions, adds to the material from his own experiences, and uses vocabulary similar to, or equal to, that of the author, the teacher has sufficient evidence to know that if the student had the necessary reading skills he could be reading and learning from subject-matter books at this level.

The highest level at which the student satisfies the several criteria just discussed is considered to be his *reading potential at this time.*

Although we have discussed the *reading-potential test* as an individual test, it may be used as a group test. Spache (9, pp. 128–32) strongly recommends this kind of measure for determining students' potential for learning content materials. Instead of the teacher reading the material aloud to one student, he may read selections to groups of students, after which they are asked questions about the material. Spache (9, p. 131) says that such testing will provide the teacher with an estimate of the level of concepts that the student can understand, the level at which he can discuss subject matter with the class, and the students who can be expected to profit from class discussion even though they lack the skills necessary for reading the text.

The Teacher Observation

A diagnosis or evaluation of a student's ability to read subject matter is not complete until the teacher had made a number of observations of the student's reactions in learning situations. Recorded teacher observations of student behavior adds meat to the skeletal profile of achievement-test scores.

The classroom teacher is in a most strategic position to observe student behavior over a period of time. His *planned* and *recorded* day-by-day observations give him insight into the student's interests, attitudes, personality, physical well-being, emotional stability, and overall developmental growth, which he can gain in no other manner. These observations are useful not only for acquiring a thorough understanding of the student's weaknesses and strengths, but for planning new learning experiences for him.

Teacher observation, because it is diagnostic in nature, must be accurate and must be pointed toward improving instruction in both *reading* and *subject-matter learning.* In order that instruction may be improved, observation must include the student's mental, physical, social, and emotional reactions in learning situation.

Following is a suggested guide that may be duplicated by the teacher for aiding him in directing his observation for student improvement.

Teacher's Guide for Observing Students Reading

1. Does the student exhibit behavior symptomatic of the fact that the material is too difficult for him to read? (Some such symptoms are: finger-pointing, vocalizing, lack of interest, fidgeting, inability to concentrate on reading for any length of time.)
2. Does the student lack interest in reading?
3. Does he get literal meaning from the textbook?
4. Can he read "between the lines"?
5. What kinds of books does he read during the independent reading period?

Discussion Period

1. Does the student participate willingly?
2. Does he participate when asked to do so?
3. Does he ask pertinent questions?
4. Does he make relevant statements?

Speaking Skills

1. Does the student use complete sentences?
2. Does he use fragments or partial sentences?
3. Does he attempt to use any of the new vocabulary peculiar to the content field?

4. Is his vocabulary specific?
5. Is it limited?
6. Does he speak clearly and audibly?

Listening Skills

1. Is the student interested in what other students discuss?
2. Is he interested in the teacher's contributions?
3. Does he interrupt the speaker?
4. Does he appear to listen to learn or does he appear to listen only to refute the speaker?

Writing Skills

1. Can the student express himself in writing?
2. Does he have a spelling problem?
3. Can he answer questions better in written than in oral form?
4. Is his writing legible?

Student's Attitude

1. Does he appear to like school?
2. Does he enjoy reading?
3. Does he appear to want to learn subject matter?
4. Does he get along with the other students?
5. Does he get along with other teachers and his teacher?

Interests

1. Does the student appear to be interested in subject matter?
2. What kinds of reading materials does he choose to read?
3. Is he more interested in the discussion period than in the reading period?
4. Does he ask for, or seek, other books in the content area?

Student's Self-Concept

1. Is the student shy, withdrawn?
2. Is he overly aggressive?
3. Does he demand attention unduly?
4. Does he exhibit self-confidence?
5. Is he uncertain, unsure, overly cautious, afraid to take a chance?
6. Is he persistent and determined to complete a task even if it is difficult?
7. Does he give up easily?

Recording Data

In order that the evaluative procedure lead to adequate diagnosis and serve as a guide for improving student learning experiences, the teacher should have a plan and materials available for recording. All student reaction and behavior cannot be recorded, but a systematic form for recording standardized test scores, informal test scores, pertinent student comments, and observed behavior should be written objectively and succinctly.

The student should be shown his test results. He has a right to know the scores he made and the significance of those scores. We want him to know what the scores indicate in order that he can assume the responsibility for improving himself. Unless he has such information and understanding, he has no guide for knowing what he is doing in relation to what he can do. After all, we are attempting to help the student to become an independent reader, learner, and thinker. Self-appraisal is an important step in this direction.

SUMMARY

In this chapter evaluation has been defined as an educated, orderly attempt to judge student's achievement in the light of specific, measurable, and attainable goals. The "good" and "poor" reader has been scrutinized and the reading terminology of developmental reader, corrective or retarded reader, and of remedial reader has been defined. To understand the student reader more thoroughly, the four reading levels have been discussed. Administering an informal reading inventory, the following levels may become apparent: (1) the basal reading level, or the independent reading level, (2) the instructional reading level, (3) the frustrational reading level, and (4) the probable capacity level.

The four steps in constructing the Informal Reading Inventory are given a detailed account: (1) selecting reading materials of same subject-matter area at different levels of reading difficulty; (2) how to develop ten questions concerning the reading material in question; (3) vocabulary, fact, and inference questions; and (4) the elimination of all types of guessing questions–answers. The steps to be taken and followed by teachers in Oral Reading at Sight, in Silent Reading, and in Oral Rereading have been explained and illustrated by the example of "Mary." This is a thorough practical application of what has been expounded theoretically.

To improve teacher observation, a guide for observing students' reading includes discussion period, speaking skills, listening skills, writing skills, students' attitudes, interests, self-concept, and the recording of the data obtained.

SELECTED REFERENCES

1. Anderson, Vernon E. *Principles and Procedures of Curriculum Improvement.* New York: The Ronald Press, 1965. Chaps. ix, xvii.
2. Barbe, Walter B., and Carr, Jack A. "Research Report: Listening Comprehension as a Measure of Potential Reading Ability," *Reading in Action.* International Reading Association Conference Proceedings, Vol. II. New York: Scholastic Magazines, 1957.
3. Betts, Emmett Albert. *Foundations of Reading Instruction.* Cincinnati: American Book Co., 1957.
4. Dolch, Edward W. *Methods in Reading.* Champaign, Ill.: Garrard Press, 1955.
5. Ebel, Robert L. "Measurement and the Teacher," *Educational Leadership,* Vol. 20 (October, 1962), pp. 20–24, 43.
6. Harris, Albert J. *How to Increase Reading Ability* (4th ed. rev.). New York: David McKay Co., Inc., 1961.
7. Kress, Roy A. "When Is Remedial Reading Remedial?" *Education,* Vol. 80 (May, 1960), pp. 540 ff.
8. Smith, Nila Banton. *Reading Instruction for Today's Children.* Englewood Cliffs, N.J.: Prentice-Hall, Inc., 1963.
9. Spache, George D. "Classroom Techniques of Identifying and Diagnosing the Needs of Retarded Readers in High School and College," *Better Readers for Our Times.* International Reading Association Conference Proceedings, Vol. I. New York: Scholastic Magazines, 1956.

SUGGESTED ADDITIONAL READING

Baron, Denis, and Bernard, Harold W. *Evaluation Techniques for Classroom Teachers.* New York: McGraw-Hill Co., Inc., 1958.

Bond, Guy L., and Wagner, Eva Bond. *Teaching the Child to Read* (3d ed.). New York: The Macmillan Co., 1960.

Dressel, Paul L. "The Evaluation of Reading," *The Reading Teacher,* Vol. 15 (March, 1962), pp. 361–65.

Durrel, Donald D. "Learning Difficulties Among Children of Normal Intelligence," *Elementary School Journal,* Vol. 55 (December, 1954), pp. 201–8.

Gates, Arthur I. *Reading Attainment in Elementary Schools: 1957 and 1937.* New York: Bureau of Publications, Teachers College, Columbia University, 1961.

Henry, Nelson B. (ed.). *Reading in the High School and College.* The Forty-seventh Yearbook, Part II, National Society for the Study of Education. Chicago: The University of Chicago Press, 1948.

HITCHCOCK, ARTHUR A., and ALFRED, CLEO. "Can Teachers Make Accurate Estimates of Reading Ability?" *The Clearing House*, Vol. 29 (March, 1955), pp. 422–24.

JOHNSON, MARJORIE SEDDON. "A Study of Diagnostic and Remedial Procedures in a Reading Clinic Laboratory School," *Journal of Educational Research*, Vol. 48 (April, 1955), pp. 565–78.

JOHNSON, MARJORIE SEDDON. "Evaluation in Reading as an Intellectual Activity," *Scholastic Magazine*, International Reading Association Conference Proceedings, Vol. 8, 1963, ed. J. ALLEN FIGUREL, 1963.

LINDVALL, C. M. *Testing and Evaluation: An Introduction.* New York: Harcourt, Brace & World, Inc., 1961.

ROBINSON, HELEN M. "Corrective and Remedial Instruction," *Development in and Through Reading.* The Sixtieth Yearbook of the National Society for the Study of Education. Chicago: The University of Chicago Press, 1961.

ROSENHECK, VIOLA. "The Use of Reading Test Results in Counseling," *Personnel and Guidance Journal*, Vol. 42 (November, 1963), pp. 290–94.

RUSSELL, DAVID H. *Children Learn To Read* (2d ed.). Boston: Ginn & Co., 1961.

SHAW, PHILLIP. "Setting College-Bound Students Into Orbit," *Reading in a Changing Society*, ed. J. ALLEN FIGUREL. International Reading Association Conference Proceedings, Vol. 14. New York: Scholastic Magazines, 1959.

SMITH, HENRY P., and DECHANT, EMERALD V. *Psychology in Teaching Reading.* Englewood Cliffs, N.J.: Prentice-Hall, Inc., 1961.

TRAXLER, ARTHUR E. "Critical Survey of Tests for Identifying Difficulties in Interpreting What Is Read," *Promoting Growth Toward Maturity in Interpreting What Is Read.* Supplementary Educational Monographs, No. 74. Chicago: The University of Chicago Press, 1951.

WALKER, FREDERIC R. "Evaluation of Three Methods of Teaching Reading, Seventh Grade," *Journal of Educational Research*, Vol. 54 (May, 1961), pp. 356–58.

6

A DEVELOPMENTAL READING PROGRAM

What Is a Developmental Reading Program?

At present, there is no clear-cut definition of a developmental reading program. Artley (1, pp. 321–28), Betts (2); Fay (4); Strang, McCullough, and Traxler (9); and Super (10, pp. 301–9) are among those who have discussed the need for such a program that will provide for the systematic, sequential development of a students' reading skills at all grade levels.

This book defines a developmental reading program as a planned, systematic program of reading designed to produce independent readers. It begins at the first grade and continues through the sixteenth grade. It is based upon two fundamental principles: (1) each student has the right to receive as much instruction in reading as is necessary for him to learn to read to the limit of his reading potential; (2) each student has a responsibility to himself and society to develop, refine, and extend his reading skills to their maximum.

Is there a need for a developmental reading program in the secondary schools? There is graphic evidence of a real need for the continued teaching of reading at both the secondary and college levels.

Following are some facts revealed by research:

1. The mentally superior students in the secondary schools and colleges are among the most seriously retarded readers.
2. There is a difference of at least 6 to 9 grade levels in the reading ability of secondary students in almost every classroom in America. At times the range of difference between the best and poorest readers in a class will be as great as 12 to 14 grade levels.

3. Approximately 15 per cent of America's adults are functionally illiterate (6, p. 56). An additional 15 per cent of the adults read and write at or below the sixth-grade level. Only half of Americas' adults read and write better than the average eighth-grader.
4. Eighteen million adults who will be among the first to lose their jobs through automation will find it almost impossible to prepare themselves for other jobs because 15 million are functionally illiterate and the remaining 3,000,000 are non-readers.
5. Lack of reading skills is one of the major reasons for the large number of school dropouts (12, p. 23).
6. An alarming number of college freshmen lack the reading skills necessary for learning at the college level. One study (3, p. 156) revealed that more than two-thirds of the freshmen who were completing their first year of college had never been taught how to concentrate on reading, how best to read a chapter in a book, or how to read critically. Sixty-four per cent of these students stated that they had never been taught to develop an awareness of problems when reading.
7. For the past eight years the writer has given the *Diagnostic Reading Test* (11) to all prospective secondary teachers enrolled in Methods of Secondary Reading at the Oregon State University. When the scores of these upper-classmen and graduate students are compared with the reading norms for college freshmen, they range from the first to the 99th percentile.

Numerous other studies show that there is a critical need for the continued teaching of reading at the secondary and college levels.

Reading Programs Now in Operation

Until recently, most secondary teachers and administrators either ignored or refused to accept the mounting evidence showing the need for the teaching of reading to students beyond elementary school. Nevertheless, a few farsighted teachers and an occasional administrator in some school systems did initiate and experiment with various kinds of reading programs. Most of these programs were limited in scope, dealing primarily with remedial readers. A few, however, were developed for corrective readers, and an occasional reading course was designed for college-bound students. During the past few years many secondary schools have realized that a developmental reading program is not only desirable but essential to the improvement of student learning.

Philadelphia and New York were among the first cities to establish developmental reading programs at the secondary level. Available information indicates that *the reading programs of both cities are similar.*

Philadelphia and New York City junior high schools provide developmental and remedial reading instruction. Both systems have developed excellent teacher's guides for reading in grades 7, 8, and 9.

Objectives of a Developmental Reading Program for Secondary Students

A developmental reading program must be based upon sound educational and psychological principles. The objectives of the program must be geared to student needs. Harris, discussing the objectives of a sound reading program, notes that the Yearbook Committee of the National Society for the Study of Education has stressed the interrelationship between reading and the school program. "The Committee," he says, "has emphasized that reading must fit harmoniously into the total plan of a good educational program" (7, p. 11).

The preceding viewpoint presents a strong case for reading for education, but it also implies that reading and learning are two different distinct processes, an implication the writer of this book cannot accept. Reading is basic to virtually all learning in school, especially to all higher levels of learning. For too long, teachers and others have looked upon reading and learning as two completely different areas of educational program, a fallacy that we must recognize. Reading and learning are not dissimilar educational processes. They are two interwoven and mutually dependent phases of the same complex, thinking process; they are never two separate areas.

Reading is not a subject that must fit itself harmoniously into the total educational program. Reading is an inherent, irrevocable, functional part of the total educational process. It is one of the facets of language. Without language, education is nonexistent. Reading must not be considered a segment of nor an appendage to the educational program. The confused thinking that so considers it has been a major deterrent to the improvement of student reading and learning.

In 1948 the Yearbook Committee of The National Society for the Study of Education (8) called attention to the need for a sound reading program in high schools and colleges. The Committee pointed out that a sound reading program must be based upon the recognition "(1) that growth in reading is continuous, (2) that the function of guidance in reading is to start with the student at his present level of reading ability, and (3) that it should carry him forward to high levels of competence in harmony with his capacity and the increasing demands made upon him when reading (7, p. 11)."

The Committee's suggestions are as relevant today as they were when first written and should be heeded by those who are developing or initiating reading programs.

Major Objectives. Two general objectives that are basic to every developmental reading program are (1) to give each student the kind of instruction and experience that are necessary for him to become a mature, independent reader and learner and (2) to provide each student with the kinds of reading experiences that will make of him a person who loves to read.

Specific Objectives. The specific objectives of a developmental reading program at the secondary level, grades 7 through 12, should be based upon student needs. Because students' needs vary greatly, it is impossible to list here all the specific objectives of a developmental reading program. However, there are specific reading skills that must be mastered before a student can read subject matter successfully. Following are some of the basic reading skills that need to be considered when objectives for a reading program are considered.

Word-recognition Clues. Many high school students and some college students have not mastered the word-recognition skills necessary for quick, accurate pronunciation of words. Word recognition is dependent upon the student's use of configuration clues, word-structure clues, phonetic skills, and context or meaning clues. Students who are unable to apply these word-recognition skills to unfamiliar words must be given the help and the practice that will enable them to do so.

Vocabulary Development. Many students will need help in improving the breath and depth of their understanding or listening vocabulary. Many high school and college students are unaware that most words have multiple meanings and that the meanings of words vary with the context in which they are used.

Dictionary Skills. Shocking as it may sound, few students, even at the college level, can use a dictionary efficiently. All students in high school should be given practice in finding words rapidly and in selecting definitions that lead to the selection of the proper meaning for unknown words as they are used in particular contexts.

Many students are unable to pronounce an unfamiliar word after they have found it in the dictionary and have noted its phonetic respelling. They are totally unaware of how to use the dictionary's pronunciation key, diacritical markings, and accent marks.

Organizing and Outlining Materials Read. Students do not learn to organize and outline materials at a particular age or grade in school. Ability in organizing and outlining develops gradually and systematically. First-graders begin receiving help in organizing and outlining when they retell stories and incidents to their classmates. Such preparation is basic to the higher-level skills of organizing information, facts, supporting details, and ideas, for the purpose of summarizing, reaching conclusions, and solving problems. Many high school and some college students arrive at faulty conclusions and are unable to solve problems because they have never learned how to organize and outline their reading assignments.

Interpretation of Reading. Students must be able to predict outcomes and anticipate what will follow logically when certain details and statements are presented in written material. They must be capable of spotting an author's biases and his use of emotionally laden words in lieu of facts. They need to learn to detect the author's purpose for writing, and to evaluate what he has said in relation to his purpose. They must be able to judge the merit of given facts and to draw tentative conclusions.

Adjusting Speed of Reading. Secondary students usually have a single rate of reading. They read comic strips, light novels, history, and mathematics at the same speed. They need to be taught to adjust their speed of reading according to their purpose for reading, their background of experience in the particular area of reading, and the difficulty of the material. They need to learn when and how to skim materials rapidly, to read rapidly, and to slow down and read critically.

All these specific reading skills have, or should have, been taught to each student before he enters the secondary school. Even though these skills may have been learned previously by most seventh-, eighth-, or ninth-graders, many students will continue to need help to relearn or to review and improve their basic reading skills. A sound developmental reading program should provide each student with the opportunity to either relearn or review these basic reading skills that are prerequisite to efficient learning of subject matter through reading.

Principles of a High School Developmental Reading Program

Following is a list of principles that should be used for guiding the planning and operation of a developmental reading program. The list is neither extensive nor complete. There is always room for adding principles that apply to a particular school situation that may not be needed in other schools. A reading program based on the principles in this list will be educationally and psychologically sound. It will be a realistic program, and it will be perhaps a bit ahead of the times. It will be a program that produces results by improving learning through improved reading. It will produce better emotionally adjusted students. It will abolish the gruesome practice of mentally torturing students because they are unable to read.

A developmental reading program must:

1. Include every subject, teacher, and student.
2. Follow clearly defined written objectives that are based upon students' needs.
3. Provide adequate reading instruction for each student at his own instructional level of reading whether he be a developmental, retarded or corrective, remedial, or non-reader.
4. Have flexibility in order that a student may move in or out of a special phase of the program when his needs dictate such movement.
5. Provide direct instruction in reading subject matter.
6. Include an adequate supply of interesting subject materials at various levels of difficulty.
7. Utilize the services of at least one thoroughly prepared specialist in reading.
8. Contain provisions for in-service reading instruction for teachers.
9. Consider reading as an integral part of the total educative process.
10. Recognize that reading must be taught at all grade levels in the public school system.
11. Provide students with numerous opportunities for wide and varied reading experiences.
12. Arrange for the continuous evaluation of students.
13. Have a permanent committee of interested persons with authority to study and recommend changes deemed necessary for improving the program. The membership of the committee must include a professional school librarian.

Planning and Organizing a Developmental Reading Program

Planning and organizing a developmental reading program is a tremendous job, but its results are even more tremendous. Because the program is designed for all the students, it must offer help and guidance to the successful reader, the mildly retarded or corrective reader, the severely retarded or remedial reader, and the occasional non-reader. Some corrective readers, and all remedial and non-readers, will require specialized help in separate classes. But before we consider these special phases of the program, let us discuss the initial planning and preparation required for the proper functioning of a developmental reading program.

Initiating the Program

The impetus for a reading program must originate in the head and the heart of a person or a group. A single teacher may be the stimulus for the program (5, pp. 37–41). He may take a course in reading or have become an expert in reading and, inspired and dedicated, may attempt to start a reading program. He may initiate such a program in his own classes. But unless his school administrator believes in a developmental reading program and gives it wholehearted support, his program will have little chance of success. For example, at a recent in-service meeting of teachers and administrators the writer heard a superintendent of schools say, "We don't have any place in our science program for the poor reader. If a student can't read, he can't take science. We don't teach reading in our high schools and we don't intend to!" Can a single teacher's suggestions and efforts be sufficient stimuli for developing a reading program in a high school under the jurisdiction of this kind of an administrator? Probably not, but occasionally an unsympathetic administrator becomes sympathetic when he becomes better informed about reading and sees the results of developmental reading programs.

Fortunately the unsympathetic and uninformed administrator is disappearing, and in some instances the initial action for the organization of a high school reading program originates in the superintendent's office. And such action should be initiated from his office.

Problems When Introducing a Reading Program

Teacher Objections. Ask any secondary teacher, "What is one of your biggest problems in teaching subject matter?" Invariably the answer will include a comment about the lack of students' reading skills. Ask any administrator what one thing contributes most to the poor learning of students and he will tell you that learning is hampered most by poor reading. Ask any reading consultant what is the major obstacle to overcome in developing a reading program in the high school and he will tell you that it is teacher objection to participation in such a program. These answers don't agree, do they? However, they represent some of the major problems that hamper the development of reading programs in high school.

Why do secondary teachers object to taking part in a developmental reading program? The writer's opinion, based upon lengthy experience as a teacher and as a reading consultant working with secondary teachers, is that secondary teachers are actually apprehensive about their ability to teaching reading. They are afraid to try to teach reading. Most secondary teachers recognize the need for teaching reading and seriously desire to help students in their classes, but they appear to be fearful of doing the wrong thing. Apparently they feel it is better to do nothing than to attempt to do something about which they know little or nothing.

Time for Planning a Program

Most secondary teachers do an excellent job of preparing subject matter for their students despite their being continually pressed for time by such responsibilities as serving on numerous committees and performing other tasks in addition to their classroom teaching. Any suggestion, therefore, that may take a teacher's time from teaching, from preparation for teaching, or from marking students' papers, may receive a cool reception. The suggestion that they teach reading in their subject matter meets not only with coolness but many times with determined opposition.

Planners and initiators of a reading program must consider such problems and must take steps to alleviate them. First, one must provide teachers with some extra time for learning about a reading program. There are persons who argue that it is difficult to arrange time for teachers to attend meetings concerned with improving the teaching of reading. These same persons, however, know that arrangements can always be made to provide teachers and students with time for observing special events and attending important athletic contests. Likewise, when reading is recognized as being important for learning, arrangements can be made to provide teachers with time to think about a reading program, time to see demonstrations of how to use reading techniques to promote learning in subject matter, time to learn how a reading program benefits teachers and students, and time to serve on a reading program committee. When such arrangements are made, the most obstinate objectors to a reading program usually become staunch supporters.

Materials for the Program

Any reading program must have an adequate supply of reading materials. An adequate supply of materials means that subject-matter teachers must have a number of supplementary reading materials covering the same topics as the textbook but at various levels of reading difficulty. A teacher of American history, for example, who is teaching students about the problems of writing the Constitution of the United States must have, in addition to the textbook, materials that are easier to read, but that cover the same ideas. He cannot teach problems of the writing of the Constitution to one group, the French and Indian Wars to another, and The Westward Movement to a third group simply because these are the only materials available that will meet the reading needs of different students.

Procuring supplementary materials that cover the same areas that are included in the regular textbook is not an easy task. It takes time, effort, and some additional funds, but if subject-matter teachers are ever going to improve their students' learning of content through reading, teachers must have the necessary reading materials. Publishers have followed an almost inexorable policy of producing subject-matter textbooks at one prescribed level of readability. For example, most biology or a social studies textbooks used in the ninth grade will be written and published at only a ninth-grade reading level. Therefore, at best, only 50 to 60 per cent of the ninth-graders can read the text with varying degrees of ease and success. An additional 10 to 20 per cent *may* be capable of reading it with much teacher help, but somewhere between 30 and 40 per cent of the students will be so frustrated by the difficulty of reading level that they may as well be given a textbook written in a foreign language.

In order that we do not leave our reader, with any false impressions about publishers, it is necessary to note that publishing textbooks is an expensive venture. Publishers, like other businessmen, must show a profit or go out of business. Consequently, they try to publish the kinds of books that teachers will buy and use. *If teachers demand and use multilevel textbooks for teaching subject matter, publishers will produce the books.* At least one company is now publishing a series of easier-reading pamphlets in American history* and world history. There are nine pamphlets in each series. The accompanying guide for teachers specifies that the materials are written for students classified as low-ability groups. Each lesson includes the introduction of four or five vocabulary words, purposes for the reading, and exercises for checking comprehension. Although these pamphlets are not *the* answer to various levels of reading difficulty, they are a beginning. It is highly probably that within a decade a number of publishers will be

* Jack Abramowitz, *American History* (Chicago: Follett Publishing Co., 1963).

producing similar materials in most subject-matter areas and at various reading levels.

Deciding When and Where To Begin

Let us suppose that the administrators and teachers at a school we shall call West High School have expressed an interest in organizing a developmental reading program. What procedure should they follow in order that the program be most beneficial to the teacher, parents, and students?

Experience indicates that, when a group of secondary teachers under the leadership and support of an enthusiastic administrator becomes interested in improving the reading skills and achievement of students, they are apt to be like a small, hungry boy at a Thanksgiving dinner; they may take on more than they can handle. A wise administrator can maintain teacher enthusiasm and insure the success of a developmental reading program if he leads teachers to recognize that a complete reading program cannot be accomplished in the first year. A simple guide might be: "Start small and grow big."

Because the reading program is concerned with every student, there is much leeway in where and how to start giving students needed help. You must decide whether you want to begin your program by helping remedial, corrective, or developmental readers. In most instances teachers decide to begin with the remedial reading phase of the program. Unfortunately, this is seldom the wisest choice. There are several valid reasons why it is best not to begin with the remedial phase: (1) although there are fewer remedial readers than there are corrective and developmental readers, remedial readers are more difficult to teach; (2) a remedial reader is *remedial* because he has psychological and/or neurological problems that require the help of a reading specialist; (3) the remedial reader must be taught on an individual basis or in a group of no more than three or four; (4) because the remedial reader has severe reading problems, his progress is generally very slow. Now this does not mean that he will be overlooked or by-passed simply because he has severe reading problems that require intensive and extensive help. All we are suggesting is that in the beginning it is more prudent to help students who will require less time and effort and who can be helped in greater numbers with the least personnel. For example, at best, a reading specialist can help no more than twenty remedial readers in a day, and remedial readers need help daily. In contrast, a reading specialist may work with from one to four or five teachers in one day. The help that the teachers receive may be used to help several hundred less severely retarded readers. However, the purpose of this discussion is *not* to tell you how to run your program. The purpose is to point out the strong and weak points of where to begin a reading program. You must choose where and how you will initiate your program. Your needs at West High School may differ from those of East High School, and your needs should govern your choice.

Helping the Corrective or Retarded Readers

In this book the term "corrective reader" is used instead of "retarded reader" because of the connotation that is often implied by the term "retarded."

Corrective readers may be helped in several ways: (1) by the regular classroom teacher using the techniques of teaching reading discussed in previous chapters, and (2) by a special reading teacher in a separate classroom. In some instances it may be most beneficial for a student to receive both kinds of help for a limited period of time.

Because the techniques of teaching reading are discussed in detail in other chapters, here we shall merely outline the steps necessary for a teacher to follow in helping a corrective reader in the regular classroom.

1. Provide the student with reading materials at *his* instructional level in reading.
2. Use the assignment period to motivate the students to read, to set purposes for the reading, to develop concepts, to introduce new and difficult vocabulary.
3. Determine the student's ability to pronounce words used in the material and his understanding of the material.
4. Provide time for the student to practice and review previously learned reading skills.
5. Encourage the student to learn new vocabulary words by himself.
6. Keep a brief record of particular reading needs of the student and occasionally give him special help with these needs.
7. Inform the student of noticeable progress and improvement.

In some high schools a special reading class is provided for helping corrective readers improve their general reading skills. In this kind of class all students are helped to improve their reading skills by a special reading teacher. Classes are composed of students from all grade levels in the school, and students are taught in small groups according to each one's instructional reading level. In some schools students receive credit for attending these reading classes and other schools do not.

Some of the advantages attributed to teaching corrective readers in a special class are: (1) students receive instruction from a specially prepared teacher; (2) students receive a psychological lift when they see that other students have problems similar to theirs; (3) students receive help when they need it; (4) subject-matter teachers freed of the responsibility for teaching reading to these kinds of students can concentrate on helping students learn subject matter. Some of the arguments against the special reading class for corrective readers are: (1) the reading specialist is limited to teaching *general* reading skills and not the skills, vocabulary, and concepts needed for reading subject matter; (2) a student may make progress in the special reading class but regresses when he returns to his original class; (3) a student may be emotionally upset by the stigma attached to having to attend a special reading class; and (4) students often do not receive credit for taking a special reading class and therefore do not put forth their best efforts.

There is insufficient research for one to arrive at any valid conclusions about the particular strengths and weaknesses of special reading classes for corrective readers. Experience shows that students benefit from help with reading whether such help be given when in special classes or within the regular subject-matter classroom. If a subject-matter teacher is unable to help a corrective reader in his class, the student certainly should receive help in a special reading class. However, the availability of special reading classes for corrective readers does not relieve the subject-matter teacher of his responsibility for helping students to improve their reading of subject matter. The subject-matter teacher must introduce and encourage student use of a technical vocabulary, help students to learn to set purposes for reading, develop new concepts and correct faulty ones, and provide students with materials at their instructional reading levels.

Reading Instruction for the Remedial and Non-reader

The remedial reader and the occasional non-reader must receive individual instruction from a competent, thoroughly prepared reading teacher. His reading problems are so severe that he cannot be helped by anyone except a clinically educated specialist. The kind of treatment he needs can be determined only by a complete evaluation and careful diagnosis of his problem.

Remedial and non-readers do not fail to learn to read effectively because of lack of intelligence, nor because of lack of attempts by teachers to teach them. The reasons for a student being a remedial reader or non-reader are multiple. Only in extremely rare cases can the reason be traced to a single causal factor. By definition, a remedial reader has some kind of neurological impairment or severe psychological upset. In some instances the problem can be traced to brain damage or to some abnormality in the functioning of the brain.

Diagnosing a remedial reader as brain-injured is outside the realm of a teacher or reading expert and can be done only by a competent neurologist. Similarly, clinical psychologists or clinical experts in reading are the only persons qualified to diagnose psychological problems as being major contributors to reading problems. Teachers, however, can be alert to symptoms of excessive retardation in reading and can report such students to the administration for further appraisal.

Following are symptoms peculiar to remedial readers: (1) The student is unable to recognize a word even after receiving help from the teacher. For example, the student reading the following sentence, "He jumped into the wagon but the wagon did not move," may need help in pronouncing *wagon* and forgets or cannot recall *wagon* when he sees it the second time in the same sentence; (2) the student can understand subject material read to him but is unable to read the material himself; (3) the student learns content without difficulty when he does not have to read to learn; (4) the student receives an average or superior score on an individualized test of intelligence.

Help in Reading for the Highly Intelligent Student

Many highly intelligent or gifted students need help with reading. A fact that is too easily overlooked is that the intelligent student needs guidance, especially in reading, as much as, if not more than, the average or below-average student. However, the amount of time needed by the intelligent student will be much less than that needed for other students. He often needs only a hint or suggestion from the teacher to overcome his difficulty. He benefits greatly from a minimum of help.

The intelligent student does best when he is given special assignments that require wide and thoughtful reading. One of the surest ways to dampen his enthusiasm for learning is to force him to drill on meaningless detail or to assign him extra work simply because he is capable of doing it.

Some schools are organizing special reading classes for gifted students. One small high school in Oakridge, Oregon, developed a special reading class for 17 college-bound students. The students met two or three times a week as a group and spent the other days of the week in doing individual reading. During the group meetings they gave and discussed special reports, book reviews, and critiques of books and articles they had read.

During the year-long program, students were taught to write some of their critiques. Some students spent part of the time in improving their vocabularies, some learned to spell better, and others worked on critical reading. In brief, much of the work the students did was of their own choosing. According to the teacher, there was a minimum of structured reading activities except those that the students developed themselves. In this instance the students were fortunate in having one of those rare persons, an understanding teacher who was also an excellent teacher of reading and English.

The results of the program measured by standardized reading test scores were amazing. Students' written reactions about the value of the course were laudatory. Such a program or class is only a part of a developmental reading program, but it is an important phase that meets the needs of certain students and should be considered when organizing a total reading program.

A Brief Summary

At this point, let us summarize briefly our discussion of a developmental reading program. We have:

1. Defined a developmental reading program as an overall reading program that meets the needs of all students in school.
2. Established that there is a need for a developmental reading program at the high school level.
3. Shown the necessity for, and suggested some definite objectives or goals for a developmental reading program.
4. Provided a minimum list of principles that must be observed when organizing a developmental reading program.
5. Noted that although there are problems in initiating a reading program, they can be solved.
6. Shown that a developmental reading program must include provisions for helping *all* students to improve their reading skills.

The Role of Personnel in a Developmental Reading Program

The first part of this chapter showed that a developmental reading program provides for the continuous teaching of reading, and that it is vital to student learning. The remainder of the chapter is concerned with the role of each person who participates in the program.

Role of the Administrator

The high school administrator is a leader for improving the school's curriculum and teaching procedures. Because he is responsible for improving the learning of students and teachers, he must initiate the movement for a developmental reading program. But supplying the impetus for a reading program is merely the beginning of his involvement. The following list defines some of his duties. As an administrator he must:

1. Furnish the original stimulus for a developmental reading program.
2. Have a knowledge of reading and continue to broaden his knowledge through wide reading and study.
3. Know the reading achievement of students in his high school.
4. Secure the support of the school board for a reading program.
5. Inform and acquaint parents and students about the purposes and procedures of the program.
6. Obtain a budget that is sufficient to cover the expenses of a reading program.
7. Provide for needed in-service education of staff.
8. Locate and hire at least one full-time reading specialist.
9. Secure additional consultants when they are needed for special problems and instruction.
10. Insure coordination and cooperation between the school's guidance and counseling services and the reading program.
11. Arrange for released time for teachers who are working on major committees or other assignments.
12. See that funds are available for additional reading materials, including those in subject-matter areas.
13. Schedule and maintain classrooms needed for special reading classes.
14. Make certain that professional reading books, magazines, and pamphlets are available to teachers.
15. Keep his staff, students, and parents advised about the program.

A cursory reading of the duties of an administrator shows the need for the delegation of authority to different staff members and committees.

One of the administrator's first tasks will be that of arousing teachers' interest for the program. To say that some teachers will not be interested in participating in a reading program is an understatement. In the beginning, a number of teachers will offer excuses for not participating that would appall the school's most adept truant. However, appointing many of these persons to important committees may have positive and remarkable results. Once teachers begin working on the various reading committees, many of them become interested because they discover that the program has value for them and their students.

Three committees that are essential for the success of a developmental reading program and that need to be appointed early are the committee for *evaluation, objectives,* and *materials.* A brief discussion of their duties follows.

Committee for Evaluation

The committee for evaluation is one of the most important committees of the reading program and should be one of the first that is appointed. The committee's purposes include compiling and interpreting data about the reading achievement of each student. It may be that there is no regular program for testing students' reading. In this case the committee will develop, with the help of the reading specialist, a program for testing the reading achievement and the intelligence of each student.

The committee will also devise some means for ascertaining if the objectives of the reading program are being reached. If the objectives are not being met, it should attempt to determine why they are not and make recommendations for changes that will result in producing the desired results.

The committee should also develop questionnaires or other instruments for determining how parents, teachers, and students feel about the program. It should keep the administration and staff informed about its findings and progress.

An effective committee will work out a program for evaluating student growth in reading and learning. This would include (1) obtaining objective data of student growth in reading based upon standardized reading test scores, (2) securing evidence of student improvement in learning subject matter, (3) noting changes in student interest in reading, (4) checking on the general mental health of students, especially those with reading problems.

Committee on Objectives

The committee on objectives should be acquainted with recent research in reading. Its members will need to review principles of learning and become aware of recent changes in the thinking of leading psychologists because objectives of a developmental reading program must be based upon student needs, sound principles of learning, and principles of reading.

The objectives should be specific and measurable. They should be written clearly and succinctly, and subjected to continuous appraisal.

Committee for Selection of Materials

Membership of the committee for selecting materials should include the school librarian and teachers from each of the subject-matter areas. The committee should be fairly large for it has much work to do. Its major purposes is to find adequate materials at different levels of reading difficulty that will meet the needs of (1) students who lack the reading skills for learning from the regularly assigned textbook and (2) students who have superior reading skills and are not challenged by the textbook. Other duties might include (1) aiding staff members in selecting basic textbooks and (2) helping teachers to order textbooks at several levels of difficulty rather than ordering one copy of the same book for each student.

Role of the Reading Specialist

A competent reading specialist is one of the key persons in the organization and operation of a successful developmental reading program. Many a budding program in reading has failed to flower because it lacked a professionally educated and experienced reading specialist. A qualified reading specialist can help the staff realize that getting a reading program into operation requires time and total teacher cooperation.

What Is a Reading Specialist?* *A reading specialist is* (1) *an experienced classroom teacher,* (2) *specially prepared in the field of reading, and* (3) *dedicated to the task of helping all persons to read more effectively.*

A reading specialist does not become an expert in reading by self-proclamation or official appointment; nor does he become a specialist simply because he has taken a specific number of courses or because he has taught school for a particular length of time. A reading specialist understands the reading process and can teach reading because he has an educational background in reading and allied fields. He has a *minimum* of 18 quarter-hours in reading courses at the graduate level, and at least 12 hours of graduate work in psychology and evaluation. His educational preparation includes at least one year's clinical experience. In addition, he is a successful, experienced classroom teacher.

A reading specialist, as we have defined him, is an extraordinary

* The International Reading Association's Committee on Professional Standards has developed a "Minimum Standards for the Professional Training of Reading Specialists." A copy of the Standards may be had by writing the International Reading Association, Newark, Delaware.

teacher. He is competent to work with developmental, corrective, and remedial readers, their teachers, and administrators. He is prepared to test, evaluate, and diagnose reading problems, to develop a program of instruction in reading for individuals and groups, to help teachers of content to use reading techniques for improving learning in subject-matter areas, to demonstrate what can be done rather than talk about what should be done.

An adequately prepared specialist will work to insure staff cooperation by becoming acquainted with teachers and their methods for helping students to learn. He will note techniques that teachers use in helping students to improve their reading skills. Many a secondary teacher uses reading techniques without realizing that he is teaching reading and subject matter. That he is using reading techniques for improving student learning in subject matter should be made known to him and to other teachers.

Preparation of Teachers for Teaching Reading

Because very few secondary teachers ever have had a course or experience in teaching reading, the reading specialist must help prepare them. He will need to design a program for teaching teachers that is functional, and that can be understood by them. He must introduce concepts of reading and use demonstrations whenever possible. He must use the same or similar techniques with them that he used with students when introducing technical vocabulary.

During one of his first meetings with the staff he should invite teachers to ask questions about students' reading problems and thereby get the group involved in discussing reading and learning. Teacher's questions and discussion will furnish him with a guide for a number of future meetings.

Meetings should be held during the regular schoolday. They should be relatively short, to the point, and supplemented with demonstrations. Teachers, like students, need to be shown more and told less. For example, the specialist might discuss briefly how to use an informal reading inventory for determining a student's reading instruction level and then demonstrate *how* it is done. After the demonstration, teachers may discuss intelligently *why* it is important to determine each student's reading level.

Whenever possible the reading specialist should work with teachers in their classrooms. Demonstrating *how* students are prepared for reading and learning during the assignment period is one example of how the specialist can help teachers to improve student learning through reading.

Selecting the First Teachers for Initiating the Reading Program

After the first few meetings with the staff, the specialist will have a nucleus of interested teachers with which to begin the developmental reading program. He and the administrator should select no more than *two* or *three* teachers who are interested in and willing to try teaching reading. The teachers chosen for the initial phase of the program will determine the number and kinds of classes that will be used for introducing the program.

If possible, the program should be introduced in two or three subject-matter classes. Limiting the number of classes allows the reading specialist sufficient time for working with each teacher in the classroom and for meeting with those teachers after class.

In some instances the most prudent beginning may be that of working with corrective readers grouped in one classroom. Sometimes the reading specialist begins the teaching of such a group while a regular classroom teacher observes the procedures and techniques he uses in this kind of a class. The observant teacher gradually takes over the class and develops understanding of the reading process and techniques of teaching reading. At other times, a secondary teacher may have sufficient background in reading to assume responsibility for teaching the class with a minimum of help from the specialist.

Sometimes teachers want to start the program by using a group of highly intelligent students who need to be challenged by reading difficult materials. If an interested, capable teacher is available, such a class should be offered. In this kind of a class, students work best with a minimum of help, but they must have the right kind of help when it is needed.

In-Service Education of Teachers

We have previously described some of the kinds of help given teachers by a reading specialist. Such help comes under the heading of in-service education. However, teachers need more education and preparation for teaching reading than can be gained from attending a few meetings and seeing several demonstrations. In-service education must be continuous, planned, and evaluated

One of a reading specialist's responsibilities is that of planning and providing for continued in-service reading education of teachers. He works closely with the administration in securing reading experts for needed consultation and discussions with teachers. He plans reading workshops and arranges for college extension courses in reading.

Role of the Classroom Teacher

With minor exception, the teacher of subject matter in high school and college is among the most knowledgeable persons in his content field. He knows its concepts, basic ideas, vocabulary, and resources. He recognizes the contribution that his area of learning has for mankind. Because he is a teacher, he also hopes to inspire others to learn, understand, and use the available knowledge. The classroom teacher, however, is usually so occupied with teaching and its attendant chores that he seldom pauses to reflect on the extreme importance of his position. When society selects him as one capable of educating its youth, it places its total in his hands. When he accepts a job of teaching, he also must accept and assume the awesome responsibility that goes with it.

It is imperative that the teacher realize the role he plays. It is only when he realizes the significance of his position that he will do everything humanly possible to provide students with an opportunity to develop themselves to the maximum of their abilities. By helping students to improve their reading skills, he is aiding them in becoming independent learners and critical thinkers. But before he is capable of rendering such aid to students *he* must (1) understand the reading process, (2) use techniques of reading when assigning written materials for learning, (3) anticipate student needs in reading, (4) encourage students to use their previous experiences for learning new materials, and (5) arouse student's curiosity about the specific vocabulary of his content field.

SUMMARY

What a developmental reading program is and should be, what the general and specific objectives are, and how to organize it on the secondary-school and college level sounded its echo throughout this chapter. The principles of such a developmental reading program are to include subject-matter teachers, and students, to base objectives on students' needs, to begin instruction on students' instructional reading level, and to observe flexibility of the developmental reading program.

Additional facts that must be taken into consideration by teachers and administrators are:

1. Time for planning the program
2. Materials for the program
3. Decision of when and where to begin the program

4. Decision of how to help the corrective readers, the remedial readers, and the highly intelligent readers.

Furthermore, teachers' and administrators' attention has been drawn to the important functions of the reading specialist within the setting of a school, a school system, and the college. It is the reading specialist as we have identified him in this chapter who is in the unique position of helping students, teachers, and administrators in solving problems and shortcomings in reading.

SELECTED REFERENCES

1. Artley, A. Sterl. "The Development of Reading Maturity in High School; Implications of the Gray-Rogers Study," *Educational Administration and Supervision,* Vol. 43 (October, 1957), pp. 321–28.
2. Betts, Emmett Albert. *Foundations of Reading Instruction.* Cincinnati: American Book Co., 1957.
3. Carter, Homer L. J. "Effective Use of Textbooks in the Reading Program," *The Eighth Yearbook of the National Reading Conference for Colleges and Adults.* Fort Worth: Texas Christian University Press, 1959.
4. Fay, Leo C. *What Research Says to the Classroom Teacher: Reading in the High School.* Washington, D.C.: Department of Classroom Teachers and American Educational Research Association of the National Educational Association, September, 1956.
5. Freudenreich, Carl J. "How Can a Junior High School Staff Get a Schoolwide Developmental Program Underway?" *Improving Reading in the Junior High School,* ed. Arno Jewett. Department of Health, Education, and Welfare, Bulletin No. 10. Washington, D.C.: Government Printing Office, 1957. Pp. 37–46.
6. Gray, William S. "Frontiers in Preparing Teachers of Reading," *Frontiers in Teacher Education.* Normal, Ill.: Illinois State Normal University, 1957.
7. Harris, Albert J. *How To Increase Reading Ability* (4th ed. rev.). New York: David McKay Co., Inc., 1961.
8. *Reading in the High School and College.* The Forty-seventh Yearbook. Part II, National Society for the Study of Education. Chicago: The University of Chicago Press, 1948.
9. Strang, Ruth, McCullough, Constance M., and Traxler, Arthur E. *The Improvement of Reading.* New York: McGraw-Hill Book Co., Inc., 1961.
10. Super, Donald E. "Education and the Nature of Occupations and Careers," *Teachers College Record,* Vol. 58 (March, 1957), pp. 301–9.
11. Triggs, Frances Oralind, *et al. Diagnostic Reading Tests.* New York: Committee on Diagnostic Reading Tests, Inc., 1947–1963.
12. Witham, Anthony P. "Techniques for Identifying the Underachiever in Grades Four Through Eight." *The Underachiever in Reading,*

compiled and edited by H. Alan Robinson, Supplementary Educational Monographs, No. 92. Chicago: The University of Chicago Press, 1962.

SUGGESTED ADDITIONAL READING

Foster, Guy L. "Freshman Problem: 44% Couldn't Read Their Tests," *The Clearing House*, Vol. 29 (March, 1955), pp. 414–17.

Halfter, Irma T., and Douglas, Frances M. "Inadequate College Readers," *Journal of Developmental Reading*, Vol. 1 (Summer, 1958).

Jewett, Arno (ed.). *Improving Reading in the Junior High School*, Bulletin 1957, No. 10. Washington, D.C.: Department of Health, Education & Welfare, 1957.

Karlin, Robert. *Teaching Reading in High School.* Indianapolis: The Bobbs-Merrill Company, Inc., 1964. Chap. xiv.

Strang, Ruth, and Bracken, Dorothy Kendall. *Making Better Readers.* Boston: D. C. Heath & Co., 1957.

Traxler, Arthur E. "What Does Research Suggest About Ways To Improve Reading Instruction?" *Improving Reading in the Junior High School*, ed. Arno Jewett. Department of Health, Education, and Welfare, Bulletin No. 10. Washington, D.C.: Government Printing Office, 1957. pp. 5–15.

Wheeler, Keith. "Big Labor Hunts for the Hard Answers," *Life*, July 19, 1963.

Wilson, Rosemary Green. "What's Happening in Reading in Philadelphia," *The Reading Teacher*, Vol. 11 (February, 1958), pp. 185–88.

7

TEACHING SPELLING

It is not difficult to find fault with the spelling proficiency of large numbers of American students at any grade level, including college and university. Instead of ridiculing the ludicrous and pathetic orthographic distortions of the poor speller, or charging previous teachers with having failed to teach properly, schools need to establish programs for improving spelling.

It is not the writer's purpose to criticize the American public school unjustly or indiscriminately, but weaknesses in the teaching of spelling must be recognized. Not only must weaknesses be recognized, they must be accepted and steps taken to help the poor speller. More important than remediation, however, is *prevention.* Programs for spelling improvement can *prevent* many spelling problems.

Teachers, administrators, educational writers, and others often try to justify many of the current practices in the teaching or lack of teaching of spelling. Comparing spelling scores of yesterday's students with today's and concluding that "Johnny spells about as well as, or better than, his grandfather" *is not* an answer for the critics.

Pointing out that more children are attending school now than at any previous time and that they are younger at each grade level, although true, does not alter the facts; large numbers of students do not spell well. Nor do such statements appease parents, salve teacher's wounds, or help the student. Teachers need to face the facts, and make them known to the public. Teachers know that in addition to the many poor spellers in school there are many, many efficient spellers. It would be of benefit to teachers, pupils, and parents if teachers would also make this fact known.

It is easy to produce long lists of misspelled words that appear in newspapers, magazines, notes, letters, and signs written by adults, but such lists are not an answer to the critics of poor spelling. Such lists, however, are ample evidence that incorrect orthography is not solely a schoolboy deficiency. They are also proof that mastery of English spelling is difficult.

Few adults, not excluding teachers, spell "all right" as two words. When these persons are shown that "alright" is not an acceptable spelling, they refute the dictionary with examples from newspapers, magazines, and periodicals. Such examples contribute to "juvenile spelling delinquency."

In the writer's home town, one of the largest book stores formerly had "Ed's Stationary Store" emblazoned across its front windows. But, perhaps the sign was correct since the store has not moved an inch. Before me, as I write, is a recognized professional text for the teaching of spelling; it notes that "many people have difficulty in spelling 'picknicking.'"

In the field of psychology and spelling, experts cite evidence that children in today's schools can spell as well as, or slightly better than, their ancestors, but such facts are generally entombed in professional journals and are rarely exhumed. Perhaps it is just as well that such facts are not given to the general public; spelling as well as or slightly better than their ancestors is hardly a sufficient goal for spelling in an atomic age. Every trade, business, and profession demands from its members written communications that vary from simple notes or briefs to lengthy critical reports and evaluations. The following directive given to a group of salesmen speaks for itself: "Sloppy, ungrammical writing of reports will no longer be tollerated."

Two perennial questions that everyone asks are: Why can't our pupils spell better? What can we do to improve their spelling?

A discussion of the first question should furnish background for understanding the spelling problem. Once one understands the problem, solutions are more likely to be found and *applied.*

Factors That Contribute to Misspelling

If those who teach spelling will recognize that *a spelling problem is rarely due to a single factor,* a long step will be taken toward spelling improvement.

Factors that contribute to poor spelling for one pupil may also be present in another who is a successful speller. Each student is different, and his problem must be diagnosed in the light of his own difficulties. A teacher should be wary of believing that he has discovered *the cause* of the spelling problem, and of treating all poor spellers alike.

Some, but not all, factors causal to poor spelling will be discussed. Additional references for further study will be listed at the end of this chapter.

Cole says that spelling errors generally can be attributed to three sources: defects within the pupil, difficulties inherent in English words, and inappropriate methods of teaching (1, pp. 223–49). Specific factors operating within the three major sources listed by Cole will be discussed in this chapter.

PUPIL-CENTERED FACTORS THAT INFLUENCE SPELLING

Intelligence and Spelling

Intelligence must be considered when discussing spelling achievement since it is important, but it is not all-important. Parents and teachers often are puzzled when a student with average or above average intelligence fails to achieve successfully in spelling. "I just can't understand it," they say. "Bill appears to be smart, but just look at his spelling."

The correlation between spelling and intelligence is low but positive. The correlation coefficients found in research studies vary from extremely low to fairly high, depending upon the samples of students and the kinds of tests that are used to measure achievement. Representative correlations are those of Betts (.30 to .40), Spache (.45), and Louttit (.50) (12). Of these, Louttit's correlation is probably the most widely accepted.

The low correlations between spelling and intelligence often puzzle and confuse those who have no background in statistics. A partial explanation for the low correlation is that *other factors* in addition to intelligence affect a student's spelling achievement. Two boys, for example, may have I.Q.'s of 120. One may be an excellent speller while the other is the poorest speller in the class. The better speller may have a more positive attitude toward spelling than the other; he may be a more efficient reader, or he may be more emotionally stable, or have more valid reasons for learning to spell. *An untold number of causal factors may be working for the achieving speller and against the poor speller.* The only way to arrive at any legitimate decision is to diagnose the spelling problem of the less fortunate speller. The only way we can really help the individual student is by studying the kinds of errors he makes, learning how he studies words, knowing his attitude toward spelling.

The best that can be said of the relationship (correlation) between intelligence and spelling is that a high intelligence is helpful in spelling, but it does not guarantee efficient spelling. *Intelligence will limit the extent to which a person can achieve in spelling, but it is not the sole factor.* Many university students with enviable I.Q.'s have come to the writer for help with spelling. Most of them, when measured by standardized spelling tests, rate no higher than fourth- to sixth-grade level. On the other hand, it is futile to expect a pupil with an I.Q. below 70 to become an excellent speller. It is important that teachers understand that *students who are poor spellers are not necessarily stupid* and that, in most cases, they can be helped. Good spellers are made; they are not born.

Auditory Discrimination and Spelling

Auditory discrimination appears to be of more importance in spelling for elementary pupils than for older students according to group data from research studies (14). Results from group data, however, should not rule out the fact that some high school, college, and university students need help in learning to hear likenesses and differences in sounds of words and syllables before they can improve their spelling. Some of the more common examples of faulty auditory discrimination exhibited by some students who have asked for help are recognizable from their inaccurate pronunciation of words. Some of these errors are: "pronounciation" for *pronunciation,* "perscribe" for *prescribe,* "pertend" for *pretend,* "permote" for *promote,* "amazin" for *amazing,* "is" for *his,* "than" for *then,* "an" for *and,* "modivasion" for *motivation,* "quention" for *question.*

The list of such errors is endless. A rough count of these kinds of mistakes found among college and university students who apply for spelling help indicates that approximately 50–60 per cent of the students have never heard the word pronounced in an acceptable manner. "Why," some say, "I have never heard it that way before." Others are unable to hear the difference between "pertend" and "pretend" until they listen to a recording of their voices as they mispronounce words.

Poor auditory discrimination is not an affliction that suddenly attacks the high school student; it has been with him for many years. Somehow his inability to discriminate accurately the various sounds of some words and syllables has flourished, undetected by his teachers or others. If it has been detected, it certainly has not been corrected; and, *in most cases, it is a contributor to faulty spelling.* It is fairly well established that a student at the upper educational levels *spells words as he pronounces them.*

The secondary teacher in any subject area may help a student to improve his spelling by helping him to note his inaccurate or faulty pronunciation of words.

Visual Perception and Spelling

Visual perception, like auditory perception (discrimination), is a learned skill. Primary teachers teach all children to notice likenesses and differences among the forms and shapes of letters and words. Elementary teachers above the primary grades also teach their pupils to note the structural likenesses and differences of words and letters. Despite the amount of time spent on visual perception by teachers and pupils, a number of secondary and college students have not mastered this skill. When upper-level students habitually write "seperate" for *separate,* "alright" for *all right,* "ect." for *etc.*, the error may result from several factors, *one of which may be faulty visual perception.*

A striking example of failure to perceive detail in words was demonstrated by an outstanding engineering student in college who came to the writer for help in spelling. On one of his typewritten assignments the misspelling "thay" appeared three times. The student was unable to detect the error on his paper. The writer, using the chalkboard, printed "thay" and, immediately below it, "They." The student then was asked if he saw any difference between the two words. After studying the two words, he suddenly brightened and said, "Yes, I see the difference. The bottom one starts with a capital letter."

A small "t" was substituted for the capital "T" while the student watched. He was again asked if he saw any difference between the two words. After almost a full minute of examination, he said, "I see it now. *You* misspelled 'they.' It should be t–h–a–y."

Not until he failed to find "thay" in a dictionary would he admit his error or accept *they* as correct spelling. "MY gosh," he exclaimed, "how long have they spelled it that way? I never saw it that way before in my life!"

He was right. *He* had never seen the word as *they* before.

The secondary or college teacher can get a rough, but quick, estimate of the number of his pupils who need help in perceiving words. He may give a fifty-word spelling test and then have each student correct his own test with the aid of a duplicated list of the words. He will find that a number of the poor spellers frequently fail to see as many as seven to ten of their own errors. And this failure is not intentional. Some, for example, who habitually write "surprize" never see the difference between their misspelling and the corrected form *surprise* until it is pointed out to them specifically.

Poor Handwriting and Spelling

Poor handwriting is often listed as a factor in spelling errors. Research and experience indicate that this holds true at the elementary level. Poor handwriting at the secondary and college levels, however, appears to be *a symptom of poor spelling rather than a causal factor.* It is interesting to note that, among those secondary and college students that the writer has taught, poor handwriting tends to improve as spelling competence improves. Numbers of students have told the writer that they purposely write illegibly when in doubt about the correct spelling of a word. It appears that at the secondary and college levels poor handwriting is often a defensive cover up for inadequate spelling rather than a causal factor for poor spelling.

THE ENGLISH LANGUAGE AS A CONTRIBUTOR TO MISSPELLING

English is certainly not a language conducive to easy or correct spelling. Horn notes that attempts to reduce the difficulties of English spelling have been the serious concern of many scholars for more than four hundred years (11, p. 1338). Yet an alarming number of professional and popular magazine articles give the impression that phonetic spelling is the answer to all, or almost all, spelling difficulties.

Teachers, parents, and students should be skeptical of suggested panaceas, short cuts, or "proven" easy ways to master spelling. English is not a strictly phonetic language, nor is it entirely unphonetic. This is not a dichotomy. If English were strictly phonetic, each letter would represent always the same speech sound. On the other hand, if it were not phonetic, to a large degree it would be necessary for the user to memorize each word he needs to read or write.

Phonics and Spelling

Just how phonetic is English? It appears that no definitive study has been made of the extent to which English is phonetic, but estimates range from 60 to 85 per cent. On the basis of a limited study of selected common words, Hanna and Hanna state that the language is 80 per cent phonetic (7). Hay and Wingo say that their research indicates that 87 per cent of English monosyllables and polysyllables "are purely phonetic" (8). Hildreth (9) says that approximately 85 per cent of the language is phonetic although she gives no reference for these figures.

Regardless of the exact degree to which the English language is phonetic, teachers and students need to know two relevant facts. First, a large number of English words are irregular and cannot be spelled phonetically. Such words as "rhythm," "women," "knight," "foreign," and numbers of others *must be memorized.* Second, it is impossible for anyone to memorize all the words he may need to spell to express his thoughts in writing. An efficient speller must understand the phonetic regularities within the language, and he must be able to apply this knowledge to spelling.

HELPING THE STUDENT LEARN PHONETIC SKILLS

Large numbers of high school students do not understand the use of vowels or consonants in English. In fact, practically all students can glibly recite the vowels—*a, e, i, o, u.* A few will add, "and sometimes *y* and *w.*" But when asked to attach meaning to these symbols they are at a complete loss. With this type of student it is necessary to begin with simple phonetic words such as "pan," "hat," "can." The student needs experience in saying these words and noting the sound of the vowel *a* as used in the examples. The next step is to have him substitute other vowels for the *a* and to note the way the word sounds. For example, the student should substitute the vowel *e* for *a* in pan and say the new word aloud. He can then be given polysyllabic words in which both the short *a* and short *e* vowels are used as in "pencil," "penalty," "pantry," "companion," etc.

After the student has developed some understanding and use of vowels in phonetic words, he must learn the number of various ways in which the vowels do not always have the same sound. Using the same vowel *a* as a starter, the student should work with words in which the *a* has a different sound, for example, "catch," "rate," "alone," "dare," and "art." All of these should not, however, be introduced at one time.

Teachers as well as students are often confused by some of the almost weird combinations of letters that are used to express the same vowel sound. This is bound to happen when an alphabet of only twenty-six letters, seven of which are vowels, is used to express at least 44 different sounds.

When students know that many of the irregularities in spelling are a result of a changing pronunciation of words and a relatively fixed orthography, they appear to have a greater interest in learning spelling. Giving students examples of words such as "knife" and "comb" and explaining that both the *k* and *b* were formerly pronounced is preferred to having pupils merely learn that these letters are silent.

Students benefit from knowing that the same vowel sound is often represented by a number of different combinations. Some of the ways in which the sound of short *i* is expressed in English lead to greater student understanding of the language. Following are some examples of the way in which the sound of a short *i* is now written: pigeon (pij in), always (ol wiz), cottage (kot ij), surface (sur fis), senate (sen it), mountain (moun tin), guitar (gi tar), gypsy (jip si), women (wim in), been (bin), famine (fam in), foreign (for in), sieve (siv).

The preceding illustrations of only a small portion of the phonetic vagaries in English should preclude one's making any sweeping, generalized statement about the values of a strictly phonetic approach to teaching spelling. Teachers and students need to understand that an efficient speller must make use of phonetic principles in spelling, but to attempt to spell all English words phonetically is an illusory and nonsensical practice. For teachers, the question is not whether phonics should or should not be used in teaching spelling. English is phonetic, or phonetic in character to a large degree, but it is not a strictly phonetic one. Efficient spelling is dependent upon the *use* and *knowledge of phonetic* skills. But an overemphasis on phonics only leads to needless spelling errors, and frustrates both pupils and teachers.

Practices That Contribute to Poor Spelling

Spelling is a learned skill and is influenced greatly by factors and conditions operating in the learner's environment. Some of the common practices of parents and teachers that contribute to poor spelling performance by the pupil are: (1) excusing a pupil's poor spelling by saying, "His father can't spell, either. Poor spelling runs in the family"; (2) insisting that pupils learn to spell orally; (3) overemphasizing the value and use of rules; (4) telling students to "sound the word out," without giving them further instruction; (5) assigning long lists of words that students will rarely, if ever, need in their writing; (6) having students write misspelled words ten or one hundred times; (7) telling students to "look it up in the dictionary" before they are self-sufficient with the dictionary; (8) assuming that students will learn incidentally all the words they will need; (9) failing to diagnose student's spelling errors; (10) failing to discover how students attempt to learn spelling words; (11) requiring *all* students to study the same list of words regardless of differences in spelling ability and needs; (12) depending upon one or two restricted procedures for teaching spelling; (13) teaching spelling as a subject apart from language, or as a mere list of words to be memorized for the sake of hurdling another page in a book,

Techniques of Teaching Spelling

Spelling is considered as a regular subject in elementary schools. In far too many instances, however, spelling instruction consists of giving the students a list of words and a set of spelling rules that he is advised to learn. This technique will keep pupils busy but it teaches little spelling. Efficient spellers do not need this kind of "help," and poor or weak spellers are unable to profit from it.

In most secondary schools, spelling instruction is incidental to English classes. Until recently, little was done to help the poor speller. Subject-matter teachers condemned English teachers for pupils' poor spelling and were content that they had fulfilled their obligations by these accusations. During the past few years, however, there has been a growing awareness among secondary teachers that all spelling is not and cannot be taught by English teachers. Teachers of science, arithmetic, history, and shop subjects want to help students improve spelling, but they do not know where to begin. They ask: "How do you check on what words the student needs to learn?" "How can I show the student that spelling is important?" "What words should I teach and where do I get them?" "What is the best way of studying spelling words?" "How much time should be given for spelling?" How many times should I say the spelling word?" Can these pupils ever learn to spell?"

Secondary teachers of this type are to be commended. It is easy for a frustrated teacher who knows little about the teaching of spelling to blame others for having failed to do their jobs. It is more difficult to help the poor speller; but it is possible, and it is rewarding to both pupil and teacher.

Help for the Poor Speller

There is no one best method or program for helping retarded spellers, A *corrective* program for the improvement of spelling at the secondary level is presented in this chapter. It has produced good to excellent results with large numbers of students. It is not the *only* program, nor is it a panacea. It is a basically sound program.

Improvement in spelling at the high school level must begin with student attitudes. Few students are poor spellers by choice.

Through bitter experience, embarrassment, and frustration, many have adopted an attitude of indifference. Some are quick to point out, "My old man can't spell, but he owns two Cadillacs. Me, I'm just like him. I can't spell, but I'll hire a secretary to spell for me."

The teacher can often help dispel student indifference toward correct spelling if he gives examples of *why* correct spelling is a necessity. He may cite instances in which lack of spelling skill kept a student from getting a job or a promotion to a better job. Leaders in business and industry continually stress their need for employees who can use language accurately. They say that potential leaders are often bypassed because they cannot write a simple report without numerous misspellings.

Those who teach spelling should heed such comments and give written assignments that are meaningful to the student. Written work should not be used merely as a ruse to detect spelling errors. A letter written by the student to a friend and mailed by the teacher is a powerful incentive for improving spelling. The student who knows that his letter will be read by someone other than the teacher will exert extra effort to spell correctly. He has a personal need to write well. He can be helped.

Having students write short articles for the school newspaper is another valuable technique. Students take pride in published articles, whether they are their own or their friends'. Teachers know that when a student's story or article appears in the student newspaper, it is a powerful motivation for all students to improve their writing. Such an incentive could be used more often than it has been.

A Method for Learning To Spell

Most poor spellers have poor methods of learning to spell (15). A helpful teacher must know how each pupil tries to learn his spelling words. This can be learned by assigning some words and noting how each pupil *proceeds to study* them. Sheer memorization is one of the most common but least effective methods for learning to spell. Students and teachers must understand this. While it is necessary to memorize some words and parts of others, it is practically an impossibility for the student to memorize the majority of words he will need in his writing. A logical solution is to teach the student a more effective method for learning spelling.

Many poor spellers at the elementary, secondary, and college levels have overcome their spelling deficiencies by using the following method, which is an adaptation of Fernald's (4) approach to teaching spelling.

1. The word must have meaning for the pupil.

   Although some teachers and students will argue that they can learn to spell a word without knowing its meaning, this is sheer folly. A student learns to spell to express himself in writing. Spelling should not be used as a mental, gymnastic hurdle for learning nonsense words, and syllables. And, words without meaning for the individual are just so many nonsense syllables.

2. The word must be pronounced clearly and distinctly.

   There is no one correct pronunciation. There are accepted pronunciations, however, and one most often used in the area should be learned. Inaccurate and indistinct pronunciation of words by pupils usually results in incorrect spelling.

3. The student guesses the number of syllables in the word.

   After the student pronounces the word accurately, he guesses the number of syllables in it. This forces him to hear the separate parts within the whole. Although research is divided about the value of syllabication of words as an aid to learning spelling, *no research indicates that it is detrimental to learning.*

4. The student finds the word in the dictionary.

   After meaning and pronunciation have been determined, and syllabication guessed by the student, he checks with the dictionary. Until he has developed some skills in finding words in the dictionary, it may be that the teacher will have to write the word for him. The student writes the word from the dictionary, checks the syllabication, underlines the syllables from left to right. He should pronounce each syllable aloud as he underlines it.

5. The student studies the word.

   The word is studied both as a whole and the syllables within the whole word. When he feels that he can spell the word, he turns his paper over so the sample word is out of sight on the opposite side of paper. He then writes the word in the following manner:

   a. He says the whole word, i.e., "factory"
   b. As he begins to write the first syllable, he says that syllable aloud, "fac."
   c. He continues to say each syllable aloud as he begins to write it. He should say it as he normally speaks and not drag it out.
   d. When he completes writing the word, he underlines each syllable (from left to right) and says each syllable as he underlines it.
   e. He should again say the entire word.

6. Student verifies his spelling.

   He checks his spelling of the word against the original on the opposite side of the paper. If the word is correctly written, he repeats steps (a) through (e). He again checks his spelling with the original. If he has written the word correctly two successive times, the word is considered learned.

7. Retention check is essential.

   A retention check of the word within twenty-four hours is vital. This review, by testing, helps the student to retain the word. If he misspells a word, he should relearn it by following precisely the same steps he previously used.

Experience shows that pupils who have been unable to learn to spell generally retain 80 to 90 per cent of the words thus studied.

Word Selection

"What words should I give students when I teach spelling?" is a perennial question asked by secondary teachers. No exact answers can be given the questioners, but there is an approximate or tentative answer. Each student will need to learn words from two kinds of word lists, recognized lists of the most common words in English, and his own individual word list. Numerous research studies of most often used words, or words with the greatest frequency, indicate that there is a *basic core of words* that everyone needs for his writing. A large percentage of the words on this page, for example, can be found in lists of the most common 2,000 to 3,000 words in English. Space limits the number of recognized word lists that teachers might use as references or guides for teaching. Lists compiled by Dolch (2), Fitzgerald (5), Gates (6), Hildreth (9), Horn (10), and Thorndike (16) are excellent word lists and are usually available in most county school libraries.

Secondary and college teachers should not assume that a majority of their students have mastered the most common 3,000 to 4,000 words in English simply because they have used them many times. A quick survey of students' written work will usually suffice to dispel any such illusions. The procedure will also partially answer the questions about what words should be taught. Teach or reteach the most common 3,000 to 4,000 words in English to those students who have not mastered them. Each student who masters such a list of words has a basic or common core of words that he needs to express his thoughts.

The second word list each student should learn is compiled by him. He should be taught to keep a record of words that are peculiar to him; words that he needs to express his ideas and experiences in areas of his own particular interests.

TEACHING SPELLING AT THE STUDENT'S INSTRUCTIONAL LEVEL

Marked improvement would result in teaching spelling if teachers recognized the principle of *beginning instruction at the student's own level* rather than at grade level. It does not make sense to assign spelling words such as "secretariat," "sacroiliac," "righteous," "questionnaire," "Septuagint," and "picturesque" to students who cannot spell "secretary," "spine," "right," "question," "seventy," and "picture." The fact that such practice is more common than uncommon at the secondary level is indicative of two things: first, some secondary teachers are trying to help students with spelling; second, these teachers have not had any guidance in how to teach spelling. Therefore, the next several pages will be devoted to *how to find the students instructional level in spelling,* and *how to give spelling tests* for optimum student learning.

A student's instructional level is usually defined as that level where student learning is at its best. The material at this level is sufficiently difficult to be challenging to him, yet not so difficult that he will be overwhelmed or frustrated by it. On the other hand, the material is not so easy that it lacks face validity for the learner. For the teacher to be able to meet the student at his *instructional level* is no small task, but it is a crucial one.

FINDING THE STUDENT'S INSTRUCTIONAL LEVEL

Standardized tests and informal or teacher made tests should be used for determining a student's *instructional level* in spelling. Each has certain values that are not inherent in the other.

Standardized Tests

Standardized spelling tests are of value in any spelling program for several reasons.

1. They are developed by experts in testing and have been used with large numbers of pupils.
2. Words are selected on a scientific basis from recognized lists of most commonly used words.
3. They can be used to locate quickly both poor and excellent achievers in spelling.
4. They have norms for comparing a given class with national averages, or with other classes.
5. They can be used to get an approximate measure of a student's achievement in comparison to other students of the same grade level.
6. They have several comparable forms so that a student's rate of growth may be measured several times during the year.

7. They can be used for measuring growth in spelling over a long period of time.
8. They have specific directions for administration and interpretation of results.

Dictation-type tests should be selected in preference to tests that have the student check the correct or incorrect spelling of a word. There is a difference between a dictation, or recall, type of test and one that demands the student choose either the correct or incorrect spelling. The latter calls for a different kind of skill, which is often called a proofreading skill. Students should have practice, however, with both types of tests, but for purposes of instruction in spelling, teachers should choose the dictation-type test.

Informal Spelling Tests

Informal or teacher-made spelling tests have many values. They can be made from readily available graded spelling books or accepted word lists. Because they are composed of words that the student has studied and used in his writing, they have a high validity. At certain times and with some students, they are more valid than standardized tests that may present a sample of words that the students have *not* studied. Further, student retention of words previously studied can be checked any time the teacher considers it necessary.

Informal tests are invaluable as diagnostic tests. It is important that the teacher know what kinds of difficulties the student has with phonetic and non-phonetic words. Informal tests can be used to discover whether the student understands vowel sounds, consonant blends, the adding of affixes to known words, the addition or omission of certain syllables.

Perhaps the greatest value of a well-constructed informal test is that *it places a student at his instruction level.* It is basic that the teacher understand and know the criteria for the *instructional level* in spelling, the *achievement level,* and the *frustration level.*

Achievement Level. A student may be considered to be achieving successfully in spelling if he gets a minimum score of 90 per cent on a pretest of at least 50 words at a particular grade level. The words he missed at this level should be mastered, but to continue giving him spelling work at this level is not sufficiently challenging to him.

Instructional Level. If a student scores between 75 per cent and 88 per cent in spelling at a specific grade level, this can be taken as his *instructional level.* The teacher must continually check to see if he falls below this level or if he overcomes his difficulties and can advance to a more difficult level. As soon as a student consistently scores 90 per cent or better on pretests at a particular grade level, he should be given work at the next higher level.

Frustration Level. The student who cannot spell more than 50 per cent of the words on a pretest of spelling is completely frustrated by their difficulty. He should be tested on less difficult words until his instructional level is determined.

A student may be achieving successfully at his instructional level and occasionally score at or near the criteria for frustration level. This may be due to various reasons and should cause no undue alarm unless the pupil continues to spell at these low levels.

Making the Informal Test

Informal tests or inventories are not difficult to construct. The first task is to select a list of representative words. These may be special lists that have been developed by the particular school or district, or they may be taken from any of the accepted word lists, such as those by Dolch (2), Fitzgerald (5), Hildreth (9), and others (13). Many teachers prefer to use the graded word lists of an accepted spelling series.

Suppose that the secondary teacher chooses a popular elementary series of spellers for his word list and finds that the seventh-grade speller contains 704 words. To get a representative, 50-word test, he divides 50 into 704 and gets 14+. Starting with any word he wishes, he takes every fourteenth word until he has a test of 50 words.

Similar inventories should be made at various grade levels because of the great differences among the spelling achievement of secondary students. High school teachers should not be surprised to find a range of from ten to twelve grade levels between the poorest and best spellers in the class. Some students will need help with third-, fourth-, and fifth-grade words while others will be so efficient that they will be independent of teachers in this skill.

Review, the Key to Retention

Ebbinghaus (3), in his classical experiment, demonstrated that forgetting follows a definite pattern and is most rapid in the period immediately after learning. Review is necessary for retention except in rare instances where the stimuli are so great that one exposure suffices.

School subjects do not fall into this category. The student who has recently learned new spelling words should have numerous opportunities for using these words in writing. He should use them, and be checked on his use of them until they become so habitual that he is free to express his thoughts without fretting about the mechanical process of writing words.

Spelling Rules

Teachers are not generally in agreement about the value of teaching rules of spelling. Secondary and college English teachers whom the writer has questioned contend almost unanimously that, if students learn rules of spelling, they will become efficient spellers. Elementary teachers, when asked the same question, generally say that learning a minimum number of rules having the fewest exceptions aids correct spelling; rules, however, *should not* be overstressed.

The fact that a student knows a rule does not guarantee that he will make any use of it. The writer has long noted this while teaching secondary and university students. He recently conducted an experiment* in which he taught spelling to three different groups of university students who were average or above in all their subjects but were very poor spellers. A different method of spelling was used with each of the groups. The group which was taught with an emphasis on rules could recite the rules verbatim. Given a test of twenty-five words among which were six that followed the "ie" rule, thirteen students out of twenty-two misspelled one or more of the "ie" words† despite knowing the rule.

After the students had corrected their own papers, they discussed *how* and *why* the "ie" rule applied to each of the six words. Two days later, the same six words were included in the spelling list. *Nine* students again misspelled at least one of the same words. The misspelled words were studied again, and application of the rule was discussed by the students. The same six "ie" words were included in subsequent spelling tests. It was not until the words had been studied, reviewed, and tested a total of five times that *all* students in the group spelled all of them correctly.

Many secondary teachers have had similar experiences while teaching spelling to severely retarded spellers. Few retarded spellers need to learn rules of spelling. They need to learn to spell words. One of their major group weaknesses is that they have poor methods of learning words. Attempting to teach spelling by teaching rules to severely

* Paper presented to National Committee on Diagnostic and Remedial Reading.
† The six words are: receive, weight, deceive, perceive, grief, neighbor.

retarded spellers, who comprise approximately 30 to 40 per cent of the high school population, is fruitless and frustrating to both pupil and teacher.

On the other hand, some students who are only slightly retarded in spelling are frequently helped by spelling rules having few exceptions, if they understand the rules and have sufficient practice in using them.

Previously learned habits of poor spelling plague most inefficient spellers. These students have established patterns of misspelling, habits that must be corrected. Kinesthetic memory perpetuates the spelling pattern, whether that pattern is correct or incorrect. For this reason, the teacher should insist that spelling be learned correctly as a kinesthetic pattern. This allows for no erasures or patching of words. When an error is made, the student must *correctly respell the entire word in writing.*

Precautions To Be Observed When Teaching Rules

The following list of precautions should be observed when teaching rules of spelling:

1. Teach the student to recognize that a rule is not inflexible, and that it *usually* applies. The only rule of spelling that has no exception is that *q* is always followed by *u* in English.
2. Teach as few rules as possible, and then only those with the fewest number of exceptions.
3. Teach only *one* rule at a time. When several rules are presented at the same time or in too-quick succession, confusion is inevitable. To tell students, for example, that "ly" is added to adjectives to form adverbs and then have them memorize that rule in the hope or on the assumption that it will be used is sheer fantasy. They will continue to make such errors in writing as, "quicklly," "finaly," "roughlly," "awfuly." *After they are shown how* "ly" *is added to quick, final, rough, and awful, they can be helped to* "discover" *why and how* the "ly" rule applies to words and what it does to them. When this happens, *teachers teach, and students learn!*
4. Emphasize application and understanding of a rule rather than the parroting of meaningless words.
5. Give frequent opportunity for practicing and using the newly-learned rule.

Mnemonic Devices

Some persons question the use of mnemonic devices in teaching spelling; others make excessive use of them, and a few even think they are some new kinds of teaching machines. Many classroom teachers teach mnemonic devices, which they say helps students improve their spelling.

"Mnemonic" comes from "Mnemosyne," the Greek goddess of memory. A mnemonic device is a memory aid that helps one to remember. An example of a mnemonic device used by students to help them remember the spelling of *separate is, Se (e) pa rate* with the waitress. Another popular mnemonic that has helped many a student is, only an *ass* would spell *occasional* with two *s*'s.

The first and favorite mnemonic device that the writer recalls having seen was used by a country school teacher more than forty years ago. She introduced our class to the "ceed" brothers.

There was:

"ex" "pro" and "suc"

They are the only three who spell their last name *ceed.*

It is easy to recall that:

suc + ceed = succeed
ex + ceed = exceed
pro + ceed = proceed

The other "ceed" brother is *super,* and since he is above the rest, he spells his last name *sede.* He is the only member of the group who dares defy family tradition.

"super"

super + sede = supersede

All other "ceed" words, such as "recede," "precede," "concede," etc., use the *cede* ending. Of course, one could argue that the *sede* in "supersede" comes from a different root, *sedere,* meaning "to sit" while *ceed* comes from *cedere,* to move. Etymologically this is correct, and the teacher should know this. That the student who needs the aid of mnemonic devices should know this difference in roots, at this time, is debatable.

THE ETYMOLOGY OF WORDS—AN AID TO SPELLING

Etymology, a fascinating aspect of language has been generally overlooked by teachers in the public schools; at least, it has been sadly neglected. Few college students have had much experience with the study of word origins, but once they are exposed to it they evince great interest in this approach to understanding words. Secondary teachers might well take advantage of students' natural curiosity about words and introduce them to etymology. Few approaches to the study of language will create as much student enthusiasm and learning.

The teacher who knows about word origins develops techniques of introducing the etymology of words that immediately intrigue students.* He may give students a list of spelling words such as "villain," "cupboard," "chauffeur," "tantalyze," "weiner," "good-bye," "pinafore."

Instead of correcting misspellings, students are instructed to locate each word in the dictionary and are then helped to note the etymology of each one. "Villain" is an excellent word with which to begin for several reasons. When students see that "villain" comes from the Latin *villa,* a farm, or country house, they rarely misspell the word thereafter. In addition, their interest in words is aroused further when they see that *villain,* initially a peasant farmer or country bumpkin, has come to mean something vastly different from the original.

Another technique that has been used successfully is to ask puzzle-type questions about words. One example is to ask students how John Glenn, a fortuneteller, a typewriter key, and a flower are related. Little teacher help is needed to elicit student response that John Glenn is an astronaut. Students, however, usually need some help in determining that *astro* is the key word that ties all the words together. After they "discover" that "astro" comes from the Greek *astron* (star), they are "on their own."

The teacher who wishes to enliven the teaching of spelling, develop student vocabularies, and help students understand the English language should not overlook etymology or the study of word origins.

* Some excellent references for word study are included in the bibliography at the end of this chapter. The list is a minimum one, but can be used as a starter.

SUMMARY

Good and poor spelling is in evidence among all Americans regardless of age or schooling. Spelling, like reading, arithmetic, and speaking, is a learned process. Any student who is mentally and physically capable of attending high school, and who has an honest desire to learn to spell, can do so. Spelling seems to be learned easier by some students than others but this does not rule out the premise that all students can learn to spell.

Those who would help a student to improve his spelling should keep the following points in mind:

1. Begin teaching at the learner's instructional level.
2. Observe how he learns words. If he has a poor method for learning, teach him a better one.
3. With the student, plan a program for his spelling improvement.
4. Give him a chance to achieve success by learning words he needs to use in his writing.
5. Provide time and opportunity for consistent review.
6. Make use of mnemonic devices, etymology of words, and other devices that incite interest and aid in learning.
7. Recognize that some words must be memorized, that some words follow rules, that some words can be spelled phonetically, but that overemphasis on any of these techniques will result in more harm than good.

SELECTED REFERENCES

1. Cole, Luella. *The Elementary School.* New York: Holt, Rinehart & Winston, Inc., 1947.
2. Dolch, Edward William. *Better Spelling.* Champaign, Ill.: Garrard Publishing Co., 1942.
3. Ebbinghaus, H. (1885). *Memory, a Contribution to Experimental Psychology,* trans. H. A. Ruger and C. E. Bussenius. New York: Columbia University Press, 1913.
4. Fernald, Grace M. *Remedial Techniques in Basic School Subjects.* New York: McGraw-Hill Book Co., Inc., 1943.
5. Fitzgerald, James A. *The Teaching of Spelling.* Milwaukee: Bruce Publishing Co., 1951.
6. Gates, Arthur I. *A List of Spelling Difficulties in 3876 Words.* New York: Bureau of Publications, Teachers College, Columbia University, 1937.
7. Hanna, Paul R., and Hanna, Jean S. "Spelling as a School Subject," *National Elementary Principal,* Vol. 38 (May, 1959), pp. 8–23.

8. Hay, Julie, and Wingo, Charles E. *Reading with Phonics.* Philadelphia: J. B. Lippincott Co., 1948.
9. Hildreth, Gertrude. *Teaching Spelling.* New York: Holt, Rinehart & Winston, Inc., 1955.
10. Horn, Ernest. "The 3,009 Commonest Words Used in Adult Writing," *The Fourth Yearbook.* Washington, D.C.: Department of Superintendence of the National Education Association, 1926.
11. Horn, Ernest. "Spelling," *Encyclopedia of Educational Research* (rev. ed.), ed. Chester W. Harris. New York: The Macmillan Co., 1960, pp. 1337–54.
12. Marksheffel, Ned D. "A Spelling Improvement Program," *Elementary School Journal,* Vol. 54 (December, 1953), pp. 223–29.
13. Marksheffel, Ned D. *Spelling for High Schools.* Syracuse, N.Y.: The L. W. Singer Co., Inc., 1957.
14. Marksheffel, Ned D. *The Relationship of Auditory Discrimination to Spelling Achievement at the College Freshman Level.* Doctor's Dissertation. Stanford, Calif.: Stanford University, 1958.
15. Spache, George. "Spelling Disability Correlates. 1. Factors Probably Causal in Spelling Disability," *Journal of Educational Research,* Vol. 34 (April, 1941), pp. 561–86.
16. Thorndike, Edward L. *A Teacher's Word of 20,000 Words.* New York: Bureau of Publications, Teachers College, Columbia University, 1931; rev., 1932.

SUGGESTED ADDITIONAL READING

Ayer, Fred C. "An Evaluation of High School Spelling," *School Review,* Vol. 59 (April, 1951), pp. 233–36.

Betts, Emmett Albert. *Foundations of Reading Instruction.* Cincinnati: American Book Co., 1957.

Blair, Glenn Myers. *Diagnostic and Remedial Teaching.* New York: The Macmillan Co., 1956.

Bloomer, Richard H. "Connotative Meaning and the Reading and Spelling Difficulty of Words," *Journal of Educational Research,* Vol. 55 (November, 1961), pp. 107–12.

Brown, James Isaac, and Salisbury, Rachel. *Building a Better Vocabulary.* New York: The Ronald Press Co., 1959.

Burton, Dwight. "Spelling Can Be Taught to High School Students," *School Review,* Vol. 61 (March, 1953), pp. 163–67.

Campanale, Eugene A. "A Survey of Methods in the Teaching of Spelling," *Elementary English,* Vol. 39 (May, 1962), pp. 445–55.

Carrell, James, and Pendergast, Kathleen. "An Experimental Study of the Possible Relation Between Errors of Speech and Spelling," *Journal of Speech and Hearing Disorders,* Vol. 19 (September, 1954), pp. 327–34.

Cook, Ruth C. "An Evaluation of Two Methods of Teaching Spelling," *Elementary School Journal,* Vol. 58 (October, 1957), pp. 21–27.

Funk, Wilfred, and Lewis, Normal. *Thirty Days to a More Powerful Vocabulary.* New York: Wilfred Funk, Inc., 1942.

FUNK, WILFRED JOHN. *Word Origins and Their Romantic Stories.* New York: Wilfred Funk, Inc., 1950.

FURNESS, EDNA L. "Should Reading and Spelling Be Taught Separately?" *Clearing House,* Vol. 31 (October, 1956), pp. 67–70.

GREENE, HARRY A. *The New Iowa Spelling Scale.* Ames, Ia.: State University of Iowa, 1954.

HANNA, PAUL R., and MOORE, JAMES T. "Spelling from Spoken Word to Written Symbol," *Research in the Three R's,* ed. C. W. HUNNICUT and WILLIAM J. IVERSON. New York: Harper & Row, Inc., 1958. Pp. 309–15.

HARRIS, OLIVER E. "An Investigation of the Spelling Achievement of Secondary School Pupils," *Educational Administration and Supervision,* Vol. 34 (April, 1947), pp. 208–19.

HIXSON, JEROME C., and COLODRY, I. *Word Ways.* Cincinnati: American Book Co., 1939.

HORN, THOMAS D. "Research in Spelling," *Elementary English,* Vol. 37 (March, 1960), pp. 174–77.

LEWIS, NORMAN. *Word Power Made Easy: the Complete Three-Week Vocabulary Builder.* Garden City, N.Y.: Doubleday & Co., Inc., 1949.

LOUTTIT, C. M. *Clinical Psychology* (rev. ed.). New York: Harper & Row, Inc., 1947.

MARKSHEFFEL, NED D. "Helping Retarded Spellers," *Improving College and University Teaching,* Vol. 11 (Spring, 1963), pp. 97–100.

MARKSHEFFEL, NED D. "Composition, Handwriting, and Spelling," *Review of Educational Research,* Vol. 34 (April, 1964), pp. 177–86.

MERRIAM CO., G. & C., Springfield, Mass.: The Publisher, 1937. *Vocabulary Building, Word Study, and Bibliography.*

MORRIS, WILLIAM, and MORRIS, MAY. *Dictionary of Word and Phrase Origins.* New York: Harper & Row, Inc., 1962.

PLESSAS, GUY P., and PETTY, WALTER. "The Spelling Plight of the Poor Reader," *Elementary English,* Vol. 39 (May, 1962), pp. 463–65.

RINSLAND, HENRY D. "A Review of the Traxler High School Spelling Test," *Fourth Mental Measurements Yearbook,* ed. OSCAR K. BUROS. Highland Park, N.J.: The Gryphon Press, 1953.

RUSSELL, D. H. *Characteristics of Good and Poor Spellers: A Diagnostic Study.* Contributions to Education, No. 727. New York: Bureau of Publications, Teachers College, Columbia University, 1937. 103 pp.

SHIPLEY, JOSEPH T. *Dictionary of Word Origins.* New York: The Philosophical Library, Inc., 1945.

SPACHE, GEORGE. "Spelling Disability Correlates. 11. Factors Probably Causal in Spelling Disability," *Journal of Educational Research,* Vol. 35 (October, 1941), pp. 119–37.

STAIGER, RALPH C. "The Spelling Problem in High School." *Education,* Vol. 76 (January, 1956), pp. 280–85.

STAUFFER, RUSSELL G. "A Study of Prefixes in the Thorndike List To Establish a List of Prefixes that Should Be Taught in the Elementary School," *Journal of Educational Research,* Vol. 35 (February, 1942), pp. 453–58.

STAUFFER, RUSSELL G. "The Relationship Between Reading and Spelling," *Education,* Vol. 79 (December, 1958), pp. 206–10.

WALLACE, EUNICE E. *Programed Spelling for High School and College Students.* Corvallis: Oregon State University, 1964, n.p. (Mimeo.)

WALLACE, EUNICE EWER. *A Comparison of Two Self-Instructional Methods for Improving Spelling in High School and College: A Twenty-six Classroom Experiment.* Doctor's Thesis. Corvallis, Oregon: Oregon State University, 1964. 130 pp. Abstract: *Dissertation Abstracts,* Vol. 25 No. 10 (April, 1965), p. 5801.

8

TEACHING READING IN CONTENT AREAS

Although there is a lack of adequate information about school dropouts, it is estimated that from about 33 (13, p. 14) to 40 per cent (20, p. 5) of America's youth will never complete high school. Despite the large number of dropouts, the percentage of graduates is higher than ever before. And both dropouts and potential graduates are presenting secondary teachers with problems that previously did not concern them. Such unexpected problems often place the teacher in a awkward and disconcerting position. The problem of teaching reading in the content areas is a prime example.

Until the last several decades, the secondary schools were highly selective. Students who were unable to achieve academically dropped out of school for various reasons, including inefficient reading. The withdrawal of such students left a select group of students who generally were efficient readers. Today, the holding power of secondary schools is much greater for all students, and many inefficient readers remain in school. Few secondary teachers have been academically prepared to teach reading in content areas and are, therefore, frequently subjected to severe criticism for not helping inefficient readers improve reading skills. Is such criticism of secondary teachers warranted? Let us consider some of the more common charges, from the points of view of both critics and teachers:

The Critic's Viewpoint

Critics claim that secondary teachers are completely indifferent to students' reading difficulties. They say teachers are not concerned about whether students can or cannot read the assigned textbook. Students who are unable to read adequately are looked upon as biological anomalies or as products of inefficient elementary schools. The sooner such students are dropped from school, the better the school will be, say the critics.

The Teacher's Viewpoint

Many secondary teachers admit that in the past some teachers may have been, or may have appeared to have been, indifferent to students' reading needs simply because they did not know enough about the reading process to recognize when students needed reading help. Teachers also state that they recognize the need for different levels of textbooks but that it is impossible to provide students with multilevel textbooks and to teach reading because (1) the school administrators insist that teachers use only the one adopted textbook, (2) the course of study is designed for a single specific textbook, (3) less difficult textbooks are unavailable in the particular subject-matter field, (4) teachers rarely have had a course in *how* to teach reading, and therefore, have no idea of what is meant by teaching reading in content areas, or (5) teachers would teach reading if they knew how reading should be taught.

A Consideration of the Critic's and Teacher's Viewpoints

Careful consideration of the critic's and teacher's viewpoints indicates that the critics do have grounds for complaint. Unfortunately, the critics have overgeneralized often. Some of their criticism have been caustic and unwarranted. Nevertheless there have been legitimate reasons for criticizing the teaching of reading in the secondary schools.

Historically, the responsibility for the teaching of reading was relegated to the elementary school. Many secondary teachers felt no obligation to help students with reading. But they ought not to bear full blame for their reluctance. Until recently, parents, children, educators, and teachers considered reading to be a relatively simple skill mastered in the elementary grades. Today, such a concept of reading is unacceptable.

Research has revealed that reading is infinitely more complex than it was previously thought to be. Smith and Dechant (17, p. 378) note that the emphasis on a developmental reading program has occurred only within the past twenty years. As late as 1948, Gray noted (6, p. 47) that the two most common procedures used by high schools and colleges for attacking the reading problem of students was (1) to use reading tests to study the attainments and needs of students, and (2) to provide corrective and remedial help for poor readers.

In view of the reading help being offered in many of today's high schools and colleges, the procedures that were used in 1948 appear to be limited. There are high school administrators and teachers who do little to improve students' reading. Such relative inaction often brings detrimental criticism down upon those teachers who are attempting to improve students' reading.

Teacher-education institutions and state departments of education must bear some of the blame, inasmuch as few require secondary teachers to take a course in the teaching of reading, even though such courses may be listed in institution catalogues.

In summary, during the past ten years there has been significant change in secondary teachers' views about the teaching of reading, and many teachers are now asking pertinent questions about techniques and methods for teaching reading in the content areas. Some of the questions will be used as guidelines for the following discussion.

How Can I Teach Reading in My Content Area?

Although certain reading skills and needs are peculiar to each content area, a number of reading skills and techniques are common to all subject-matter fields. Before we discuss reading in specific areas, such as English, home economics, and science, let us look at some ways in which every secondary and college teacher can help his students to read more efficiently. At the same time, we must not deviate from the purpose of improving the learning of subject matter through reading.

Efficient learning of subject matter in the classroom is not a haphazard phenomenon. Student learning is determined greatly by the kind of guidance that is given by an adequately prepared teacher. Students must do their own learning, but learning does not proceed automatically simply because a student is in a classroom. An adequately prepared teacher understands the principles of learning and uses them to enhance student learning. Space does not permit a dicussion of learning principles.* However, the teacher who determines students' ability to read the prescribed text is following a procedure consistent with learning principles. Before he makes reading assignments from the textbook, it is psychologically sound and practical that he know: (1) which students can read the materials independently; (2)

* The student who is confused by the various theories of learning may benefit from reading Ernest R. Hilgard, *Theories of Learning* (rev. ed.; New York: Appleton-Century-Crofts, 1955).

which students can read the text with his help; and (3) which students cannot read the text under any conditions.*

Students Need Help in Learning How To Read a Textbook

Teacher observation and research indicate that students need help in learning how to use their assigned textbooks. Teachers should know the strengths and weaknesses of the textbooks their students use. The teacher should know when to warn students about particularly difficult passages and when to supply clues for understanding the materials. In many instances, textbooks covering the same materials and supposedly written at the same reading level vary greatly in difficulty of reading although they may have the same readability score. The differences in difficulty of reading may be due partly to a difference in authors' styles of writing, outline or organization of materials, and the manner in which new vocabulary is introduced. Whatever the reasons, the alert teacher recognizes the sections of material that may confuse his students and prevents such confusion by noting the difficulties when he assigns the material.

The subject-matter teacher is a specialist in his field of learning. The fact that he is a specialist may be detrimental rather than conducive to student learning. The specialist is in the precarious position of knowing his field so well that he may forget the numerous learning experiences, the hours of study, and the continual motivation that preceded attainment to his present state and knowledge. He must never assume that concepts that appear simple to him are not equally simple for students who lack his preparation, education, and maturity. The specific vocabulary that is necessary for understanding the written content of his specialty, and that he uses effortlessly and meaningfully, may constitute gargantuan semantic barriers to students. Therefore, the specialist, or teacher of subject matter, must recognize his own unique position for helping students to learn in his area of specialization.

The teacher of subject matter who recognizes that concepts develop slowly and from meaningful learning experiences will provide sequential experiences that enable students to learn content. He will seek to insure adequate learning by introducing students to some, but not all, of the key vocabulary words. He must use the words in both spoken and written form *before* students attempt assignments that use these specific words for the first time. By introducing some technical words and by setting up experiences that require students to learn additional

* See Chapter 5, *Evaluation of Reading in Subject Matter*, for a discussion of how to evaluate students' reading levels.

vocabulary, he is not only teaching subject matter but he is also using reading techniques.

What Is Meant by "Teaching Reading in Subject Matter"?

Many secondary teachers are confused and frustrated when they are told that they must teach both reading and subject matter. Because they have rarely had any preparation for teaching reading, and because they do not understand what is meant by "teaching reading," some teachers become defensive immediately and state unequivocally that they have neither the time nor the inclination to teach beginning reading or remedial reading. Whether they do or do not recognize the import of their statements, such statements are germane to the problem. Teachers and administrators should understand clearly that teachers of subject matter are no more responsible for teaching beginning reading or for teaching remedial reading than they are responsible for controlling the weather.

The teaching of beginning reading and remedial reading are specialized teaching areas to the same degree as is the teaching of mathematics and chemistry. Teachers of subject matter do not have the educational preparation necessary for teaching beginning or remedial reading. Further, if they had the preparation and experience to teach these areas of reading, they could not do so in their regular classrooms because the required time is not available. If for any reason, a secondary student needs help in *learning to read* or if he requires *remedial reading,* he is outside the jurisdiction of the subject-matter teacher. He must receive individualized instruction from a reading specialist. Subject-matter teachers, however, must accept responsibility for identifying and referring students in their classes who need specialized help in reading.

Does Teaching Reading in Subject Matter Make Sense?

Succinctly stated, teaching reading in a subject-matter area is simply *teaching that does make sense.* Sometimes, a succinct statement may be as distracting as a discursive one, especially for students who lack sufficient experiences in the area under discussion. It may be helpful to look in on a portion of a general science lesson being conducted by a Portland, Oregon, high school teacher. His students range from average to superior intelligence and are in the tenth grade.

The class is in progress as we enter the classroom. One group of students is learning how alcohol is extracted from fermenting fruit. Some of the students are already observing their gurgling jugs, and are busily making notes of the action while others are setting up similar equipment. Another group is reading textbooks and other reference materials to find answers to previously assigned questions. Several students appear to be working independently of all groups. A group of eight students is clustered about the teacher, who is wearing a butcher's apron and is expertly wielding a scalpel on a fresh beef heart that he got at the packing house early this morning.

As he steadies the heart he says, "I can handle this muscle easily by grasping it here at the *superior vena cava* and the *aorta.* Am I right in thinking that we decided to dissect this heart so that we can look at a cross-section of the *right* and *left auricles,* and their accompanying *ventricles?*" The class nods in agreement, and he continues to talk and to draw the students into the demonstration. "Where do I start cutting, Bob?" As Bob directs him, he cuts swiftly and accurately. "Now you can see the *auricles* and *ventricles.* Locate the right *auricle* for us, Mabel. How do you know this isn't the left *auricle?* Good thinking. Could you draw this heart from memory, Bill? All right, take a good look, slip into that seat and let's see what you can do. I'll bring you up on what we've covered when you finish."

Without any perceptible break in the lesson, Bill slipped into a desk and began drawing the heart while the remainder of the class continued to observe the demonstration. "If this is the left auricle what is this, Anne? Which of the *ventricles* has the thicker wall, George? Why is it thicker? Here, Mabel, feel the difference. The rest of you feel the difference in the thickness of the walls. Does our textbook agree with your statement about the left *ventricle,* Jerry? Find the author's statement and reread it to us as soon as we've finished, Anne, please."

At this point we must leave the group and review the technique of reading that the teacher used.

Had the teacher prepared the group for the demonstration? What statements give us a clue that the group had previously read about the heart? Did the teacher review the specific vocabulary during his conversation with his students? Did he check on any student's pronunciation of the terms? Did he test any student's ability to visualize what he had observed and then to reproduce his mental picture so that others might use his illustration for learning? Did he provide his students with meaningful learning experiences? Do you feel that they were interested and that they were learning? Before you read further pause to reflect on the teacher's behavior.

As the class left at the end of the period, the teacher remarked, "I'm not sure whether I'm teaching reading or not, but *my students are learning.* They can read their texts or these other books I have. They can write and spell, too!" He added with a trace of pride, "I really don't know if I'm teaching reading or not, but what I'm doing *makes sense to me.*"

The teacher's actions make sense to anyone interested in helping students to learn. He was certainly teaching *reading and subject matter.* The reading techniques he used are listed briefly. Check your answers to the above questions with the following list:

1. The teacher was prepared for teaching.
2. The students were ready for the demonstration. They had read about the heart and its functions.
3. The students knew the technical vocabulary.
4. The teacher reviewed the pronunciation of some vocabulary and checked some students' pronunciation of the new words.
5. One student was directed to find and reread a specific selection that he later read orally to the group. The teacher told us that there had been some discussion and questions about the textbook author's statements during the assigned silent reading.
6. The teacher's questions called for a knowledge of *facts,* the ability to make *judgments,* and an understanding of *vocabulary.*
7. Various groups of students were working at different tasks according to their needs for various learning experiences.

This brief example of a secondary teacher teaching subject matter and reading as an integrated process to high school sophomores deserves thoughtful consideration by all subject-matter teachers because it makes sense! It makes sense because reading and learning of content cannot be considered as separate entities, but as interwoven learning techniques.

What Kinds of Readers Can Be Helped by the Subject-Matter Teacher?

First, the teacher must understand that *developmental readers,* those who are reading at approximately their own reading potential, will continue to improve their reading skills with a minimum of teacher help. Second, *corrective* or *retarded* readers, those who are reading below their reading potentials but who are not severely retarded, will need help from the teacher but are capable of improving their reading skills. The teacher, therefore, has two kinds of readers whom he can and must help if he is to fulfill his obligations to students and to subject matter; he can help *developmental* and *corrective* readers.

What Can the Teacher Do To Help His Students Read Better?

Few secondary students are efficient, mature readers. Many of them have been exposed to a number of general and specific reading skills but for numerous reasons the exposures did not take. Reading skills, like other learned skills, usually require more than one presentation before they are mastered. Optimum improvement of student reading is dependent upon skillful teaching; practice, review, evaluation, reteaching, and motivation must be continuous from grade to grade, and from day to day. For example, by the time students reach high school most of them have had lessons in how to use a textbook. Therefore, it appears logical for secondary teachers to assume that students know how to use their textbooks to the utmost. A few minutes expended in checking this assumption will disclose the fallaciousness of such thinking. For example, during the past eight years the writer has had all the future secondary teachers at Oregon State University in his Methods of Reading classes answer a number of questions about their own reading skills and habits. Approximately 3,000 questionnaires were answered anonymously by juniors, seniors, and graduate students. The students came from every state in the Union, from every kind of a high school from private to public, from large schools and small schools, and from progressive to traditional schools.

The results of their answers are as follows: (1) Fewer than five per cent of the students ever read the preface to their texts; (2) less than 10 per cent know either the author's name, or the name of the textbook; (3) about 2 per cent know both the author and the title of the textbook after using it for about three months; (4) approximately 90 per cent of the students read the assignments by beginning on the first page of the chapter and reading sequentially until they arrive at the last page; (5) from 60 to 70 per cent of the students never look at charts, graphs, or tables; (6) 10 to 20 per cent look briefly at the charts, graphs, and tables but do not study them; (7) fewer than 15 per cent use a dictionary to check on pronunciation and meaning of words that they do not know unless they are told that they will be tested on them; (8) less than half the students use a dictionary skillfully; (9) not one in a hundred who looks up a word in the dictionary refers to the etymology of the words; (10) about 95 per cent use context clues to derive meanings of words; (11) not one in fifty knows how to set purposes for reading; and (12) 99 to 100 per cent feel that the way to improve their reading is to increase their speed.

Such reactions by university students causes one to question some of the teaching to which these students were exposed.

TEACHING READING IN ENGLISH

Every teacher of subject matter faces the problem of teaching students to read in his specialized field. Nevertheless, only a comparatively small percentage of subject-matter teachers recognize the responsibility to improve students' reading skills. It is much simpler to toss the reading problems onto the shoulders of the English teacher. It is overlooked often that the English teacher is as much a subject-matter specialist as is the biology, home economics, or mathematics teacher. There can be no denying the fact that the English teacher should teach students certain communication skills, but he should not be expected to teach students to read biology, home economics, or mathematics. His responsibility for teaching reading includes, for example, the teaching of general reading skills that are used in all kinds of reading, and the specialized reading skills required for the reading of literature.

The public, including teachers of subject matter, often has a confused, distorted, and totally unrealistic view of the English teacher's role. It is an unfortunate use of human intelligence to assume that the English teacher's job consists of assigning a few themes, teaching some rules of grammar, including diagramming, and having the students read *The Tale of Two Cities,* and "something" from Shakespeare.

One of the methods for determining any teacher's responsibilities is to examine the aims or goals of both the content area and the teacher. If we examine the goals of English that abound in the various courses of study, we discover immediately and in no uncertain terms the reasons for the public's confusion about the role of the English teacher. Hook (8) notes that in past years a researcher studied the published aims of English and found that 1,581 different aims were listed. No doubt other aims of English have been added since that time. Is it any wonder that the English teacher finds that he is unable to teach all that is expected of him? The wonder of it is that more confusion and chaos does not exist in the area of English.

The function of this discussion is not to determine or to dictate what the English teacher should teach, how he should teach, or why he should teach. The purpose of this particular discussion is to help the secondary teacher understand how and why the teaching of reading is a cardinal function of the total English program, and to help the English teacher to recognize the unique importance of his position for helping each student to improve his reading skills, and to develop a love of reading.

The Reading Table

Every subject-matter area should have its own classroom reference library, and each English classroom should have a reading table. It should be a table on which there are books of all kinds and descriptions. These should include books of poetry, philosophy, art, music, science and some books of nonsense. Somewhere among its volumes there should be stories of Greek, Roman, and old Norse mythology, animal stories, biographies, mysteries, and even a Western yarn or two. And by all means, a few mail-order catalogues, including late editions of the Sears Roebuck and the Montgomery Ward catalogues.

These books should range from very easy to difficult reading. The books are not a substitute for the school library but are merely a sample of some of the riches of reading to be found in the library. They are the 'free samples" to induce the uninitiated to try the larger stock.

A reading table can be justified on both psychological and educational principles. Many a reluctant reader learns to love to read when he finds that there are certain times that he can read what he wants to read, how he wants to read, and when he wants to read, without worrying about making a book report.

Experience indicates several precautions to be taken if the library table is to fulfill all of its functions. First, the teacher must maintain control over the table's contents and use. He can do this easily and satisfactorily by assigning student librarians who take charge of keeping the table orderly, checking out occasional books for overnight reading, and seeing that books, magazines, and newspapers are returned by the users.

Second, every student should have an equal opportunity to use the reading table. Some teachers who use reading tables allow only those students to use the table who finish all their assigned work. Such practice denies the experience of free, selective reading to those students who are often in most need of it—the slow-learner and the corrective reader. A sounder and more logical approach is to have regularly assigned times when different groups of students are permitted to use the books from the reading tables. Third, books need to be changed regularly. School librarians are usually most cooperative and helpful in suggesting and supplying appropriate books. It has been the writer's experience that students will bring from their homes an ample supply of excellent magazines. The supply of magazines kept on the table should be limited and changed often. An oversupply of magazines that are not replaced weekly sometimes tends to bring out crude artistic attempts from some students. Mustaches, false eyebrows, and other adornments tend to find their way into dog-eared magazines.

What Word-Recognition Skills Need To Be Taught?

Although the teaching of word-recognition skills is primarily the responsibility of elementary teachers, high school English teachers often need to reteach and review basic word-recognition skills. Inefficient or corrective readers usually need help in (1) building an adequate sight-word vocabulary, (2) using context clues, (3) applying phonetic skills, (4) using word-structure skills, (5) using the dictionary, and/or (6) knowing when to seek a teacher's assistance.

Because many secondary teachers have requested a review of word-recognition skills, the following chapter is devoted to developing word-recognition skills.

Reading Lengthy and Difficult Selections

The majority of high school and beginning college students display a complete lack of understanding of how to read lengthy and difficult materials. Nor do they understand the necessity for learning how to read such material in depth. Most of them feel that they can fulfill their responsibility for learning by reading assigned materials at one hurried sitting. Sometimes they "cover" the material by reading the first sentence of every paragraph, reading only the summary of the chapter, or by reading the headings of sections of the material. Occasionally, and with certain kinds of materials, cursory reading or skimming is the most efficient type of reading and is all that is required of the material or student. But too many students rely upon rapid reading and skimming to serve all of their reading needs. On the other hand, there are some students who feel that they must read every word. Any of these practices, when carried to extremes, is an inefficient method of reading.

Secondary and college students must learn that much of their outside reading is meaty and requires thoughtful mastication; it is not a placebo to be swallowed in one, almost effortless gulp. The student who is given experiences in reading thought-provoking materials that require the last ounce of the student's ingenuity in applying his previously learned skills, knowledge, and experiences, before he arrives at a conclusion, achieves the satisfaction and pride that comes only from knowing that his mettle has been tested and found not wanting. Much of the writing that we call literature demands concentrated, thoughtful reading. Without guidance from the English teacher, the student is apt to dodge literature of this type, or if it is assigned, he will grudgingly rush through it without any positive learning.

The empathetic, adequately prepared teacher denies no one the opportunity for engaging in difficult reading. But he makes certain that no one is forced into attempting to do the impossible. He recognizes that all students are not capable of reading difficult selections. With *adequate teacher help* some students may improve their reading skills and eventually read difficult material but others will never be capable of such high-level reading. For some, sixth-grade materials are about as far as they will ever reach.

Difficult reading is a learning experience that is a rewarding but an exacting taskmaster. The qualifications are difficult to meet. First, the student must possess that which we term above-average intelligence. In addition, he must have mastered all the basic reading skills, such as accurate, rapid word recognition; he must have a vast reading and understanding vocabulary; he must know how and when to adjust his rate of reading to meet his purposes; he must have a wide and varied background of experiences; he must have that inner desire to want to learn; he must have a love of reading. When he meets these minimum requirements, he is ready to meet the challenges of the author of difficult reading.

For the student who meets the qualifications, difficult reading can be an exciting adventure. But the reader must recognize and respect the author's intelligence, his ability to place words so accurately that their message is revealed to only those who are sufficiently intelligent and skilled in reading to fathom them. The reader must be aware that he will need to call upon all of his past, present, and even future experiences to interpret accurately the author's thoughts. He must pit his knowledge and skills against the author's artful presentation and thinking in order that he react prudently to the passage. He cannot remain aloof from the material, but must become an active participant in the thinking process called reading.

The reader of difficult matter must be a critical reader. He is one who accepts the challenge of new ideas but does not accept new ideas simply because they are new or fashionable. He searches his, and the author's thinking for flaws and false premises. He discards and rejects non-pertinent data, false assumptions, beguiling analogies, biases, and unfounded assertions. He deftly parries emotionally laden statements and refuses to be rushed into false conclusions by cleverly disguised opinions presented as factual evidence. He anticipates logical, sequential presentations of statements and outcomes. He considers all relevant, factual statements in their entirety before arriving at conclusions.

The understanding teacher knows that students must have numerous, varied experiences before they can tackle difficult reading. He does not assign this kind of reading to students before they are ready for it. This means that he must evaluate each student's total reading achievement and provide various learning experiences that prepare the student for such reading. He knows also that all students are not ready for difficult reading at the same time, and that some students may never be capable of such reading.

When students are ready for difficult reading, the teacher interests and motivates them for the reading by asking them purposeful questions before, during, and after the assigned reading is completed. The questions need to be critical but not captious. In some instances, the questions call for written precis about the selection; in other instances, assigning the student a written compendium may better serve the learner's needs. In any event, teacher questions help the student to set purposes for his reading, give him direction when needed, help to clarify his thinking, and insure his successful completion of the reading.

Factors That Influence Student Reading and Learning in English

Teachers of some content areas may expect to have in their classes only those students who are interested in the content and who are efficient achievers. Therefore, they may be less apt to recognize the relationship between reading and learning subject matter. This phenomenon does not apply generally to the English teacher. Experience and research show that English is the most disliked of all school subjects. Why should such a feeling exist among students? Let us look for answers by observing the student characteristics of one freshman or sophomore English class.

There are, for example, 35 students in Miss Joe's tenth grade. Among the 35 students there may be two or three who are unable to read any material above second or third-grade level. At the other extreme, there may be several who are capable of reading advanced college materials. Approximately half the class will be able to read tenth-grade textbooks. The reading proficiency of the remaining members of the class will vary from the fifth- to twelfth-grade levels.

How is Miss Joe going to find an anthology or a single literary selection that will be sufficiently challenging for the more efficient readers and yet not too frustrating for the less-efficient readers? Miss Joe says that any such idea is ridiculous. Few English teachers disagree with her. Nevertheless, in most school systems, Miss Joe is expected to do the impossible. She is provided with 35 identical textbooks with which she is supposed to teach literature and reading to 35 students of dissimilar interest, intelligence, and reading achievement.

If Miss Joe has had some preparation for teaching reading during her teacher-education years, she may be able to make some adjustments for students' differences in reading. She may rewrite some materials, get supplementary materials from the library, group students according to their reading needs and abilities, provide help with word-recognition skills to those in need of such help, and teach others how to set purposes for reading. She will not insist that all students work simultaneously on one reading level or on one reading skill. She knows that such practice can only lead to reading failures. Above all else, Miss Joe will attempt to make reading interesting and meaningful.

Apparently there are not sufficient Miss Joe's to meet students' needs since research shows that in any class similar to hers, from one-fourth to one-third of the students will drop out of school before graduation. But is poor teaching the determinant of the dropout problem? No. Actually, no one knows why students leave school, but the causes appear to be multiple. Studies indicate that social, economic, and educational factors influence a student's decision to leave school.

Some who study the dropout problem state that the dropout implies failure on the school's part (20, p. 6). Such implications deserve the consideration of all educators, administrators, and teachers, especially when we know that approximately 90 per cent of the dropouts, including those of average and superior intelligence, have reading problems.

A recent study (5, pp. 159–69) of Negro and white dropouts showed that these students were lacking in language development. As a group, they were behind their contemporaries in all areas of the language-arts. Findley (5, p. 161) notes that every dropout study points to poor reading as a significant element of the problem.

In summary, although student's reading difficulties may not be a primary reason for the dropout problem, the wide range of differences in reading achievement among students in any typical high school classroom is evidence of the need for improving the teaching of reading at all grade levels.

Questions that the English teacher might ask himself before he begins teaching his classes are: How many students may become dropouts before they complete the school year? What are their specific needs in the language-arts area? How many of these boys and girls have problems in which reading may be of value? Do they know how to use reading to help solve their problems? How many would like to read but are unable to pronounce and understand the words that are necessary for getting meaning from reading? How might I obtain materials that students can read and that they find interesting?

The use of questions like these should help a teacher to determine *how, when,* and *why* he will use the assigned textbook.

The capable English teacher knows that for various reasons some students will never be able to read as well as their classmates. It is vital that all teachers recognize those students who do not have the potential to keep up with the rest of the class, but who are working at their capacity. Such students should be given just, but not undue, praise when they earn it. Likewise, it is no less important that the teacher recognize and help those students who are *not* reading up to their potentials even though they may be achieving at the class level. The only way a teacher can determine if a student is reading at, above, or below his own capability is to *evaluate* each student's reading. For information about testing and evaluating student reading, see Chapter 5.

Briefly, the "average student" should be able to get the main idea of a paragraph after he has read it. After reading, he should recognize and use details for supporting his opinions. He should be able to follow oral and written directions, set legitimate purposes for reading, vary his rate of reading according to *his purposes, his experiences,* and *the difficulty of the material,* and derive some valid conclusions when he has completed the assigned reading. If he performs these tasks in a satisfactory manner, it is axiomatic that he must have mastered the basic skills for recognizing and pronouncing words. In addition, he must know *how* and *when* to use the dictionary efficiently, to question the author's purpose and motives for writing, to use additional references without teacher prompting.

There are some English teachers who say, "If I delayed teaching literature until my students could use the dictionary, follow directions, set purposes for reading, and do all those other learning tasks, I'd *never* teacher literature." Probably the best way to answer such a statement is to ask, if a student has not learned the basic reading skills that are prerequisite to reading literature, is he ready to read literature? It is evident that he is not and will not be ready until he learns them. Attempting to teach literature to a student who is lacking the prerequisites may be a harrowing experience for both teacher and student unless the teacher recognizes the students' weaknesses and adjusts to them.

Most students, including many who are not efficient readers, can learn to like and to appreciate literature if they are given materials at their own instructional level of reading. When students have materials at the instructional level they can learn to set purposes, learn new vocabulary, enjoy the reading, and participate in discussions.

Teaching Reading in Literature

Asking English teachers to teach reading while teaching literature often elicits a response that indicates the asker would rarely win a popularity poll. English teachers, however, are recognizing the need for teaching reading, and many who teach reading while teaching literature say that their use of reading techniques enhances student's enjoyment and understanding of literature.

Disagreement about teaching reading in literature is only one of the areas in literature in which unanimity is lacking. Much evidence in professional English journals and textbooks shows that there is wide disagreement among teachers over what constitutes good literature. Some teachers and authorities insist that literature is found only in "The Great Books." Others are just as determined that certain classics must be read by everyone. Another large group is equally vehement in saying that a combination of classics and recent books should be considered as literature. Burton (3, p. 87) defines literature "as those genres which have reference to a world of imagination, of fiction." He excludes biography, essay, letters, and speech, although he admits that there is a place for them in the reading program. Sauer (16) notes that some teachers will have nothing to do with any literature written before 1920.

The kind and vintage of writing that you consider to be literature is your decision. The writer of this book is concerned with helping teachers to improve their teaching of literature by using proven techniques of reading. English majors are adequately prepared to make their own selections of the literature they will teach. Surely students may profit from reading in any or all of the previously mentioned areas, if they are capable of reading them. Instead of English teachers spending time in discussing what is or what is not good literature, might it not be more meaningful if they were to ask, "What literary selection most nearly meets the needs of this particular group of students at this time?" It is possible that writing that is literature for the 10 o'clock group of students may be either too sophisticated or not sufficiently challenging for the 11 o'clock class members. Teachers of literature might well heed the words of Sauer (16) and others (8, 12) who say that literature should, first of all, provide students with pleasure. How many students have developed a dislike for literature because "great literature" was forced upon them before they were prepared to read the materials or before they were sufficiently mature to understand the concepts and thinking involved in the story? No matter how moral, how instructional, or how revealing a literary selection is to an efficient, mature reader, or English teacher, it may be a regrettable form of punishment to the frustrated student who is unable to comprehend the words and who is lacking the experiences and maturity necessary for reading the material.

Goals of Literature Must Be Adjusted to Student Needs and Capabilities

The teacher of English should adjust the broad general goals of literature to the kinds of students he teaches. It is no simple task to set different specific goals for different groups of students, but it is practical, worthwhile, sound, and a mark of efficient teaching.

The English teacher may better understand the enormity of his job if he recognizes that of all teachers, he is one who will have contact with every kind of student who enters the secondary school. Mentally, they will be brilliant, average, and below average; they will be the motivated, the non-motivated, and the I-dare-you-to-teach-me youngsters; they will be emotionally stable, highly emotional, and non-emotional or sluglike in their reactions; they will be the sure, the unsure, and the vascillating or pendulum type; and they will be developmental, corrective, and frustrated readers; and they will be educational cripples. Yet each one of these individuals will be expected to increase his listening, speaking, reading, and writing skills *while* acquiring aesthetic and ethical morals from the literature prescribed for his grade level.

Teaching Reading in the Study of Drama

Let us assume that you know how to evaluate student reading achievement and that you have evaluated your students. You find that this particular group of students is capable of high-level reading, and you conclude that this group is ready to learn to read drama. Are you going to begin with modern drama or are you going to start with Shakespeare? According to some experts (2), the teaching of modern drama is one kind of experience while the teaching of Shakespeare presents a number of different kinds of experiences that create or contribute to reading problems. Bernstein (2, p. 276) says that it is easier for the student to read and understand modern drama than it is for him to read and understand Shakespeare. Bernstein reasons that in modern drama the characters are more familiar to the students; the actors' choice of vocabulary is simpler and easier for students to grasp. The plot structure of modern drama involves experiences that are more akin to the students' own experiences; they are developed in action and excitement; their arrangement follows a typical pattern.

Because the vocabulary of modern drama is generally less difficult than most other literary materials that you may assign, students will be more interested in modern drama and more able to read it with ease than they can read Chaucer, Milton, and Shakespeare.

Shakespeare deals with problems that are foreign to most, if not all, beginning students. He speaks in a strange tongue. His style of writing, the poetry of his genius and his time, are unfamiliar and unusual. The customs of the characters, their beliefs, their mannerisms, are not of this world. Shakespeare's plots are highly involved and complex. The unsophisticated TV addicts who occupy some of the seats in your classroom will be no more interested in reading and knowing Shakespeare than they are in studying Beowulf.

The English teacher's job is to provide experiences that help students to understand Shakespeare. Loban, Ryan, and Squire (12, p. 342) suggest that introducing too much background material before the plays are read may be unwise. Students should be given needed background information as they read and encounter difficulty. Because the reading of Shakespeare may be difficult for even the better students, information pertinent to better understanding may need to be given briefly, quickly, and intermittently. It has been said that "Shakespeare should speak for himself—and as soon as possible."

A brief summary of teacher-student tasks that promote efficient reading of literature:

1. Teachers can help students to understand literature by reading some of the more difficult passages to them.
2. Teacher interpretation of some of the passages is necessary if students are to understand fully the power and depth of the author's language.
3. Before students become efficient readers of literature they must be helped by being given specific purposes for reading particular passages. One expert (2, p. 200) notes that extremely difficult sections of Shakespeare can be assigned as homework *when* the teacher knows how to direct students to read certain parts "line by line." Since the purposes for reading the selected lines are teacher purposes, they should be given to students as specific questions.
4. When students have read and studied assigned passages and can

pronounce the words accurately, they should be given the opportunity to read some selections aloud.

5. Students should learn that in reading drama, every word is necessary to the action.
6. Students must learn to be adept in looking for key words that give clues to future action, that reveal character, and that help to set the tone or create mood.
7. The reader must develop a wide and specific vocabulary in order that he can appreciate the fine nuances and sly innuendoes of the words of master writers.
8. The development of the preceding high-level reading skills seldom takes place without expert teacher guidance.

IMPROVING THE LEARNING OF SOCIAL STUDIES THROUGH READING

Teachers and writers of social studies generally agree that three major purposes of the social studies are: (1) growth in knowledge and understanding; (2) development of skills; and (3) development of attitudes (16, pp. 5–14). These purposes are directed to the development of a democratic citizenry. They are essentially the same purposes that the early colonizers of America apparently had in mind when they declared education vital to citizenship and made provisions for schools to provide youth with the knowledge and skills necessary for responsible citizenship in a democratic society.

In the public schools, the social studies are concerned with man's relationship to his fellow man and to his environment. Therefore, the social studies must use the facts, concepts, and knowledge from many content areas or disciplines to help students to understand the culture and society in which they live. Although several social studies classes may draw their content from the same sources, they may be vastly different from each other. Because different social studies teachers emphasize different areas or different aspects from the same content area, there has been some confusion and disagreement about the value of, and the place of the social studies. Experts in the area, however, have no doubts about the role and place of the social studies. They note that the social studies reorganize and simplify content from the social sciences for instructional purposes.

What specific disciplines are included among the social sciences? Even the professionals in the various social sciences are not in complete agreement about the specific content areas that should be classified as the social sciences. Anthropology, geography, history, economics, education, law, political science, and sociology are usually listed as being social sciences. In addition, criminology, philosophy, psychology, and religion are sometimes listed as social sciences (7, p. 1296). When one stops to reflect upon the concepts and the vocabulary necessary for reading and understanding each of the above-listed social sciences, and when he recognizes also that efficient reading is greatly dependent upon experiential background and vocabulary, he can realize why reading in the social studies is difficult for many secondary students and adults.

Because the materials of the social studies are varied, the concepts new or unusual, and the vocabulary highly specialized and different, the social studies teacher must be prepared to help students with reading if they are to grow in knowledge and understanding, develop skills, especially the skills of communication, and acquire positive attitudes. Knowledge of some of the characteristics that contribute to efficient reading of social studies materials should be of value to the teacher. Research (12, pp. 1296–1319) shows that efficient readers of high school social studies have certain characteristics that set them apart from the poor readers. Efficient readers have: (1) average or above average intelligence; (2) a liking for reading; (3) a large specialized social studies vocabulary; (4) a broad general vocabulary; (5) a good understanding of metaphorical language; (6) accurate comprehension of time and place concepts; and (7) an active interest in school and community affairs.

The Reading of Social Studies Is Difficult

Regardless of the teacher's choice of textbook and content for social studies, much of the reading will be difficult for many students and impossible for others. Reading, however, is one of the main learning experiences in most high school social studies courses because actual experiences are necessarily restricted. Teachers should provide many additional learning experiences in order that the students' learning from the textbook will be less difficult and more profitable. Supplementary materials that can be used to increase understanding of the textbook include related books at various reading levels, film strips, moving pictures, television, flat pictures, tape recorders, various kinds of maps, globes, charts, and graphs. Although many a student will be helped by using these visual and auditory aids, the aids are not a substitute for reading; they are supplementary to the textbook.

In order that teachers may help students who experience difficulty in reading the textbook, it is necessary for teachers to know and understand the causes of the difficulty. Following is a brief discussion of some of the factors that contribute to pupil difficulty in reading social studies.

First, one of the most plausible reasons why students are unable to read the textbook is that all students do not have the same reading ability. It has been noted previously that the range of reading achievement among high school students may be as great as from seven to ten grade levels. The unwarranted and inhuman practice of assigning all students to read a single textbook ignores completely the differences in students' reading ability. Such practice contributes to the lack of efficient learning of content material and the improvement of reading skills. Numerous teachers steadfastly refuse to accept this basic principle and spend countless hours fruitlessly searching for a text that presents factual material that can be read and understood by *all* students. Until teachers recognize that all students do not have the same ability to derive meaning from written materials, both students and teachers will be frustrated. Optimum learning of subject matter by all students will be an impossibility.

Factors That Make Some Textbooks Difficult

Most textbooks are excellent sources of information, facts, and ideas pertinent to learning in specific content areas. The material is usually of the highest caliber because it is written by experts in the particular area of concentration. The fact that textbooks are written by experts is at once both a major weakness and a major strength. Specialists in subject matter are usually amateurs at writing. They understand so well the materials about which they write that they appear to forget that the student has but a meager knowledge of the vocabulary and concepts necessary for understanding.

In 1937, Horn (9) noted the difficulty of the presentation of the ideas found in social studies and social science textbooks. He stated that even if the materials were written in a clear, attractive style and in untechnical language, the very nature of the intrinsically complicated concepts would be difficult to understand.

An excellent, and more recent study by Peterson (14) supports Horn's statements. Ideas, facts, concepts, details are generally jammed into compressed, abstract statements that shove and crowd every sentence. Only a highly efficient reader with wide experience in the particular content area is capable of understanding much of the material.

The majority of social studies students are completely overwhelmed by the staggering number of tightly compressed facts that authors manage to squeeze into a single written page. The student who has learned during his school years that teachers tend to stress facts in examinations can become suddenly "fact slappy" when he first begins to read social studies materials.

Students must learn how to select pertinent facts from irrelevant facts. They must have some way of determining which facts are considered so important that they must be learned and retained, and which facts merely help them to get an overall view or main idea of a selection. Such learning is not easy, it requires concentrated thinking.

The number of concepts introduced on a single page of a social studies text can be staggering to students. For example, a single paragraph of 154 words selected at random from one of the leading tenth-grade social studies texts contains the following referents: The Pyrenees, Spain, Mohammedan invaders, eighth century, subdued by armies of little Christian kingdoms, crusade, knights, fellow Christians, Reconquest, 1492, Ferdinand and Isabella, Granada, Castile and Aragon, Navarre, united politically, strong national state, little Portugal, a separate national state. Not only are some of the proper names difficult or impossible for some students to pronounce, they are utterly devoid of meaning. In order that a student derive any positive learning from these words, he must have more than a meager idea of history, geography, and time sequence.

To understand "Pyrenees" and its relation to the remainder of the paragraph, the student must know something about the location and the ruggedness of this range of mountains. What countries does it separate? What is its general direction? How far does it extend? What is its approximate elevation? What are the three main sections of this range?

Knowledge of both history and geography is required of the student if he is to understand the reference to "Mohammedan invaders." Who were the Mohammedans? From where did they come? Why were they invaders? How many were there? Were they successful? Were they repelled? Why were they so feared? What finally happened to them?

So far we have merely mentioned some of the questions concerning but two words, "Pyrenees" and "Mohammedan," in the 154-word paragraph about which a student must have some knowledge if he is going to get meaning from the paragraph. No mention was made of the terrain, weather, and geologic formation of the Pyrenees. The influence of Mohammed (Muhammad), his religion, his origin, his place in history, his followers were not even considered in our brief example. The intent of this example is to alert teachers to some of the concepts, vocabulary, and word-recognition skills students must have if they are to read and learn social studies.

Arguments Favoring the Use of a Single Textbook

Some authors of professional textbooks on the teaching of social studies contribute, wittingly or unwittingly, to the use of a single text by attempting to be objective and present the advantages and disadvantages of using a single textbook for instructional purposes. Their attempts at objectivity usually present arguments in favor of a single text that have a strong emotional appeal for teachers, but they are arguments that are neither psychologically nor educationally sound. Following are some of the reasons often proposed in favor of using a single textbook.

The use of a single textbook saves valuable teacher time. The authors of the textbooks search through numerous facts, ideas, and content areas to bring to the teacher a single volume containing a well-written, carefully planned, selected, and organized body of facts. Because various authors use different approaches and criteria for selecting and organizing facts, the teacher has a choice of a number of bodies of facts compressed between two book covers. The teacher has only to select the textbook that contains the facts that he feels students should know. For a busy teacher with large classes, much preparation time is saved by using one text.

In addition, it is argued that in a single text the instructional aids, such as maps, charts, graphs, and pictures, have been selected to go with the prepared materials in order that students get more meanings from the printed material. Further, since all students are exposed to the same reading materials, the teacher can expect all of them to be familiar with the same information. When all students are familiar with the same information, they will be interested in, and capable of, discussing the materials. Furthermore, teacher time is saved by having students discuss the author's questions that are found at the end of the chapter.

Arguments Against the Use of a Single Textbook

The most direct and valid argument against the use of a single textbook for teaching subject matter to students is that all students are not capable of reading material written for one grade level. Numerous studies show the wide range of reading ability among students in any average American classroom, but it is difficult to get teachers to shake the dust from these studies in the library and to use the findings for improving student learning. However, the busy teacher who has little time to read research evidence needs only to step inside almost any classroom in the American high school and he will see the live data—students who cannot read the text. Teachers will testify to the fact that numbers of their students cannot read the assigned text and yet they continue to order books at the same reading level for all students. Why? When teachers and future teachers discuss reading levels, they are quick to say, "But if all students in one class don't read at the same level, to order all books at the same level doesn't make sense." Then, after momentarily considering their statement, they ask, "Does it?" No. It is more realistic to order books at various reading levels. The question that is most important is, how are you going to order textbooks? Your selection of appropriate textbooks is critical to your students.

No teacher or any other individual has the right to deprive a student from learning subject matter in any area because the student is unable to read a particular textbook. The student who is unable to read the assigned textbook, regardless of the causal factors for his inability, should not be humiliated and frustrated by being assigned a task from which he cannot escape, and from which he can expect only failure. It is axiomatic that one learns to read only by reading. But being forced to pretend to read material that is totally incomprehensible does not improve a student's reading. In fact, a student who is placed in such a situation actually regresses in reading skill.

Let us examine the proposition of using a single textbook in light of the three major purposes of the social studies. Can the first purpose, *student growth in knowledge and understanding*, be served by the teacher who believes in and who uses a single textbook for teaching social studies? Can the student who is unable to read the text grow in knowledge and understanding if he is unable to interpret and get meaning from the printed symbols?

The second major purpose of the social studies is *the development of skills*. If these skills include the skills of communication, will the student who is unable to read the material improve his use of vocabulary, develop needed word-recognition skills, learn new concepts, and develop others? Will the student be able to discuss intelligently those facts, events, and ideas that he is unable to read?

The third major purpose of the social studies is *the development of attitudes*. What kinds of attitudes are being developed by students who continually meet failure in the classroom because they cannot read the material? Do these students develop positive attitudes toward the rights and responsibilities of others? Are these students developing a feeling that an independent, enlightened citizenry is vital to the survival of a democracy? How many of these students will support education after they finish their sentence of twelve years at hard labor in the public schools? How many of these students will develop positive, professional attitudes about the schools, education, democracy, and mankind? How many will continue to read and to learn after the doors of the high schools close behind them?

Is the Use of a Single Textbook a Good Practice When the Student Is Able To Read the Material?

Even for those students who are capable of reading the material, a single textbook has many limitations. Writers, because of their experiences, preparation, and interests, do not interpret the same set of facts in the same way or with the same results. The writer's purposes will influence his conclusions and the facts he uses to present the content. A writer's viewpoint, no matter how objective he may desire to be, will be affected by certain predilections or prejudices that worm their way into much of his material. For example, political expressions and conclusions by two different writers, but based upon the same available facts may be, and usually are, poles apart with little hope of their being reconciled. Would you, as a social studies teacher, feel that you were meeting your professional obligations to your country, school, and students if you deliberately limited students to the point of view of a single textbook? This is the question that you must decide for yourself after you have pondered all available facts.

A DIRECTED READING LESSON IN SOCIAL STUDIES

The following illustration of a directed reading lesson may help to clarify the manner in which reading skills contribute to the learning of subject matter. No single textbook has been used in this example, inasmuch as we have previously discussed the necessity for using various levels of reading materials. Even though some teachers are still bound to a single basic textbook by conditions beyond their control, experience indicates that teachers collect numerous materials for supplementary reading. Many of these materials, newspaper and magazine articles and pamphlets, are written at a level below that of the regular textbook and may meet the reading requirements of less capable readers.

Teachers' Manuals

Most manuals that accompany subject-matter textbooks provide teachers with an overview of the contents and an explanation of the general plan of the text, including suggested teaching procedures. Teacher opinions about the use and value of manuals vary markedly, but many state that the manuals they use are most helpful.

Objectives. Listed in the Teachers' Manual or determined by the teacher.

1. Man has used past progress to make improvements in the areas of travel and communication.
2. Many people from different cultures contribute to the welfare of mankind through their ideas, inventions, and discoveries.
3. Appreciation of man's struggle to improve his living conditions.

Phase I: Assignment or Readiness Period* During this period the teacher is first concerned with developing interest in the material and providing motivation for reading. His second concern is the development of reading skills and the learning of content. In order that students comprehend what they read, he introduces some of the new words. He also asks pertinent questions to determine the meanings his students have for some of the new vocabulary. His final procedure is that of helping students set purposes for reading by asking them questions *before* they read.

New Words and Abbreviations To Be Introduced:

disrupted	transcontinental	inducements
synthesized	integrated	CAA
ICC		

Questions used for Directing the Silent Reading:

1. What kinds of communications are discussed by the author?
2. In what ways does the government use communication?

Phase II: Silent Reading.

Group 1. Regular textbook, pages 107–19.
Group 2. Alternate textbook, pages 88–90, 271–76.
Group 3. Supplementary materials assigned as needed.

Phase III: Question and Discussion Period. Teachers should always ask for answers to the questions he used in directing the silent reading.

* A detailed discussion of the assignment period is presented in Chapter 2, "Readiness for Reading Subject Matter."

1. What kinds of communication were mentioned by the author?
2. How does the government use communication?
   Answers indicate students' abilities to: (*a*) read for purpose, (*b*) recall details.

Additional Teacher Questions.

1. What might happen if communication between the government and the people were suddenly *disrupted.*
   Question tests: (*a*) Students' understanding of new vocabulary word *disrupted,* (*b*) Students' abilities to make judgments from details given.
2. How have communications affected man's way of life? (Main idea.)
3. What are some of the weaknesses in communications among backward nations? How might communications be strengthened in these nations? (Ability to make use of present knowledge to solve problems—associational and inferential thinking.)

Provide time for students to ask questions.

Phase IV: Rereading (Silent or Oral). If there are no reasons for rereading, this part of the directed reading lesson may be omitted. If there is, for example, disagreement about facts given by the author, inaccurate comprehension of author statements, or other evidence of superficial reading, rereading may be highly beneficial for students.

Phase V: Special Improvement. This phase of a directed reading lesson has been given various names by different writers. The intent of the phase is the same, however, whether it is called "Enrichment," "Additional Reading," "Skill-Building Period," or "Following up the Reading."

During this time the teacher develops and assigns activities designed to alleviate students' needs that were noted during the preceding phases.

In some instances, an entire group of students may need additional help in understanding a concept, or in developing a needed reading skill. At times, certain students from several instructional groups may need to develop the same reading skill and will form a new group for that single purpose. Most of the time, however, this is the period in which students do individual work in different areas of learning.

Some Learning Activities

Independent reading for:

1. Enriching one's own background or for sheer enjoyment

2. Developing speed of reading while retaining comprehension
3. Making special reports to class
4. Presenting differing points of view about the unit being studied
5. Learning about important individuals who contributed to the area
6. Enlarging vocabulary

Building skills:

1. Improving dictionary skills
2. Using reference materials
3. Learning to recall details
4. Making inferences from own background, plus facts given
5. Improving faulty or inadequate word-recognition skills
6. Practicing following directions
7. Improving comprehension skills, summarizing short articles, and adjusting speed of reading to different types of materials
8. Reading and making maps, charts, and graphs

Summary

This brief outline of a directed reading lesson in social studies was presented to illustrate how reading is used in learning subject matter. The general plan may be used, with minor adjustments, in most other content areas. Other social studies lessons and different subject-matter units might require diverse and various emphases, and stress different reading skills, but the overall plan, as presented, is a sound one.

TEACHER PRACTICES THAT CONTRIBUTE TO STUDENT LEARNING OF SOCIAL STUDIES THROUGH READING

1. Determine the approximate reading ability of each student and provide him with materials at his own reading and learning level.

2. Teach students how to read the textbook.

3. Teach pupils how to set purposes for reading and teach them why it is necessary to set purposes for efficient reading and learning.

4. Help students to learn how to skim or read rapidly those portions of the textbook that are not especially difficult.

5. Help students to understand that certain sections of the text that are difficult require purposeful study-type reading. Study-type material requires active, thoughtful, associative reading that does not permit fantastic skimming rates of thousands of words per minute.

6. Teach students to make use of author clues; italics, bold-faced headings, and word clues such as, "on the other hand," "for example," "in order of importance," "therefore," "furthermore," "because," etc.

7. Refrain from trying to "cover the book." If the book must be covered, do this little chore the first day and then proceed to teach students according to their needs and abilities.

8. Provide adequate time for student discussion of the materials they have read. Allow time for students to disagree and then to reread the same and other materials for clarification of points about which they disagreed.

9. Teach students to listen, to read, to discuss, and to think about all of the available facts before arriving at conclusions.

10. Insist that students learn precise meanings of words rather than getting only a vague generalization of words.

11. Use as many visual aids as possible in order that students be helped to get meaning from the materials that they have read.

12. Recognize that concepts do not sprout like radishes, but are slow in developing and are dependent upon facts, experience, and maturity.

IMPROVING THE LEARNING OF MATHEMATICS AND SCIENCE THROUGH READING

That the reading of mathematics and science is an exceedingly difficult task for many students is a truism. If students are to improve their learning in mathematics and science, they must first be helped to improve their reading in these important subjects. Few students are capable of learning the specialized vocabularies of mathematics and science without the assistance of a teacher. Teachers, therefore, should know the various factors which make the reading of a subject difficult.

Vocabulary and Concepts

The vocabulary and concepts of mathematics and science make them difficult subjects for students to read and learn. Much of the vocabulary and many of their concepts have little relationship to students' past experiences. Their language contains so many new, unfamiliar words that learning the language of science and mathematics is like learning a foreign language.

The vocabulary of mathematics and science is exact and precise. Technical vocabulary has specific meaning. There can be no loose generalization about connotation. A hazy idea of the word is inadequate because context is of little or no help. The student may have some general meaning of the word "point," for example. To him it may be a point of departure, a sharpened point, a point of land, a point to be considered, a score in a game, or a point in the stock market. The industrial arts student may recognize it as a part of the electrical equipment that breaks or makes a circuit. The student of home economics may associate "point" with the mark on a pattern, or a particular kind of embroidery called *needle point.* The student of mathematics must have a much more abstract and specific concept of point. Many students in mathematics have difficulty in trying to conceive of a point as being *an undefined, unseen, but postulated element.* This is evident when they are asked to define a point. Some are unable to recognize that the little round dot on the chalkboard or piece of paper is not a point but merely a graphic representation of an abstraction. Although teachers may tell students that a point does not exist in a material way, this concept is almost impossible for some youngsters to comprehend. Concept development is a process that is dependent upon numerous experiences, facts, and the student's ability to organize his experiences in order that he can generalize.

It has been shown on numerous occasions that the concepts and the vocabulary of science and mathematics are frequently introduced to students too rapidly and briefly. Because there is so much for students to learn in these areas, there is the ever present tendency to "cover the material" in too brief a period of time. Teachers might seriously consider taking more time to develop broader concepts of mathematics and science.

Techniques for Teaching Vocabulary

Teachers can do much to create a positive learning attitude among students by discussing with them the importance of learning the new vocabulary of mathematics and science. Bamman, Hogan, and Greene (1) have pointed out that some of the symbolization and vocabulary of mathematics are used in science but with different meanings. They call attention to the confusion that may result if the mathematical meanings of "inversion," "base," "solution," and "radical" are applied directly to science materials. According to Leary (11) research shows that, although teachers expect students to understand the specific vocabulary of their courses, few attain this goal. In fact, many teachers have only a vague idea of the limited technical vocabulary of students in their classes.

Student Use of Technical Terms Does Not Denote Meaning

It is poor practice to assume that students understand the vocabulary of science and mathematics even when they use the terms correctly. Many students memorize formulas and definitions of words that often make no sense to them, but the memorization is not always in vain. Students discover quickly that repeating these vacuous words in order may suffice for an answer to some teacher's questions. Following is an illustration of what happens often when a student substitutes senseless memorization for learning and gets away with the deception.

Recently the writer was asked to check the reading achievement of a high school student who confused and vexed his teachers. According to his intelligence test scores and to some of his teacher's statements, he was highly intelligent. However, he was also an enigma in many ways. His teachers said that he read well but could get little meaning from his reading, nor could he seem to apply what he did get.

The boy readily agreed to read a selection from his textbook. He chose a selection about photosynthesis. He pronounced the words accurately and clearly. When he finished he looked up and said, "Well?" Accordingly he was asked to relate briefly what he had learned. Without hesitation he said, "Photosynthesis is a process in which the energy of sunlight is harnessed. Carbohydrates are formed from carbon dioxide and water. This is often called the assimilation of carbon." His teachers nodded in agreement and then turned quizzical eyes toward the examiner.

The examiner asked the boy to explain in his own words what was meant by the formation of carbohydrates. He replied weakly, "You know. Carbohydrates are formed from carbon and water." Looking at the trees, lawn, and shrubs just outside the window, the examiner said, "Take a look out here and tell me where photosynthesis is taking place at this moment." The boy looked for long minutes and then said, "I'm not sure, but it must be somewhere. Could it be in the trees —the leaves I mean?"

The student was able to pronounce and memorize words about photosynthesis. He was an excellent example of a *verbalizer.* His performance was akin to that of a human tape recorder. He repeated words that were as empty and devoid of meaning as if they were sired by a vacuum. Apparently, somewhere in his school experiences he had been rewarded for being able to recite the words from the book. He had become so proficient in memorizing and repeating upon command senseless bits of the language, which he pawned off as learning to unsuspecting teachers, that at first he refused to accept the examiner's diagnosis of his problem. Because he had above-average intelligence, he finally realized and accepted the idea that he could learn and that sheer memorization of "nonsense syllables and words" was not learning. He has not developed into an excellent student in the few months he has been receiving help in reading, but he is now getting meaning from his reading, and appears to be much happier in the classroom.

He continues to be bothered by the thought that sheer memorization is not learning.

Teachers and students who know of other cases similar to the one just discussed are reluctant to believe what they observe. "How can such a thing happen?" they ask. "Why doesn't someone help these students? What can teachers do to prevent this kind of problem?"

Many of these students do receive help from competent teachers but little mention is made of such help. It is expected that teachers will produce "minor miracles" in the classroom. Some students, however, like the one cited as an example of a verbalizer, escape detection and continue to substitute memorization for understanding.

There are various hypotheses about why some students resort to memorization as a form of learning. It is possible that students, lacking the mental and emotional maturity for understanding the material at the time it is presented, memorize formulas, definitions of key words, and textbook phrases with the hope of passing a test. Other students may be mentally lazy and find that it is simpler to memorize than to work for meaning. And in certain instances teachers may unwittingly contribute to student memorization by insisting that students use the author's exact words when answering questions. Whatever the factors are that contribute to student memorization of material, teachers must be on the alert for signs that indicate students are substituting memorization for understanding. There is no valid reason why an intelligent student should engage in this sort of educational masquerade for nine or ten years before he is unmasked.

Relationship of Vocabulary and Concepts in Science and Mathematics

Vocabulary and concept development are often discussed separately by writers and teachers. Such a practice permits a close examination of the area being discussed, but it may give the reader the impression that vocabulary and concepts are unrelated and separate entities. This is not the case. When a person's vocabulary is improved, clarified, or expanded in any manner, his ability to think is helped. Although there is not complete agreement, most linguists, psychologists, and others who work with words agree that thinking without using language is either limited or impossible. If such a conclusion is valid, a student's understanding of a new word is not limited to that one new word. The new word represents a new idea, a new facet of thinking, a new or expanded concept.

Vocabulary and Concept Development Are Closely Related Processes That Must Be Developed Simultaneously

All concepts are not of equal value, nor are they of equal weight. They range from the simplest of ideas to the most difficult of abstractions. The student in mathematics or science first learns basic, simple concepts and then enlarges, alters, and refines them. He moves from concrete to abstract thinking at high levels. Concepts allow the scientist and the mathematician to save time and effort because they permit generalizations. Two physicists may use the terms "mass," "energy," "fusion" with complete understanding. They need not wade through the development of the concepts of these words. Likewise, "integer," "chord," "segment," and "ratio" convey meaning to the mathematics student who has learned the concepts associated with these words. The beginning student may be spellbound and lost when he first hears them. Words, then, may convey thoughts or ideas, and they may also confuse thoughts or, as in the case of the student and *photosynthesis,* they may hide the lack of thought.

"A concept is the amount of meaning a person has for any thing, persons, or process . . . A concept is a word or other symbol which stands for the common property of a number of objects or situations" (4, p. 154). The preceding brief definitions of a concept by Burton concurs with the view presented previously that concept and vocabulary development are interrelated processes that do not develop separately or independently of each other.

Techniques for Developing Vocabulary and Concepts of Mathematics and Science

There is nothing esoteric about teaching vocabulary and developing concepts, but one must have an understanding of what he is attempting to do. A teacher's task is predetermined by definition; he is attempting to improve student learning. It is his job to teach students how to set goals and to reach these goals. Telling a student to set goals and to strive to achieve them before he is sufficiently mature and experienced to understand what is meant by *a goal* is folly.

The teacher who decides to encourage student learning will read the literature of vocabulary and concepts and develop a simple, effective plan for helping students to help themselves. Instead of saying, "Look up the words you don't know," he may distribute a list of difficult and seldom-used words with the admonition, "Learn these and be able to write a definition and spell them." He thus *introduces some of the pertinent words during the assignment period.*

The Assignment Period Is the Readiness Period for Learning Subject Matter

At this time the teacher introduces *some* of the new words in sentences. He also *writes* the new words on the chalkboard. For example, the class may be studying *water as a solvent.* Certain of the words will have no meaning for some students nor will they be able to pronounce them. The teacher may say, as he writes *solvent* on the chalkboard, "We are going to read about water as a solvent. Who knows what *solvent* means?"

By writing and pronouncing the word, the teacher helps the student to associate the spoken word with the printed symbol. In addition, he helps to arouse student interest by encouraging those who know some meanings of solvent to discuss the word. Those who have no understanding of the word get some idea of what it means by listening to their classmates. They learn and become interested in this and other new words. It may be that *solute* needs to be introduced; the relationship of *solute* and *solution* may be explored. Some students will discover that the *solution* of a problem is not the same as a *solution* of salt and water. In fact, to give students more meaning about *solution* as it is used in a chapter about *water as a solvent,* the well-prepared teacher might have some salt and a glass of water available. Other words that might need to be introduced to the class in this selection are *concentration, suspension,* and *saturated.*

Teachers should not attempt to introduce *all* the new words, but some of the key words that may cause confusion and contribute to faulty learning need to be presented to students *before* they begin reading. There are those who claim that this is "spoon-feeding" and that such practice takes too much time from learning.

The same people who claim that the introduction of *some* of the new technical vocabulary to students is time-consuming and spoon-feeding, often take much care in teaching students how to use laboratory equipment that is new and strange to them. Is the proper use of equipment of greater importance and more difficult than is the proper use of unpronounceable and strange technical vocabulary? Is the claim of spoon-feeding a valid one? Again, you must answer the question for yourself.

Why Teachers of Mathematics and Science Must Teach Reading

One of the major problems facing teachers of mathematics and science is that of improving the reading skills of mentally capable, highly motivated students who lack the reading skills necessary for comprehending the written materials of the two fields. Many students who enter high school come from schools where the formal teaching of reading ended somewhere between the fourth and sixth grades. Unless these students receive reading help from secondary teachers, the world may lose some potentially great mathematicians and scientists.

Lest we appear to be overly optimistic about the importance of reading for learning mathematics and science, let us clarify this point. Without question there is much more to the learning of these content fields than the reading of a textbook. Much critical thinking and problem-solving occurs outside the reading process, but efficient reading is basic to all higher levels of learning in these areas.

Learning and Using Special Vocabulary, Abbreviations, and Symbols

A student in any branch of science must be capable of many kinds of reading that are not required in other areas. In addition to the highly technical vocabulary, scientific writing is filled with abbreviated forms and symbolic language. "Sulfuric acid," for example, may be written as $H_2 SO_4$, or it may be referred to as *oil of vitriol.* But before a student can begin to understand any of these three symbols they must have meaning for him. He must have some knowledge about the acid. He should know, for example, that sulfuric acid is a water *solution* of *hydrogen sulfate.* He must have some knowledge of the acid's *gravity, boiling point,* and its heat *liberating quality.*

In some instances, symbols such as $\rightarrow$, $\rightleftharpoons$, and $\uparrow$, may be no more than doodles, or direction markers in a parking lot. To the uninitiated student in chemistry, they may be meaningless, but when they are used in a formula they are logical, meaningful language, which must be learned.

The abbreviations and symbols of arithmetic are equally difficult for students until they are explained and made meaningful by the teacher. It is probable that some of the readers of this book ordinarily do not use some of the more common arithmetical symbols and abbreviations and symbols these youngsters need to know, note the following samples: $\div \times > <$ cwt. gr. yd. mi. hr. min. ans.

The preceding examples indicate the necessity for teaching symbols and abbreviations by subject-matter teachers. Because they are symbols, or stimuli for meaning, they are reading skills. Students lacking these reading skills will have difficulty in solving problems or equations until these needed skills are learned.

ADJUSTING SPEED OF READING

Many students believe that the faster they read, the more they comprehend. These same students usually experience difficulty in solving problems and conducting laboratory experiments because they try to read too rapidly. In some content areas, rapid reading has certain advantages, depending upon the reader's purpose. He may read rapidly to get a quick overview of the material or he may skim words quickly to find a particular name, date, or location. In some reading, words that are unknown may be skipped, and often are, without distorting meaning. Such practice, however, will not produce accurate meaning in science and mathematics. These content areas must be read slowly and accurately. Sometimes they must be reread several times before the full import of their meaning is perceived. A science or mathematics teacher may improve students' reading by teaching them how and when to *adjust* their rate of reading to (1) the *difficulty* of the material, (2) the amount of *experience* they have in the area, and (3) the *purpose* for which they are reading.

SELECTING READING MATERIAL

Teachers have long known that some textbooks are more difficult to read than others. Teachers also know, for example, that a student may read one general science book without too much difficulty but will be completely frustrated by another general science textbook that is supposedly written at the same grade level. It is possible that both books may be of the same difficulty, according to a sample of readability. But mechanical measures, readability formulas, are only *guides* to reading levels, and as such, are useful. Readability formulas, however, do not take into account the author's style, his sentence structure, or organization of material. Teacher judgment of the difficulty of a textbook, therefore, has a definite place in the selection of readable textbooks for various members of each class.

Teachers are beginning to select simpler written materials for the less efficient readers when easier reading materials are available. Teachers sometimes rewrite the materials in less complicated language and thereby help students to improve their reading and learning of subject matter. Nevertheless, some students read and learn from simplified materials only slightly better than from more difficult textbooks.

Teachers must be prepared for such student reaction. Simplifying reading material will not inevitably improve all student learning. Easier, or more commonly known words may be substituted for the more difficult vocabulary, but *concepts cannot be simplified.* Nor can all students reason at the same level and with the same efficiency. Selecting materials that students are capable of reading is most important, but giving students materials they can read is not a guaranteed solution for all learning problems.

Inefficient readers who are capable of high-level reasoning may lack both background experiences and the necessary reading skills for reading and learning from the regular textbook. In such instances, simplified reading materials and numerous activities for developing meaningful experiences may produce surprising improvement.

SUMMARY

There are sufficient data that show the need for teaching reading in high school and college. There is increasing evidence that subject-matter teachers can promote student's reading skills, and consequently the learning of content, by analyzing the reading skills needed in their content fields. Surveys and experience indicate that selecting materials that are based on students' reading achievement levels, teaching vocabulary and concepts, helping students to adjust their speed of reading to the kinds of materials being read, and asking questions that require students to apply the ideas they have gained from reading can be used effectively by subject-matter teachers to advance students' reading.

SELECTED REFERENCES

1. Bamman, Henry A., Hogan, Ursula, and Greene, Charles E. *Reading Instruction in the Secondary School.* New York: David McKay Co., Inc., 1961.
2. Bernstein, Abraham. *Teaching English in High School.* New York: Random House, Inc., 1961.
3. Burton, Dwight L. *Literature Study in the High School.* New York: Holt, Rinehart & Winston, Inc., 1959.
4. Burton, William H., *et al. Education for Effective Thinking.* New York: Appleton-Century-Crofts, Inc., 1960.
5. Findley, Warren G. "Language Development and Dropouts," *The School Dropout*, ed. Daniel Schreiber. Project: School Dropouts. Washington, D.C.: N.E.A., 1964. Pp. 159–69.
6. Gray, William S. "Nature and Scope of a Sound Reading Program," *Reading in the High School and College.* The Forty-Seventh Year-

book, Part II, National Society for the Study of Education. Chicago: The University of Chicago Press, 1948.

7. Gross, Richard E., and Badger, William V. "Social Studies," *Encyclopedia of Educational Research* (3d ed.), ed. Chester W. Harris, with the assistance of Marie R. Liba. New York: The Macmillan Co., 1960. Pp. 1296–1319.
8. Hook, J. N. *The Teaching of High School English* (3d ed.). New York: The Ronald Press Co., 1965.
9. Horn, Ernest. *Methods of Instruction in the Social Studies.* New York: Charles Scribner's Sons, 1937.
10. Jarolimek, John. *Social Studies in Elementary Education.* New York: The Macmillan Co., 1963.
11. Leary, Bernice E. "Meeting Specific Reading Problems in the Content Fields," *Reading in the High School and College.* The Forty-seventh Yearbook, Part II, National Society for the Study of Education. Chicago: The University of Chicago Press, 1948.
12. Loban, Walter, Ryan, Margaret, and Squire, James B. *Teaching Language and Literature.* New York: Harcourt, Brace & World, Inc., 1961.
13. Miller, S. M. "Dropouts—A Political Problem," *The School Dropout,* ed. Daniel Schreiber. Project: School Dropouts. Washington, D.C.: N.E.A., 1964, pp. 11–24.
14. Peterson, Eleanor M. *Aspects of Readability in the Social Studies.* New York: Bureau of Publications, Teachers College, Columbia University, 1954.
15. *Reading in the High School and College.* The Forty-seventh Yearbook, Part II, National Society for the Study of Education. Chicago: The University of Chicago Press, 1948.
16. Sauer, Edwin H. *English in the Secondary School.* New York: Holt, Rinehart & Winston, Inc., 1961.
17. Smith, Henry P., and Dechant, Emerald V. *Psychology in Teaching Reading.* Englewood Cliffs, N.J.: Prentice-Hall, Inc., 1961.
18. Strang, Ruth, McCullough, Constance M., and Traxler, Arthur E. *The Improvement of Reading.* New York: McGraw-Hill Book Co., Inc., 1961.
19. Strang, Ruth. "Progress in the Teaching of Reading in High School and College," *The Reading Teacher,* Vol. 16 (December, 1962), pp. 170–77.
20. Tyler, Ralph W. "Background," *The School Dropout,* ed. Daniel Schreiber. Project: School Dropouts. Washington, D.C.: N.E.A., 1964. Pp. 5–8.

SUGGESTED ADDITIONAL READING

Belden, Bernard R., and Lee, Wayne D. "Readability of Biology Textbooks and the Reading Ability of Biology," *School, Science, and Mathematics,* Vol. 61 (December, 1961), pp. 689–93.

Bentley, Ralph R., and Galloway, R. Edward. "A Comparison of the Readability of Vocational Agriculture Reference Books with the Reading

Ability of the Students Using Them," *Journal of Experimental Education,* Vol. 29 (June, 1961), pp. 373–83.

BOND, GUY L., and KEGLER, STANLEY B. "Reading Instruction in the Senior High School," The Sixtieth Yearbook, Part I. National Society for the Study of Education. Chicago: The University of Chicago Press, 1961.

DAWSON, MILDRED A., and BAMMAN, HENRY A. *Fundamentals of Basic Reading Instruction* (2d ed.). New York: David McKay Co., Inc., 1963. Chap. xv.

DE BOER, JOHN J., and WHIPPLE, GERTRUDE. "Reading Development in Other Curriculum Areas," The Sixtieth Yearbook, Part I. National Society for the Study of Education. Chicago: The University of Chicago Press, 1961.

GATES, ARTHUR I. "Reading Abilities in the Content Subjects," *Readings in the Language Arts,* compiled by VERNA DIECKMAN ANDERSON, PAUL S. ANDERSON, FRANCIS BALLANTINE, and VIRGIL M. HOWES. New York: The Macmillan Co., 1964.

GRAY, WILLIAM S. "Increasing the Basic Reading Competencies of Students," *Reading in the High School and College.* The Forty-seventh Yearbook, National Society for the Study of Education. Chicago: The University of Chicago Press, 1948.

HENRY, NELSON B. (ed.). *Reading in the High School and College.* The Forty-seventh Yearbook, Part II, National Society for the Study of Education. Chicago: The University of Chicago Press, 1948.

MCGINNIS, DOROTHY J. "The Preparation and Responsibility of Secondary Teachers in the Field of Reading," *The Reading Teacher,* Vol. 15 (November, 1961), pp. 92–97, 101.

MARKSHEFFEL, NED D. "The Use of Reading in Subject-Matter Areas," *The Portland High School Curriculum Study,* Vol. 10. Speaking, Writing, and Reading in Courses Other Than English and Speech. School Dist. No. 1, Multnomah Co., Ore., 1959. Pp. 35–48.

PARKER, DON H. "Reading in Science: Training or Education," *Science Teacher,* Vol. 30 (February, 1963), pp. 43–47.

PODENDORF, ILLA. "Accent on Thinking in Science for Children in the 60's in the Classroom Through Reading and Research," *Science Education,* Vol. 46 (March, 1962), pp. 184–85.

SPRIETSMA, LEWIS R. "Reading Skills Should Be Taught at All Levels," *Journal of Secondary Education,* Vol. 37 (April, 1962), pp. 252–55.

STAUFFER, RUSSEL G. "A Study of Prefixes in the Thorndike List To Establish a List of Prefixes That Should Be Taught in the Elementary School," *Journal of Educational Research,* Vol. 34 (February, 1942), pp. 453–58.

THORNDIKE, EDWARD L. *The Teaching of English Suffixes.* New York: Bureau of Publications, Teachers College, Columbia University, 1941.

9

WORD-RECOGNITION SKILLS

Efficient readers in high school seldom encounter words in their reading that they are unable to recognize immediately. When they do meet an unfamiliar word, they are usually capable of identifying it immediately and associating the proper meaning with it. The corrective, or retarded reader, however is not so fortunate. He meets many words that have no meaning for him because of his inability to pronounce them. Unless he can pronounce written words, he is powerless to associate meaning with them.

The exact number of high school students with reading problems is unknown since there are no accurate overall data. But there have been a number of estimates by reading researchers and reading authorities that indicate the number of such readers is greater than most people realize. Gray (8, p. 390) notes that it is an unpleasant fact, but unless the teaching of reading is greatly improved, 20 per cent or more of the children now beginning school will develop reading problems before they enter high school. Other estimates of reading retardation vary from as low as 20 to as high as 50 per cent. Although estimates, as well as the reading competencies of students, will differ within school districts and among states, it is more realistic to expect that from 30 to 40 per cent of the high school students will not be reading as efficiently as they are capable of doing.

Some Word-Recognition Problems of a College Freshman

Let us examine a sample of word-recognition errors made by Jan, a college freshman, during an informal reading test, since her pattern of errors reveals the kinds of word-recognition skills that need to be learned by many inadequate high school readers. We need to know that she (1) graduated from high school with a "B" average, (2) achieved an IQ of 117 on the Wechsler Adult Intelligence Scale, (3) repeated the second grade because of difficulty with reading, (4) decided to seek help in reading when she was "unable to remember" anything she read in her college textbooks, and (5) exhibited no visual anomalies.

Jan read orally from an interesting magazine article of approximately seventh-grade difficulty. In a 204-word sample, she made 22 errors in word recognition for a score of slightly over 89 per cent. She omitted *the* once, and inserted it on two occasions. She was unable to pronounce three words, *prodigious, fugitives,* and *ingredient.* She also misread figures. The stimulus *1,700* was called *170,* and *1,200,000* was called *12,000.*

Following is a list of the words that she mispronounced:

Stimulus		*Jan's Response*
giveaway	**	gaveaway
response	*	responses
effectiveness	+	efitiveness (corrected later)
is	**	as
heard	*	heed
implicit	* +	implicated
intelligence	*	intelligent
voice	*	voices
global	+	globial
ground-wave	+	grounded-wave
dimension	*	diminishing
means	*, **	seems
weep	**	sweep

Do you note any particular pattern of errors in the above list? In eight words (*), errors were made in either the final or the two final letters. In four words (**), errors were made in the initial part of the word. Four errors (+), were made in the middle of words.

It is apparent that Jan (1) depends greatly upon *configuration clues* as one method of attacking words, (2) needs help with *phonics clues,* and (3) makes little use of *context and structural clues.* Her *sightword vocabulary,* words recognized immediately, is flagrantly insufficient to meet her reading needs at the college level. In fact, a diagnosis of her reading problem revealed that her instructional reading level was sixth grade. Her low score of 89 per cent in word recognition in the example given indicates she is frustrated by her inability to pronounce words at seventh-grade level. Further evidence of her frustration was her score of 40 per cent in a comprehension test based on her reading.

The example of Jan's difficulty with word recognition was cited since her word-recognition problems are typical of many secondary students who are not competent readers but who have the potential to become effective readers if they receive adequate help. Contrary to what has often been said about it being too late to attempt to improve the reading of a student after he reaches high school, most incompetent high school readers can be helped.

While the lack of adequate word-recognition skills contributes to reading problems, such a deficiency is not *the* reason for all inefficient reading. In previous chapters, we have shown that there are *many reasons* why students fail to achieve success in reading. We also mentioned that *verbalizers* are able to pronounce innumerable words with accuracy, yet they are not competent readers. In summary, good readers who have minor problems in word recognition and corrective readers who are word-recognition cases may improve their reading efficiency when they receive adequate instruction in word-attack skills. Therefore, techniques of word recognition will be discussed in the following order, which is not necessarily the order of importance but rather the order in which we discussed some of Jan's word-analysis deficiencies: (1) configuration clues, (2) phonics clues, (3) context or meaning clues, (4) structural clues, and (5) dictionary skills.

CONFIGURATION CLUES

Configuration clues refers to the patterns or forms of words. There is a difference between the shapes of the words "father" and "son." If the two words were outlined, the general form of *father* would be much different from that of the rectangular shape of *son. Father* has three ascending letters and one descending letter, while *son* has no irregularities in height of letters.

The use of configuration clues as one means of word analysis requires the reader to note carefully the pattern of words, and also to use context clues in combination with word forms.

Individuals, however, differ in the amount and degree to which they use configuration clues. Oftentimes students may be misled, as Jan was, into making errors in pronunciation by excessive reliance on word forms. The following sample illustrates some of the words that confuse corrective readers who overuse configuration clues:

want, went, won't
fell, full, fall, fill
his, him
house, horse
was, saw

Summary

Most elementary teachers teach children to use configuration clues as an aid in recognizing words. Some authorities believe that the use of configuration clues for learning to pronounce words has much value and has not been stressed sufficiently (1, p. 611). Others state there is no real evidence for emphasizing the forms of words (11, p. 90), while still others maintain that both beginning readers and adults make frequent use of configuration clues to identify words (4, p. 190).

At this time, available evidence and the judgment of authorities indicate that the use of configuration clues for identifying and recognizing words is of value to both beginning and mature readers, although the manner in which the clues are used may differ between the two kinds of readers.

PHONICS AND READING

The teaching of phonics in America provides interesting and controversial reading. The first truly phonetic system in America was developed by Noah Webster primarily for patriotic reasons and secondly for pedagogical purposes.

A Brief History of the Phonetic Method of Reading in America

Noah Webster was a highly patriotic and important figure during the time when the United States was becoming a nation, and he contributed greatly to both the teaching of reading and nationalism. At the same time he unwittingly planted the seed of many a bitter discussion concerning methodology and techniques of teaching reading by introducing phonics to America.

Webster was graduated from Yale with a degree in law, but turned to teaching. It was during his travels as an itinerant teacher that he became alarmed at the differences in speech among the peoples of villages and hamlets that were separated only by a few miles. He could foresee that a young nation of many tongues would not lend itself to solidarity but rather to diversification. America, he felt, was destined to become another Europe of many small nations instead of a single strong nation unless a common language bound the people together.

Not only did Webster recognize the need for a common language for all the people, but he also helped to foster such a phenomenon by writing a series of three books based upon a phonetic system which he felt would insure the same pronunciation of words by all the people. The most famous book of the series, the *American Spelling Book,* was actually a reader but became affectionately known to millions as, *The Blue Back Speller.* He taught not only spelling but pronunciation, common sense, morals, and good citizenship (17).

Horace Mann, who has been mentioned previously in this book, was a severe critic of the alphabet method of teaching reading. Through his reports to the Board of Education in Massachusetts and numerous speeches he did much to arouse public opinion against this faulty concept of teaching reading. But old customs and habits have a way of perpetuating themselves. When discussions arise about the alphabetic-phonetic method in the writer's classes, anywhere from two or three, to as many as seven or eight students insist that they were taught to read by saying, "k - a - t, *cat.*" Others say they were taught to read by saying, "c - k, a - ă, t - tuh, *cat.*"

During the 1880's a number of phonic systems were introduced into the schools. One of the most popular and best known of the *synthetic* methods was the Pollard System. The sounds of consonants and vowels were taught and then combined into families that were the bases for words. Miss Pollard did not believe in teaching whole words before giving pupils instruction in sounding letters. She believed it was more sensible to lay a foundation from which words were built.

Other important and well-known methods that can only be mentioned here were, *The Rational Method,* 1894; *The Gordon System,* 1902; and *The Beacon Method,* 1912.

The Analytic Approach to Phonics

The analytic approach to teaching phonics, first developed by Anna D. Cordts, is a distinct departure from the previous synthetic methods of phonics (3, p. 220). Children using this method of phonics start with whole words and learn consonant and vowel sounds in words as they occur in reading. Pupils are taught to discover phonetic units within new words or syllables from a known word. In Cordts' (3, p. 220) own words:

> The children discovered each "phonetic" unit themselves from a word they already knew and which had become the key word for the unit. The word *candy,* for example, was the key word for the beginning (*ca*) as in *cattle, calendar, camera, cavities, castle, California.*
>
> The vowel (*ir*) was discovered from the key word *bird,* the diphthong (*ou*) from the key word *mouse,* and the consonant sound (*p*) from the key word *sheep,* for example. [3, p. 220.]

Although there are many phonics methods, they may be classified under two main headings: (1) the *synthetic* approach and the (2) *ana-*

lytic approach. It is difficult to say how many teachers use the synthetic approach. Spache (13, p. 229) says a survey by Russell shows most reading authorities recommend the analytic approach and that only 15 per cent of today's teachers use a synthetic approach.

Most reading authorities favor the analytic approach because (1) the elements that comprise words are learned as syllables or words and not as isolated letter-sound combinations, (2) phonics becomes a part of word-recognition skills in reading rather than becoming a method of reading, (3) phonics becomes an aid to getting meaning from reading, (4) students learn to make generalizations for pronouncing words rather than memorizing separate sounds of words and trying to blend them into words, and (5) more children learn to love reading instead of developing a dislike for it.

Phonics or Phonetics?

Should the term "phonics" or "phonetics," be used in discussing the relationship of sounds and letters? Both terms are used interchangeably by writers, teachers, educators, and the public. Usage, Gray (8, p. 301) says, has determined that *phonics* is most accepted in the public mind. In this book, *phonics* and *phonetics* are both used to denote the association of sounds with letter symbols.

In the past, there has been much confusion about the role of phonics in teaching reading. And there have been numerous claims that both the lack of teaching phonics and the overemphasis on phonics as a method of teaching reading have been the main reasons for reading failures among children. Unfortunately, there is *no one reason* for reading failures and neither is there *any one system* that has *the* answer to word recognition and other reading problems. It may be true that the lack of phonetic skills is *one of the factors* contributing to a child's reading difficulty.

On the other hand, many children are inefficient readers because their instruction in beginning reading overemphasized phonics, and they have never learned to use other word-recognition skills. Some children have developed an excessive dislike of all reading because of the difficulty they experienced in learning to read by a particular system of phonics. Teachers must be continually aware of the "medicine man" of reading. He has a product to sell that may cause much damage to children under the guise of being the *system that makes sense* or *the only correct way to teach.* For one who might be tempted to try an untested or psychologically unsound approach to word recognition, Gray (8, p. 221) has a word of warning:

> For every beginner who survives the unpsychological rigors of the alphabet-phonics approach, there may be thousands who never fully recover from the confusing ordeal, and spend the remainder of their lives with an intense dislike for reading. [8, p. 221.]

It is indeed a rare school system that does not include the teaching of phonics in the teaching of reading. Naturally, the amount of phonics and the particular phonetic approach being taught will vary among schools and among teachers in the same school. Teachers recognize that if students are to become independent readers they must develop phonetic skills, regardless of disagreement whether the approach is *analytic* or *synthetic.*

Disagreement About Phonics Adds to Teacher Confusion

We know from teachers' comments and experience that most secondary teachers claim to have little or no knowledge about phonics clues or how to teach pupils how to use phonics in pronouncing words, although these same teachers use phonics many times in their own reading. Secondary teachers, however, are not alone in their uncertainty about phonics. Elementary teachers, who are normally responsible for developing children's phonetic skills are in much the same position. They are uncertain whether or not they are teaching phonics correctly (5, p. 227) because few of them have had little preparation for teaching phonics (3, pp. 1–3). In addition, the numerous controversies over the way reading should be taught indicate that "misconceptions concerning phonics and methods of teaching sounding are fairly common" (10, p. 26).

Gans (7, p. 1) writes that *phonics* is of much interest to many people, yet many of those who become excited about the role of phonics know little more about the subject than, "It has something to do with learning to pronounce words." Cordts (3, p. 242) notes that, "the layman has little knowledge of what the phonetic approach really is." She further states (3, pp. 251–52) emphatically that laymen and educationists often overlook the fact that the ability to pronounce unfamiliar words "is not synonymous with knowing how to read."

Is it any wonder that secondary teachers are in a quandary about helping students with phonics clues for pronouncing words? Past experience indicates that secondary teachers develop confidence in themselves and help students with word-recognition skills when someone takes time to provide these teachers with an understanding of phonics, and other word-attack skills, and shows them some of the procedures for teaching such skills.

What Can the Classroom Teacher Do About Teaching Phonics?

A teacher cannot rely too heavily on research evidence for procedures best suited to teaching phonics. It has been pointed out (6, p. 13) that, while numerous studies are reported in the literature, few of the data have sufficient quality to justify using any special techniques or methods in the classroom. Until sufficient valid data is available, teachers must rely upon their own and other teachers' experiences, keen observation of classroom behavior of youngsters engaged in learning and using phonics, research from other areas of learning, thoughtful analysis (6, p. 14), and their own knowledge of phonics.

Secondary teachers should learn some of the more applicable *generalizations* that may be used in analyzing words. Therefore, examples of some of the more common phonic generalizations will be presented. The word "generalizations" is used here in place of "rules." Most authorities agree that *rules* of phonics do not exist, because the make-up of English allows for too many exceptions to the rule.

Consonants

Consonants are those letters of the alphabet that are not vowels. One of the easiest ways to get this idea across to students is to ask them to name the vowels, and then ask, "What are the other letters of the alphabet called?"

Students should be taught that consonants are generally consistent in the sounds they represent. The consonant *p* for example, has the same recorded sound in "pen," "pamphlet," "partner," "picture," "put," and "pot," although the vowel following a consonant produces the real difference in the sound that an individual hears. He hears that "pet," "pest," and "pen" sound alike in the beginning, but it is more difficult for him to hear the similarity in the initial parts of "potato," "pickle," and "pumpkin."

Hard and Soft Sounds of *c* and *g*

Some high school students are confused as to when *c* should take the hard sound (*k*) as in "cake," or the soft sound (*s*) as in "certain" and "century." Asking students to give examples that may then be written on the chalkboard is one technique that allows students to associate the hard and soft sounds of *c* with the visual stimuli. Few have any difficulty in making the generalization. Some examples of soft *c* words follow:

city	cyclone	bicycle	citrus	circumference
ceiling	cement	cemetery	cite	circulate
center	ceramic	cynic	cylinder	citation

Soft *g* sound is found in many similar combinations but is not as consistent in taking the soft sound (*j*).

gypsy	giant	gem	gesture
gyroplane	gist	gin	geometry

Consonant Blends

Consonant blends of two or more letters must be taught as a single unit in a word as the *str* in "string." When pupils are taught to sound separately each consonant in the *str* blend, as: *s - t - r*, they are apt to call "*string*" "stirring."

Some examples of consonant blends that may need to be taught in the manner just described are:

br as in branch, brunch, brown
cl as in climb, cling, close
cr as in crash, crack, crazy
dr as in drive, drink, drop
sk as in skate, skin, skunk
st as in steam, stop, stay
spr as in spring, sprout, sprain
str as in strike, street, strong

Short and Long Vowels

Short vowels are usually taught before long vowels, but this is not a definite procedure. Some teachers prefer to teach long vowels before they teach short vowels. Long vowels are usually sounded as their names indicate—*a, e, i, o, u.*

When Do Vowels Have a Short Sound?

Children who have no difficulty with phonics learn to generalize that vowels usually take the short sound when they are followed by a consonant; for example, "is," "it," "as," "and," "if," "end," or when they appear in words like "hit," "him," "hat," "sat," "trap," "trick," "bank," and "ran."

The preceding examples of short vowels are also examples of *closed syllables*. Can you make a "rule" for a closed syllable from these examples?

Vowels with the Long Sound

A vowel in an *open syllable* is usually long: "I," "me," "he," "we," "go," "she," "my."

A vowel that is followed by a single consonant and a final "silent" *e,* is usually long: "time," "kite," "ate," "late," "hate," "pine," "cute," "plane."

When two vowels are together (*a vowel digraph*), the first is usually long. The vowels in the following words can be used to form the preceding generalization: "rain," "mail," "seat," "see," "chain," "queen," and "boat."

Students should be advised that this generalization is not as consistent as we would like. When an unfamiliar word is being sounded and the result sounds incorrect to the learner, suggest that he try sounding the second vowel long and then making the first vowel the silent one. The *ie vowel digraphs* in the words: "grief," "believe," "piece," are examples of digraphs in which the second vowel is long.

Vowels That Are Neither Short Nor Long

The consonants *l, r, u,* and *w,* change the sounds of some vowels. When *a* is followed by: (1) *l* as in "tall," "always," and "also"; (2) *r* in "far," "argue," and "market"; (3) *u* in "caught," "nautical," and "taught"; and (4) *w* in "lawful," "awl," and "brawl," *a* is neither long nor short.

The vowels *e, i,* and *u* sound the same when followed by *r,* as in "fur," "fir" and "transfer."

TECHNIQUES OF TEACHING PHONIC GENERALIZATIONS

Teachers should determine if the students who need phonics help have learned to listen discriminately. Many high school students, for example, have never heard the word "protect" as it should be pronounced. For some of them "protect" has been heard as "pertect," "pertek," and "pretect." In these instances, a teacher's first job becomes one of teaching these students to learn to listen discriminately. Once students hear the sounds of "per" in "person" and "pro" in "protect," for example, they need to associate these sounds with their written forms.

The time to teach the letter sounds with syllables or words is when the student is having difficulty with a particular word. It is a better choice to *ask him* the part of the word that is giving him difficulty rather than trying to guess the trouble spot.

Duplicated work sheets may be used to give students practice in seeing how many of the generalizations are applied after they have been discussed. Following are several examples of work sheets that one teacher used to help groups of high school students who could hear long and short vowel sounds accurately but who were having difficulty in identifying them in printed words.

"Silent" e Exercise

What is the purpose of "silent" *e*? If you are not sure what "silent" *e* does, you will find out after you have completed the following exercise:

1. Pronounce these words aloud:

sam ______	bit ______	sit ______	hug ______	tap ______
kit ______	cut ______	man ______	min ______	pet ______
hop ______	rat ______	fat ______	tam ______	mat ______

2. Now, in the space provided, add an *e* to each word.
3. Pronounce each word aloud with the "silent" *e* added to it.
4. Did you notice that the "silent" *e* made the first vowel long?
5. Write a "rule" for "silent" *e* words.

Hard c Sound

The letter *c* sometimes has the sound of *k*. Sometimes it has the sound of *s*. Here is a rule that will help you in pronouncing words that contain *c*'s.

> When *c* comes before an *e*, *i*, or *y*, it is usually soft, or pronounced like *s*. At all other times the *c* is pronounced as *k*.

Copy these words in the blanks below: center, circus, city, ice, dance, nice, once, cent, bicycle.

__________ __________ __________ __________ __________

__________ __________ __________ __________

Draw a circle around the *c* and the vowel that makes the *c* soft, or sound like *s*.

Did you notice the two words that had both the soft and hard sounds of *c* in the same word? Now, draw a line under each of the two words containing both soft *c* and hard *c* sounds.

HISTORY OF PHONICS

The history of phonics in America is an interesting and controversial one. At times, phonics has been the most popular of all techniques, or methods, of teaching reading. On other occasions it has been held in utter disrepute by most people.

Today phonics is recognized as being an important and useful aspect of any reading program. It is an area in which most people are interested and one in which few people, excepting some experts, have any real knowledge.

Numerous systems of phonics are presently being marketed. Sponsors of some systems "guarantee that no child will fail to learn to read in the first grade *if* our system is properly used." The onus of any pupil failure, therefore, is not that of the system, but of inadequate teaching or uncooperative pupil effort. Such a viewpoint disregards all laws of child psychology and learning.

Advocates of other systems are more modest in their claims although they do not deny that their particular systems are best. Still others have programs that authorities consider to be sound and which deserve to be tried and tested in classrooms.

Phonics is an important aid in reading that should not be slighted, overstressed, or expected to make every child an efficient reader. While word recognition is vital to reading, the pronunciation of written words is only the beginning, not the final or total activity of the reading process.

DEFINITIONS OF PHONIC TERMS USED IN THIS CHAPTER

PHONICS. The application of phonetic principles for pronouncing words in reading.

PHONETICS. The term for designating the science of speech sounds, the vocal reproduction of speech sounds, and the relationship of speech sounds to language.

INITIAL CONSONANTS. Consonants that are at the beginnings of words: *m* in "mother," "me," and "my."

CONSONANT BLENDS. Two or more consonants blended in such a manner that they *may sound* as one, but each letter in a *blend* maintains its own identity. The *br* in "bring," *tr* in "tree," *str* in "street," and the *bl* in "blend" are examples of consonant blends.

DIGRAPHS. Two vowels representing one speech sound. The double *ee* in "speech," *ea* in "sea," and *ai* in "paid" are examples of vowel digraphs.

DIPHTHONGS. Two vowels blended so closely that they *may sound* as a single vowel. Some examples of vowel *digraphs* are: *oi* in "oil," *oy* in "boy," *ou* in "out," *ow* in "how."

AUDITORY DISCRIMINATION. The ability to differentiate between differences in sounds of letters and words, and to note the similarity of sounds of letters and words.

VISUAL DISCRIMINATION. The ability to perceive the similarity of letters and words, as well as to note the dissimilarity.

CONTEXT CLUES

The use of context clues has often been referred to as guessing, and guessing has an unfavorable connotation for many people. An educated guess, however, is important in numerous fields other than reading. Spache (14, p. 315) says that most context clues require a certain degree of inferential thinking, and other authorities (12) agree with this viewpoint. Bond and Wagner (2, p. 171) state that if the use of context clues is not the most important means of recognizing words, it is one of the most important. Although all reading authorities may not make such a strong statement in defense of context clues, few would disagree that the use of context clues is of help to many students in recognizing words and associating meaning with them.

Nevertheless, there are authorities who say that context clues give students only a hazy or approximate clue to the intended meanings of unknown words and do little by way of aiding word recognition. And each group can cite examples that point out the correctness of its statements.

Context clues, when used in conjunction with other word-recognition clues, appear to have much value and are widely used by readers at all levels. In many instances, the use of context clues stops a reader short when he has incorrectly perceived a word. A child, for example, reading the following sentence: "Jack rode a horse while at his uncle's ranch" may incorrectly perceive the word "horse" as *house.* If he is reading for meaning, he immediately recognizes his error through the use of a context clue. If he is merely pronouncing words and is not using context clues, he may never notice his error.

At higher levels of learning context clues may be of little value when the material is heavy with unfamiliar words, and the student is lacking experience in the particular context area. However, college students rely heavily on the use of context clues for recognition and understanding and unfamiliar words. In the writer's classes, for example, approximately two hundred out of every three hundred students who were questioned about their use of context and other word-recognition clues during silent reading said they used context clues far more than any other kinds of clues for analyzing and learning unknown words.

Like other word-recognition skills, context clues should not be overemphasized nor used exclusively for identifying and recognizing words. Most readers use a number of word-recognition clues simultaneously and without consciously thinking about the process they are using.

If students are to use context clues to advantage they should be taught how to use such clues. It is suggested that the teaching of context clues begin early by having children read meaningful materials beginning at the first-grade level.

One of the techniques often used by teachers in helping children use context clues is to ask a child who is having difficulty with a word, "What word would make sense in this sentence?" Such help often elicits the correct response. If the child's response is incorrect, the teacher may agree that the answer is a meaningful one but asks if the suggested word begins like the one in the book. The additional teacher suggestion directs the child to use phonics as an additional aid for identifying the word. This kind of teaching of word-recognition skills produces positive results.

STRUCTURAL CLUES

The teaching of the use of word structural clues as an aid for pronouncing and understanding words is one of the most important word-recognition skills that *can* be taught successfully to high school students.

Seven Reasons for Teaching Structural Clues

There are seven legitimate reasons why word-structure clues should be taught in high school. All of them are based on student needs.

1. Corrective readers in high school generally know little about the structure of words.
2. High school textbooks contain many polysyllabic words (words of more than three syllables), and inefficient readers usually skip over polysyllabic words without ever trying to pronounce them.
3. The use of structural analysis is usually a quicker method of identifying and recognizing words than phonetic analysis is.
4. Students have little difficulty in learning to recognize prefixes, suffixes, and root words.
5. Many students have no idea of what is meant by *syllables* or the role syllables play in word structure.
6. Syllables transfer to many words.
7. A knowledge of roots, prefixes, and suffixes contributes not only to improvement in word recognition, but also to improvement in spelling, speaking, and writing.

Syllabication Skills

A basic need of corrective readers in high school is that of knowing how to syllabicate words. Harris (9, p. 341) gives a hint as to why many students lack knowledge of syllabication skills when he notes that many students are unable to grasp the rules of syllabification when such skills are normally introduced in the fourth and fifth grades. He suggests that it may be unwise to spend much time in teaching syllabication skills below the sixth grade. Since the teaching of reading, prior to the past several years, generally ceased at about the fourth grade, there is little need to look further for a legitimate reason why many students lack skill in syllabicating words.

Learning Syllabication Skills Through Hearing

In the past, those teachers who taught the syllabication of words spent much time on the learning of rules. Today, the heavy emphasis on teaching syllabic rules is questioned by many. Actually, there is little need to spend hours learning rules whose transfer is of doubtful value. It is a simple task to pronounce a word and ask students to tell how many parts or syllables they hear. Even first- and second-graders hear syllables readily when they are taught to listen for them.

Those few students in high school who fail to grasp the idea of noting syllables in spoken words may be helped by having them repeat a word and note how many times they open their mouths during the process. Each time they open their mouths to release the vowel sound, the opening denotes a syllable. Some students are helped in recognizing syllables by placing one of their hands lightly around the front of the throat when saying the word. When words are spoken, the kinesthetic movement of the muscles can be felt easily when the student's hand is in such a position. As the vowels are spoken the student's lower jaw will exert pressure on his hand and thereby aid him in identifying syllables.

The transfer of knowledge of spoken syllables to printed syllables requires little practice, in most instances. The important point to make with students is that each syllable must have one vowel sound although the syllable may contain two vowels. Examples of vowel digraphs as in the words "see" and "boat," or in the syllables *pre* and *per* may be used to clarify any confusion between the number of vowels and vowel sounds in a single syllable. Diphthongs like the *oi* in "boil," and *ou* in "shout" should also be explained.

Exercises

Students may be given practice in locating and underlining syllables in words. At this stage of learning a few simple rules may be of value. Students' attention may be directed to noting that in words having two consonants between two vowels, the syllable is divided between the double consonants. Examples:

happy	hap - py
willow	wil - low
letter	let - ter

Teaching Affixes

Prefixes and suffixes should be taught to those students who do not understand them. Students need to learn that the meanings and usage of words are changed by the addition of suffixes and prefixes. One pitfall that is better avoided is that of having students memorize lists of prefixes, suffixes, and roots, which practice, it is sometimes claimed, will unlock thousands of new words for them. It is best to teach affixes in meaningful situations.

Students may, for example, have difficulty in pronouncing "rediscovering." The mere matter of length frightens many inefficient readers. In this instance, the teacher might ask for volunteers to point out the prefixes. Once these are located few students have difficulty in pronouncing them as individual syllables—*re,* and *dis.*

Finding the suffix *ing* is the next step. After this has been done, the root word "cover" is easily recognized.

Exercises, group and individual, may be used to strengthen students' skills in noting and using affixes as aids in pronouncing words.

Prefixes

An excellent study by Stauffer (15) of the most common prefixes found in the first 20,000 words of *Thorndike's Teacher's Word Book* shows that almost one-fourth (24 per cent) of the first 20,000 words have prefixes. The 15 commonest prefixes comprise 82 per cent of the total number of prefixes used in the Thorndike list. Because the 15 prefixes are used regularly, teachers and students should know them. However, a word of caution is necessary. Prefixes are not limited to one meaning—they *usually* have several meanings.

The most widely used prefix *com* is used to illustrate how a prefix shifts in meaning and changes in spelling. *Com,* from the Latin *cum,* meaning "with," also has the meaning of "together" and "very." Likewise, the spelling of *com,* and other prefixes change according to the spelling of the roots to which they are attached. For example, *com* is spelled *com* in "companion," "committee," and "community," but it changes to *col* in "collapse" and "collect." *Com* becomes *con* in "concur," "condense," and "confuse."

Following is a list of the most common prefixes found by Stauffer:

ab - from	dis - apart	pre - before
ad - to	en - in	pro - in front of
be - by	ex - out	re - back
com - with	in - into	sub - under
de - from	in - not	un - not

Suffixes

The teaching of suffixes is neglected more often than not, but neglect does not detract from their use and importance. Thorndike's (16) monograph, *The Teaching of English Suffixes,* published in 1941, is an excellent reference.

A suffix is a syllable added to the end of a word to show a change in meaning. The addition of a suffix, however, does not always add a syllable to the pronunciation of a word. This fact sometimes confuses teachers as well as students. For example, the suffix *er* when added to "walk," "talk," or "shop" means "one who walks, talks, and shops," and these become two-syllable words. But when the syllable *ed* is added to "walk," "talk," "shop," and other words, it is not pronounced as a separate syllable, but is pronounced as *t,* as in "dropped," "stopped," "walked." With words ending in *t,* however, the addition of the suffix *ed* is pronounced as a separate syllable as in "accepted," "parted," and "started."

Root Words

Students will benefit from guided practice in locating root words. This instruction should be given concurrently with that given in determining affixes. Lists of words may be given students with directions for them to underline root words. Later, students may be assigned root words to which they add meaningful prefixes and suffixes.

A sample list of root words with affixes follows:

urge	- urgent	dark	- darkening
observe	- observer	port	- exporter
length	- lengthening	nation	- international
vision	- envision	function	- malfunctioning
distribute	- redistribution	employ	- unemployment

Syllables Transfer to Other Words

When a student is shown how syllables work in words and how they transfer to other words, he is more confident in his ability to pronounce and understand unfamiliar words. And chances are that he will develop an interest in learning words if he is not pushed too fast.

The syllable *per* in "person" may be used to illustrate how a syllable often retains the same sound when used in numerous words. The following list of words might be used to show students how *per* transfers. The list may also serve as a guide in finding similar words with the aid of a dictionary.

perhaps	per - haps
perfect	per - fect
paper	pa - per
hamper	ham - per
permission	per - mis - sion
intemperate	in - tem - per - ate

Summary

Time spent in teaching inefficient readers the use of structural clues for rapidly identifying words is time well spent. The student learning that takes place during such instructional periods has both immediate and lasting benefits. Students have immediate opportunities to use their learning in listening, speaking, reading, spelling, and writing.

DICTIONARY CLUES

Learning how to use a dictionary for pronouncing words and understanding the meanings associated with them is one of the most valuable skills a student can acquire. While many high school students use a dictionary with a dexterity that amazes their elders, many of their classmates demonstrate no such skill or willingness, but use the dictionary only when they are assigned to do so.

Students who dislike using a dictionary usually have an excuse for their antipathy. They lack the skills required for using it.

Teaching dictionary skills can be an interesting and rewarding experience for both teachers and students when the teaching is begun at the student's own level. The instructional level for some high school students will be equivalent to that of fourth- or fifth-graders. Some of these students previously felt it was necessary for them to commit the alphabet to memory, a task they now must master since knowing the alphabet in sequence is a prerequisite to efficient use of the dictionary.

Many of these same students, however, upon entering high school become acutely aware of their deficiencies and sincerely desire to make up for the time they may have frittered away when dictionary skills were previously taught in the elementary grades. Other students may have missed such instruction, or for other reasons failed to benefit from lessons in dictionary usage. Whatever the reasons for their lack of acquiring dictionary skills, they now have an honest desire to learn them.

Teaching Procedures

One of the teacher's first steps should be that of determining which students need to learn the alphabet in its sequential order. Teachers are often advised to have students memorize the letters that are contained in the first, second, and third sections of the dictionary. Experience indicates that the time expended in such activity could be better spent in developing other dictionary skills. Students quickly learn, for example, that entries beginning with *e* are near the front of the dictionary, while those beginning with *m* are near the middle, and those starting with *s* are located near the end of the book. Does it really matter that one knows if these entries fall within the first or second quarter of the dictionary?

Examples of Exercises That Teach Alphabetization

Some students will need practice in alphabetizing words. For those who are weak in this aspect, exercises similar to the following may be helpful.

Exercise. Write the letters that go between the following groups of letters:

a ___ c	c ___ ___ f	k ___ ___ n	v ___ ___ y
b ___ d	g ___ ___ j	q ___ ___ t	w ___ ___ z
m ___ o	o ___ ___ r	t ___ ___ w	j ___ ___ m

Exercise. Alphabetize these words (first letter alphabetizing):

depth	beauty	cart
hygiene	lizard	quarter
yearly	absent	freedom
jealous	stream	percentage
operate	important	mountain

Additional exercises in alphabetization should include words that are placed in sequential order according to beginning two- and three-letter patterns.

Example.

whip	height	ruthful	material
wheel	heaven	rutty	mathematics

Locating Words Rapidly

The next step might be that of teaching students how to thumb the pages of a dictionary. The teacher should first demonstrate how words may be found rapidly by opening the dictionary at approximately the right location and, using one hand, thumb the pages until the guide words indicate he is near the desired word. He may then use his other hand to help him stop on the exact page. This kind of demonstration creates a positive reaction within students.

In order that students locate words rapidly, they must make use of the guide words that are in bold-face type at the top of each column of word entries. Numbers of students say they have wondered about the bold-face words but felt they probably were not important.

Although students know how to use guide words and why they should be used, they may continue to scan each column of words on several different pages in search of a word only to discover finally that the word is several pages away. The implication of such action is clear, students need guided practice in using the dictionary after they have learned how it should be used.

A well-worn but late edition of a dictionary on the teacher's desk is one of the best indicators of the kind of an example the teacher sets for his students. When students observe that even teachers need to use a dictionary, they appear to accept the idea that using a dictionary is not an indication of ignorance, but an accepted practice.

Learning the Pronunciation of Words

After a student has found the word for which he has been searching, he often needs to learn to pronounce it accurately. He can do this by using the pronunciation key used in his particular dictionary providing he knows how to use the key. Acquiring this ability also demands practice with teacher direction.

Locating Needed Definitions

Many high school students will need to be taught that the first definition under a word is not necessarily the one they need. Students should be taught to read all the definitions until they locate the one that helps them to associate the proper meaning to the previously unknown word. This means that they need to use the context in which the word was used before they can decide upon the needed definition.

One technique that helps students to realize that words may have many meanings associated with them is to have students look up several small words like "run," "foot," and "band," and to note the number of different ways each of these may be used meaningfully.

SUMMARY

Many intelligent youngsters enter high school without having learned to use a dictionary effectively. Although it may appear to be a simple task to know the alphabet in sequential order, some students have not done so. To help students become efficient users of the dictionary, it is necessary to begin at the level of instruction that they need.

In this chapter we have emphasized techniques of using different word-recognition clues for identifying words and associating them with meaning. The word-recognition clues discussed were primarily sound and visual clues. There are some students who need the additional help of kinesthetic techniques for identifying and recognizing word symbols. For a detailed discussion of kinesthetic techniques, the reader may refer to Chapter 7, "Teaching Spelling."

SELECTED REFERENCES

1. Betts, Emmett A. *Foundations of Reading Instruction.* New York: American Book Co., 1957.
2. Bond, Guy L., and Wagner, Eva Bond. *Teaching the Child To Read* (3d ed.). New York: The Macmillan Co., 1960.
3. Cordts, Anna D. *Phonics for the Reading Teacher.* New York: Holt, Rinehart & Winston, Inc., 1965.
4. Dechant, Emerald V. *Improving the Teaching of Reading.* Englewood Cliffs, N.J.: Prentice-Hall, Inc., 1964.
5. Dolch, E. W. "Am I Teaching Phonics Right?" *Elementary English,* Vol. 34 (April, 1957), pp. 227–234.
6. Durkin, Dolores. *Phonics and the Teaching of Reading.* New York: Bureau of Publications, Teachers College, Columbia University, 1962.
7. Gans, Roma. *Fact and Fiction About Phonics.* Indianapolis: The Bobbs-Merrill Co., Inc., 1964.
8. Gray, Lillian. *Teaching Children To Read* (3d ed.). New York: The Ronald Press Co., 1963.
9. Harris, Albert J. *How To Increase Reading Ability* (4th ed., rev.). New York: David McKay Co., Inc., 1961.
10. Hildreth, Gertrude. "Some Misconceptions Concerning Phonics," *Elementary English,* Vol. 36 (January, 1957), pp. 26–29.

11. Karlin, Robert. *Teaching Reading in High School.* Indianapolis: The Bobbs-Merrill Co., Inc., 1964.
12. McCullough, Constance M. "Context Aids in Reading," *The Reading Teacher,* Vol. 11 (April, 1958), pp. 225–29.
13. Spache, George D. *Toward Better Reading.* Champaign, Ill.: Garrard Publishing Co., 1963.
14. Spache, George D. *Reading in the Elementary School.* Boston: Allyn & Bacon, Inc., 1964.
15. Stauffer, Russell G. "A Study of Prefixes in the Thorndike List To Establish a List of Prefixes That Should Be Taught in the Elementary School," *Journal of Educational Research,* Vol. 35 (February, 1942), pp. 453–58.
16. Thorndike, Edward L. *The Teaching of English Suffixes.* New York: Bureau of Publications, Teachers College, Columbia University, 1941.
17. *Webster's New International Dictionary of the English Language* (2d ed., unabridged). Springfield, Mass.: C. & G. Merriam Co., 1948.

SUGGESTED ADDITIONAL READING

Burton, William H. *Reading in Child Development.* Indianapolis: The Bobbs-Merrill Co., Inc., 1956.

Dawson, Mildred A., and Bamman, Henry A. *Fundamentals of Basic Reading Instruction* (2d ed.). New York: David McKay Co., Inc., 1963.

DeBoer, John J., and Dallman, Martha. *The Teaching of Reading* (rev. ed.). New York: Holt, Rinehart & Winston, Inc., 1964.

Gray, William S. *On Their Own in Reading* (rev. ed.). Chicago: Scott, Foresman & Co., 1960.

Heilman, Arthur W. *Phonics in Proper Perspective.* Columbus, Ohio: Charles E. Merrill Books, Inc., 1964.

Russell, David H. "Teachers' Views on Phonics," *Elementary English,* Vol. 32 (October, 1955), pp. 371–75.

Russell, David H. *Children Learn to Read* (2d ed.). Boston: Ginn & Co., 1961.

Smith, Nila Banton. *American Reading Instruction.* Newark, Del.: International Reading Association, 1965.

Strang, Ruth, McCullough, Constance M., and Traxler, Arthur E. *The Improvement of Reading* (3d ed.). New York: McGraw-Hill Book Co., Inc., 1961.

Tinker, Miles A., and McCullough, Constance M. *Teaching Elementary Reading* (2d ed.). New York: Appleton-Century-Crofts, Inc., 1962.

10

STUDY SKILLS

What Are Study Skills?

Writers have used numerous and various terms to describe study skills and most of the skills so listed by them are also regularly taught as reading skills.

At present, practically any technique students use in learning school assignments may be found on some writer's list of study skills. Some of the regularly listed skills are: following directions, reading, listening, outlining, locating materials, writing reports, organizing, remembering, reviewing, making study schedules, summarizing, and taking examinations. A complete tabulation of all the specific skills, such as: (1) identifying main ideas and topic sentences; (2) determining relationships between or among paragraphs; (3) using tables of contents, indexes, and library card files; and (4) reading and interpreting cartoons, charts, and graphs, would be a wearisome, never-ending, cataloguing of limited value.

A workable grouping of skills under several main headings is a sounder and simpler approach for the purpose of discussion and for students' practical use. The selection of major areas for teaching study skills is usually based upon the opinions of experts, judgments of teachers who are teaching study skill courses, and the experience of the selector. We have followed the common procedure in making the selection in this book. In previous chapters, we have discussed the development of certain skills and understandings that might normally be included in study skills programs. It should be kept in mind that any selection is primarily a guide and not a prescription. In view of the preceding qualifications, we have chosen the following areas for discussion:

1. Following directions
2. Locating, selecting, and evaluating information
3. Organizing information

What Does Research Tell Us About Study Skills?

The specific techniques that should be taught in study skills courses are not clearly defined at this time. Methods or techniques stressed are numerous and mainly based upon "expert opinion" (3, p. 243) and psychological principles of learning. Despite the lack of unanimity of skills taught, a large number of research reports (3, p. 243; 13, p. 335; 14, pp. 675–68) indicate that teaching students how to study is beneficial and is reflected in better student adjustment and improved grades. One intensive investigation of study skills courses at the college level (3, p. 250) revealed that when student participation was *voluntary*, quite impressive gains were made. In all reports of courses that included follow-up studies of students' achievement, it was noted that the gains they made during the courses were maintained. Glock and Mallman (4, p. 289), however, after studying a group of high school students with above-average grades reported that *required* study skills courses for these kinds of students were not advisable.

Research, as spotty, contradictory, and inconclusive as it is in this area, indicates that the teaching of study skills is helpful for improving the learning of a large number of students. This is particularly true when students *volunteer* to take the courses, when they are *motivated* to improve their skills, and when they are not above average in achievement.

Are Study Skills Learned Without Guidance?

Study skills must be taught. Few students learn how to study efficiently without directed practice and guidance by a teacher. And there are basic study skills that students must learn and use for successful classroom learning.

Any program of study skills should be flexible and based upon student needs. A rigid, systematized program in which all students do a prescribed number of specific exercises without due consideration of individual differences in achievement cannot help but be a failure. To consider study skills primarily as a set of mechanical procedures is to limit one's view of study, and to oversimplify; study skills, when properly taught, include a systematic, sequential approach to learning.

A functional study skills program should provide teachers with sufficient time to test, diagnose, evaluate, and give students guidance both individually and in small groups. There should be provision for discussions about motivation, self-motivation, anxiety, and students' goals. There is little doubt that many students may become self-motivated and develop an interest in learning when they are given an opportunity to talk with a teacher about their objectives, interests, weaknesses, and strengths.

On the other hand, a highly motivated and interested student may achieve little learning in school unless he has developed the required learning skills. Such a student, however, may be taught how to learn and to develop the skills in which he is weak. Thus it appears logical to assume that a study skills program must be organized in such a way that individual and group needs may be met, whether they be in the area of attitudes or skills, or both.

A reasonable approach to determining the kinds of skills that should be taught might appear to be that of determining how good and poor students differ in the ways they approach school learning tasks. Although there has been some research in this particular area, Strang (14, p. 676) notes that such research is inconclusive because there have been no accurate means devised to determine how good and poor students differ. Answers obtained from giving questionnaires and checklists to students have proved to be interesting but for many reasons the results are questionable. It is well known, for example, that most students tend to answer surveys and checklists in the way they think the researcher wants them to answer unless they are positive that they are in a completely free and anonymous situation. In one study (1, pp. 92–128), the researchers asked students who were studying what skills they were using and found that those questioned were using many different and often unique approaches.

Many students have been taught a number of basic study skills before they enter high school or college, but for various reasons fail to use them properly. For some, the major reason for not using study techniques appears to be a lack of sufficient practice in using previously learned skills. The efficient use of study skills requires guided practice until such use becomes habitual. Others lack understanding of when to apply the skills they apparently know. It is, for example, easier to underline a sentence that appears to be important than it is to recognize how the sentence fits into the total organizational pattern of the content that is being studied. Such indiscriminate practices may prove to be more confusing than helpful. Most study skills courses are based upon the premise that students will benefit more from an orderly plan of learning than they will from a hit-or-miss approach. Some courses place heavy emphasis on improving students' attitudes, motivations, and interests while others emphasize a particular technique or plan. Experience indicates that overemphasis on either the psychological aspects of learning or the skills is not the most fruitful approach. A successful study skills program is one in which a competent teacher has time to meet with students, provide extrinsic motivation when it is needed, supply students with numerous interesting materials at their own reading levels, and teach them the skills they need for learning.

A Study Method

Robinson's (10, pp. 13–48) SQ3R method of study is known to most everyone who teaches a study skills course. It is generally recognized as being an efficient and effective method, especially at the high school and college levels. The five steps of his method are titled, "Survey, Question, Read, Recite, and Review."

A brief outline of the five steps follows. For a more detailed account of this sound technique, the reader is referred to Robinson's *Effective Study* (10).

SURVEY: *Step 1.* Surveying the material—getting a general idea of the overall content of the assigned material by reading rapidly the headings, subheadings, topic sentences, summary sentences, introduction and summary.

QUESTION: *Step 2.* Questioning the material—using the headings to make questions for guiding one's own reading.

READ: *Step 3.* Reading for understanding, guided by the questions previously determined in step two.

RECITE: *Step 4.* Reciting—testing one's ability to recall information from the reading by answering his own questions.

REVIEW: *Step 5.* Reviewing—testing one's self by recalling the main ideas obtained from reading and notetaking.

FOLLOWING DIRECTIONS

The inability to follow directions is a familiar weakness among students of all ages and grade levels. This disability, according to several authorities (16, p. 192) is not limited to children, but is also common among adults. In addition, high school and college teachers regularly note that the learning of many of their students is limited because students fail to follow directions accurately. There is no question that many laboratory experiments have gone awry, or that numerous mathematical problems have remained unsolved, simply because the directions for solution were mishandled.

The preceding statements—immediately give rise to several questions: (1) Are not pupils taught to follow directions? (2) Why should such a simple task as *following directions* be such a bane to both students and adults?

In answer to the first question, children are taught early to follow directions. Almost as soon as pupils enter the classroom they are introduced to a planned program designed to develop their abilities to follow directions. At first, all directions must be given orally, but as children begin to learn to read they are gradually taught to follow written directions.

Primary-grade teachers devise many different kinds of games that require children to listen and to follow directions. In the beginning, such games are relatively simple. The teacher, for example, may say, "Who can tiptoe to the door and return to his seat without speaking?" After the children learn to follow similar simple directions, the procedure becomes more complex. One child may be asked to go to the chalkboard, pick up a piece of chalk, mark an *X* on the board, give the chalk to the teacher, and return to his seat. Later, children may learn to draw simple boxes, or houses, according to directions given by the teacher. They must follow the directions only as they are given if they are to complete the drawing accurately.

Children do receive guided practice in learning to follow directions. Those who visit the primary grades are often surprised at the efficient manner in which children arrange chairs and get their books for a reading lesson, select the materials needed for drawing, or prepare for lunch without any lengthy set of directions from the teacher. These children demonstrate that they have learned to follow directions according to certain needs or purposes.

Answering the second question, "Why should such a simple task as *following directions*, especially written ones, be a bane to both students and teachers?" may provide some clues for improving students' abilities to follow directions.

First, it may well be that following directions is not such a simple task as most people assume it to be. The demonstrated inability of many to follow directions indicates that *following directions* is a more difficult and complete task than most people, including teachers, realize.

Oral Directions

Because the successful completion of oral, written, or a combination of both oral and written directions requires an exchange of information between at least two people, the giver and receiver, each party has definite commitments in promoting accurate communication.

The person giving the directions must use language that is clear, specific, and concise. If the directions are given orally, he must speak distinctly, accurately, and unhurriedly. Needed information must be given in an orderly, sequential manner. The directions should not be unnecessarily long nor detailed.

The receiver of oral directions must learn to concentrate upon what the speaker is saying. He must screen out distractions in order that he can hear and understand what he is required to do. He must practice remembering details in sequence so he will be able to recall them as they are needed. He should also learn to ask questions only when such action is necessary to clarify his understanding. He must learn to listen to the complete directions before interrupting to ask about a point not yet reached by the person giving the directions.

Written Directions

Students and adults fare no better when dealing with written directions than with oral directions. And as students advance from the elementary grades to high school to college and adult life, their need for following written directions increases. The inability to follow written directions accurately may limit the professional or vocational education of some, keep others from accepting or holding better jobs, and may even cost some their lives. Therefore teachers should make every attempt to help students develop this vital skill.

Gray (5, p. 58) provides us with several reasons why students make errors when following written directions. She points out that this kind of reading is tedious and demands that the reader pay strict attention to detail. Facts must not only be understood, but they must also be kept in sequential order. This means that much *rereading* may be required.

We have previously stressed that reading must be purposeful, and reading to follow directions is no exception. The reader must have his purpose(s) clearly in mind before he reads or rereads directions. He must understand that this kind of skill requires accurate reading whether it be used for solving an arithmetical equation, performing a laboratory experiment, comparing data, selecting relevant detail for solving a problem, or gathering information for a paper.

Teachers may help students develop their skills in reading directions by giving them practice in (1) detecting and understanding the roles of modifiers that indicate quality, amounts, comparisons; (2) recognizing sequential clues, such as "meanwhile," "first," "last," "before"; (3) understanding that directions follow an orderly, sequential pattern; and (4) realizing that rereading is often necessary to insure accuracy (8, pp. 336–37).

LOCATING, SELECTING, AND EVALUATING INFORMATION

Developing Skills in Reading Textbooks

Many secondary teachers realize the importance of teaching students how to utilize the assigned textbook. They take time to acquaint students with the organization of the text, the author's purpose in using bold-face headings, and other clues that help them better understand the written material. They have students read the preface to the text in order that students may obtain some knowledge about the author's purpose, the reasons for his emphasis on certain areas, and the rationale for his selections.

Sometimes teachers have students answer duplicated questions that are useful in determining whether time need be spent on teaching or reteaching students certain information about using textbooks efficiently. Such questions include those pertaining to the importance of the date of publication of a book, the author's experience and qualifications for writing, and the publisher's reputation. Other questions are designed to reveal each student's skill in using the glossary, index, table of contents, headings, and subheadings.

If a student, for example, does not know how indexes differ from tables of contents, how they are similar, and how each should be used, his learning will not be enhanced by this lack of skill. The high school or college student who is unable to use cross references or to read efficiently charts, diagrams, tables, and maps needs instruction in these vital skills regardless of his grade level.

High school and college students' study is not limited to a single textbook. Students must learn how to use reference materials in both the classroom and library. One of the best sources for teaching students how to use a library effectively is the librarian. But as cooperative as they are, librarians do not have the time to teach students *how* to use all the materials. They may acquaint students with the card files, catalogues, and reading indexes that aid students in locating sources of information. Teachers have the responsibility of giving students the necessary instruction for selecting needed information once it has been located.

Teaching students how to skim and to read for main ideas not only helps them in selecting materials and information, but it also provides practice in skills needed for organizing knowledge.

What Is Skimming?

Skimming is the name given to a particularly rapid and versatile kind of reading skill. Above all, it is not a substitute for reading, nor is it a superficial kind of reading. Reading authorities say that it is the most productive and versatile of reading skills (9, p. 29), a most useful but much-abused technique for getting information quickly (15, p. 379), and one of the most important types of comprehension skills (6, p. 434).

Skimming is a particular kind of reading skill that enables a skillful user to rapidly locate specific information that he needs. It helps him to get a quick overview of an article, chapter, or book. It is a skill that saves the student much valuable time by permitting him to locate dates, answers to specific questions, and descriptions without wading through material that is irrelevant to his immediate purposes.

It is credited with promoting students' interest in various areas since it encourages them to sample many areas that they might otherwise leave untouched because of lack of time.

The student who has learned the skill of skimming is more capable of reading extensively, organizing his ideas about a topic or certain area, and then reading intently those selections that are interesting and pertinent to his understanding. It could also be argued that the use of skimming skills aids concentration by focusing an individual's attention to the task at hand.

Rate of Skimming Varies According to Purpose

How rapidly one skims material is determined primarily by his purpose for skimming. Finding a telephone number or an individual's name in a directory is accomplished almost immediately, whereas, skimming an index to locate study skills or critical reading skills may require slightly more time. If the student's purpose is to get a general idea of the contents of a book on gardening, he will need to vary his speed. He may skim portions of the contents swiftly until a particular sentence, paragraph, or section catches his attention. At such times, he may read the entire portion at a high rate of speed and then reread particular sections intently, pausing occasionally to take notes. He may also skim the contents of a number of similar books for the purpose of locating additional material or substantiating statements from books previously read.

Techniques of Teaching Skimming Skills

Teaching proper techniques of skimming is relatively simple, but this fact in no way diminishes the importance of teaching, and using these skills. Students who have not learned to skim efficiently may be helped by observing the teacher demonstrate how skimming is used to locate needed information. The demonstration should be followed immediately by a class discussion of when and how skimming may be used most profitably. But knowing how to skim, and understanding why skimming is a productive skill, does not imply that students will use or be capable of using the skill. Students, therefore, should be given practice in using skimming to locate specific kinds of information.

Teachers may have a list of questions that are designed to promote skimming. The questions should be relatively simple and specific at first, and should be based upon materials that are being used in the classroom. Following are several examples of questions taken from a classroom text in general science:

How fast do tornadoes travel?
What is a *waterspout?*
What is the speed of light?
What kind of a building is particularly lightning proof?

Questions requiring the use of local newspapers should also be used. Examples:

What were the high and low temperatures in our city yesterday?
How much rain fell in our city during October?
What film is being shown at "The City Theater?"
Find two telephone numbers that may be called for ordering a cord of wood.
How many points was the stock market up or down yesterday?

After students have learned to quickly locate specific bits of information, they should be given practice in skimming several books to locate information that requires them to use varying rates of reading speed. They need to learn when to skim, when to slow down and read more intently, and when to reread. Examples:

Why do plants produce seeds? (rapid skimming)
How are seeds scattered. (rapid to intent reading)
Name some animals that hibernate. (rapid skimming)
Describe what happens to an animal during hibernation. (intensive reading after needed information has been located)

Another technique that teachers may use profitably is that of giving students timed practice in skimming a chapter to discover the main points the author stresses, and his general conclusion. Experience indicates that two-minute practice sessions are sufficient for a lively class discussion of what the author covers in a chapter. The amount of information that students obtain through this kind of reading is often surprising to both teacher and student.

Locating supporting details, preparing a list of references for a term paper, getting a general impression of a book, and understanding the organizational pattern of a textbook chapter are some of the many uses that may be made of skimming skills. Skimming, however, should never be looked upon as a substitute for study type reading. It is an important aid to efficient reading, but it is not the total reading process. When used improperly, skimming may be more detrimental than beneficial to efficient reading.

Reading for Main Ideas

Most elementary teachers give students instruction in how to read for main ideas, but for numerous unknown reasons many high school and even college students have little more than a vague idea of what is meant by reading for main ideas. Secondary teachers need to be alert to signs that indicate that a student may need help in this type of reading. A symptom of a student's faulty or inadequate concept of a main idea of a paragraph is his inability to select the most important idea contained in the paragraph. Such a student may be able to recall many or all of the details of a paragraph yet fail to understand the message. He becomes bogged down with detail. He lacks the skill and understanding required for selecting relevant from irrelevant detail, and for seeing the relationship of ideas among sentences in a paragraph.

What Is a Main Idea?

A main idea actually leads a double life, as Shaw has adroitly noted: "It is a *whole* idea (main idea of a section), and a *part* of a whole idea (one item of the author's outline)" (11, p. 347). And it is this cogent point that may cause difficulty for some students. They may be confused that a main idea in a particular paragraph is not always the main idea in a number of related paragraphs. They may lack both understanding of the role of main ideas and practice in selecting main ideas.

Techniques of Teaching Main Ideas

Teachers may call students' attention to main ideas by having them pay particular attention to bold-face headings and then read to note the relationship between a heading and the content that follows it. Some teachers have students read newspaper headings and the accompanying first paragraph to help build understanding of main ideas. Other teachers give students several newspaper articles from which the heading have been removed. Students read the articles and select a proper heading for each article from a list that the teacher has written on the chalkboard.

Other techniques often used are: (1) having students read or listen to a paragraph and then write one sentence summarizing the paragraph; (2) giving students a simple question to answer by reading a single paragraph; (3) asking students to find sentences in a paragraph that might be omitted without seriously affecting the total meaning; and (4) giving students several simple paragraphs in which sentences containing the main ideas have been removed and listed on a separate sheet of paper. Students then find the missing topic sentences from the list and place each in its correct paragraph.

ORGANIZING INFORMATION FOR LEARNING

Students who have not been taught the meaning and skills of taking notes, summarization, and outlining have no way of knowing the worth of these skills in organizing learning. Organization of learning requires reaction from the learner. When a student is effectively taking notes, outlining, and summarizing, he is also drawing upon his total previous learning. He must rapidly integrate and synthesize new thoughts, ideas, and facts with his previous experiences. The new vocabulary and additions to his concepts must be systematized in order that he understand and use the new information to evolve new ideas and to increase his knowledge.

Many high school and college students, however, have definite, albeit often inaccurate, opinions about the values of outlining and summarizing. Some students, for example, say that, "outlining takes too much time," "it doesn't work," and "underlining is easier." On the other hand, many students claim that outlining is the *key* to learning, while others are equally insistent that underlining the textbook is most effective. Because all of these students' expressions are based upon their experiences in using the skills cited, let us also review briefly the views of teachers, experts, and research.

Available evidence about the superiority of outlining over underlining is meager and inconsistent. The way in which underlining is done is perhaps the major weakness attributable to this practice. Students tend to underline indiscriminately and excessively because they underline as they read. Many seemingly important statements may be repeated by the writer and are duly underlined each time by the student; and, even though these statements may be in opposition to the major emphasis of the author, they are underlined no differently from the others. This kind of underlining often confuses a student when he rereads for review because it is excessive and often contradictory. Robinson supports this viewpoint and says, "Furthermore, students tend to underline complete sentences, but the long sentences that authors use to state clearly what they mean cause much more reading than will brief phrases used in notes" (10, p. 38).

When underlining is done without much thought about the overall importance and relationship of the underlined statements, as is often the case, the value of underlining is questionable. When students preread or preview materials *before* underlining, the practice undoubtedly has merit. If the reader also attempts to make an outline of his underlined statements by numbering them, or by making notes in the margins of the book, or by using some other technique for indicating the relationship of underlined statements, there is little doubt that underlining may be a valuable learning skill. Many of America's recognized scholars say that they often use this kind of underlining as an aid to their own learning.

Authorities generally agree that note-taking is a skill of critical importance (12, p. 346), and that there is no more essential skill for students to develop than that of writing an effective summary of what is read (6, p. 450). There is also evidence that outlining aids students in both oral and written recall of information (10, p. 20; 13, p. 340). The general conclusion that can be drawn from what is known about note-taking, outlining, and summarizing is that these skills are important techniques of learning that should be emphasized more than they have been in the past. Strang, however, after a thorough review of the research in this area says there is no real evidence that taking notes in outline form is any more efficient than using the same amount of time in careful reading (14, p. 676).

Many teachers not only recognize that students, including the academically advanced, need additional guidance in developing study skills, but they go a step farther and provide students with the necessary instruction. Unfortunately, only a limited number take another important "third step" and report what they do in order that other teachers and students might benefit from their knowledge. Heavey (7, pp. 39–43) is one of those who took the third step. She reported on a study skills program that she developed to meet the specific needs of a group of her gifted tenth-graders who were working on research-type papers. She found that these students of exceptional potential and qualifications needed additional instruction in locating references, taking notes from readings, organizing notes into outline form, using the notes properly in writing, and giving appropriate credit for the sources of information. She concludes that when gifted students are not given needed instruction in writing reports, their concepts of learning may be distorted, creativity stifled, and unwitting plagiarism encouraged.

The relationship between a student's mental health and his development of the study skills necessary for organizing information is rarely mentioned in study skills courses. In the writer's opinion, it is one of the most important aspects in the total school learning process. While we cannot overgeneralize about the effects of anxiety (17, p. 71), we know that students who lack the skills and understanding for organizing their learning efforts often become *anxious students.*

An anxious student is a disorganized individual who works himself into a state of extreme tension because he knows he is not achieving efficiently or satisfactorily, and he does not know what to do about his predicament. No one knows exactly how many high school and college students suffer mental breakdowns due to extreme anxiety, but the number is sufficiently large to be of serious concern to school counselors and mental health people.

While psychological research indicates that mild anxiety is conducive to the learning of most students (18, p. 169; 2, p. 595), it is also recognized that extreme motivation may lead to extreme anxiety and disorganization. Two conclusions about anxiety that teachers should keep in mind and which psychologists consider to be permissible are (1) anxiety once established, perpetuates itself and becomes its own reinforcer; and (2) anxiety is generalized (17, pp. 71–72). This means that a single event may arouse anxiety that affects the individual's total behavior. Thus, the high school student who is upset and extremely anxious in one subject-matter area because of repeated failures may become extremely anxious in all other school subjects. Even his behavior outside school may be adversely affected.

Although the real causes for a student's extreme tension may not be due primarily to the classroom situation, a number of psychologists, teachers, educators, and medical doctors believe there is a significant relationship between a student's extreme nervous tension and his inability to achieve successfully in school. Teachers, therefore, should be alert to symptoms of anxiety and seek adequate help for students who exhibit such behavior. Anxious students usually have difficulty in settling down to work finding and selecting materials, reading intently, and organizing their learning into a workable whole that is meaningful. They often fret about minor details, distrust themselves, become confused easily, become aggressive physically and verbally, blame their problems on others, and waste time seeking magic formulas for completing assigned learning tasks.

Techniques of Teaching Outlining

Students should be shown how the author of their textbook has outlined the contents of the text by his selection of chapters. By noting the chapter headings they may get a rough overview of what is contained in the book. The next step is to work through a chapter with students, showing them how the author has noted major parts in his outline by having them set in major bold-face headings. Sometimes the author centers all major points and indents all minor points under each main heading. Some authors use a numbering system and italicized print to distinguish between main parts and supporting materials. The different approaches authors use in outlining may be confusing to students unless they have previously discussed the role of main ideas in paragraphs, and how to read for main ideas. Even though students may be skilled in selecting main ideas, they may need further instruction in noting that main ideas in paragraphs may also be supporting statements for major ideas.

Teachers may have students outline a chapter from the regular textbook based upon the preceding information. After each student has outlined an assigned chapter, time should be taken to discuss the outlines and answer questions about the procedure. This exercise should be followed up by giving students practice in outlining several other chapters of the same book before they attempt to outline a chapter that may not follow the same system used by their present author.

It is important that students learn to see the relationship between major and minor points in the outline, and to see how each one fits into the total pattern of the chapter.

Note-Taking

A student who understands how to outline a chapter has an understanding of the organization of information that will aid him in taking notes from supplementary reading or listening to lectures. When taking notes from reading, he has the advantage of being able to set his own pace and to reread when necessary. When taking notes from a speech, he no longer has this advantage and must develop the ability to listen attentively and critically. He must select immediately those statements which he considers important. He should, therefore, be taught to write brief phrases that may be expanded later. He should be cautioned to be alert for such relationships and make note of them. After he has had an opportunity to rework his notes, he should discuss them with the teacher who may point out their strengths and weaknesses. Efficient note-taking is not easy and requires much guided practice.

Summarizing

Summarizing is the process of distilling information, facts, main ideas, and relevant detail into one concise unit. It demands that the student focus his attention on only the most important information gained from his study. It makes use of a student's previously learned skills in selecting main ideas, evaluating the selections, and retaining only those that are most significant.

Students who have learned to select the main idea of a paragraph and restate it in their own words, have learned a basic prerequisite for writing a summary of an assigned selection. Students who need extra time and practice in developing the skill of summarizing may need to be given instruction in summarizing no more than three or four paragraphs. They may also be helped by reading the author's summary of a chapter in their own textbooks and analyzing what the author has said and what he has omitted.

SUMMARY

Following directions, locating, selecting, and evaluating information, and organizing information have been chosen as the main areas of discussion in this chapter. The importance appears to be found in the statement that study skills must be learned and practiced by the student. In fact, if study skills do not become a habit then they are probably of little or no effect to the student. Study skills must be learned and practiced under the guidance of experienced teachers who themselves do not only know about these skills but who practice these skills. In this respect Robinson's SQ3R method has been outlined step by step.

To follow directions, students must be taught to do so because it is a more difficult and complex task than teachers may realize. To locate information, a student must be taught similarities and dissimilarities of indexes and table of contents; of reading diagrams, charts, tables, maps; and other illustrative materials, as well as to use reference materials effectively.

To select materials, skimming has been analyzed as to its definition, its rate and its techniques. This has been followed by reading for main ideas, what a main idea is, and various techniques used to select a main idea.

To organize information for learning, outlining, underlining, and note-taking have been discussed and their respective strengths and weaknesses pointed out. It may be emphasized again that the lack of sufficient and efficient study skills may well contribute to a student becoming an anxious student, a disorganized individual who does not know how to cope with his predicament.

Teaching and learning study skills have the purpose of helping the student to become an independent reader and learner.

SELECTED REFERENCES

1. Brownell, William A., and Hendrickson, Gordon. "How Children Learn Information, Concepts, and Generalizations," *Learning and Instruction*, The Forty-ninth Yearbook, Part I, National Society for the Study of Education. Chicago: The University of Chicago Press, 1950. Pp. 92–128.
2. Cronbach, Lee J. *Educational Psychology* (2d ed.). New York: Harcourt, Brace & World, Inc., 1963.
3. Entwisle, Doris R. "Evaluations of Study Skills Courses: A Review," *Journal of Educational Research*, Vol. 53 (March, 1960), pp. 243–51.
4. Glock, Marvin, and Millman, Jason. "Evaluation of a Study Skills Program for Above-Average High School Pupils," *Journal of Developmental Reading*, Vol. 4 (Summer, 1964), pp. 283–89.
5. Gray, Lillian. *Teaching Children To Read* (3d ed.). New York: The Ronald Press Co., 1963.
6. Harris, Albert J. *How To Increase Reading Ability* (4th ed., rev.). New York: David McKay Co., Inc., 1961.
7. Heavey, Regina. "Teaching the Gifted To Teach Themselves," *The English Journal*, Vol. 50 (January, 1961), pp. 39–43.
8. McKim, Margaret G., and Caskey, Helen. *Guiding Growth in Reading* (2d ed.). New York: The Macmillan Co., 1963.
9. Pauk, Walter. "Does Note-taking Interfere with Listening Comprehension?" *Journal of Developmental Reading*. Vol. 6 (Summer, 1963), pp. 276–78.
10. Robinson, Francis P. *Effective Study* (rev. ed.). New York: Harper & Rowe, Inc., 1961.

11. Shaw, Phillip. "Reading in College." *Development in and Through Reading*. The Sixtieth Yearbook, Part I, National Society for the Study of Education. Chicago: The University of Chicago Press, 1961.
12. Smith, Henry P., and Dechant, Emerald V. *Psychology in Teaching Reading*. Englewood Cliffs, N.J.: Prentice-Hall, Inc., 1961.
13. Spache, George D. *Toward Better Reading*. Champaign, Ill.: Garrard Publishing Co., 1964.
14. Strang, Ruth M. "Homework and Guided Study," *Encyclopedia of Educational Research* (3d ed.). New York: The Macmillan Co., 1960. Pp. 675–80.
15. Strang, Ruth, McCullough, Constance M., and Traxler, Arthur E. *The Improvement of Reading* (3d ed.). New York: McGraw-Hill Book Co., Inc., 1961.
16. Tinker, Miles A., and McCullough, Constance M. *Teaching Elementary Reading* (2d ed.). New York: Appleton-Century-Crofts, Inc., 1962.
17. Townsend, Edward Arthur, and Burke, Paul J. *Learning for Teachers*. New York: The Macmillan Co., 1962.
18. Travers, Robert M. W. *Essentials of Learning*. New York: The Macmillan Co., 1963.

11

VOCABULARY, CONCEPTS, AND CRITICAL READING

In previous chapters we have discussed basic reading abilities that are fundamental to critical reading in any content area. Students cannot be taught to read critically until they have acquired these basic skills that include the ability to understand the literal meaning of what they read, to set purposes for reading, and to react to what they have read.

In this chapter we are concerned with the interrelatedness of the roles of thinking, language, vocabulary, concepts, and critical reading. Let us, therefore, begin with a discussion of *thinking*.

What Is Thinking?

Teachers are warned regularly by the press, parents, and educators to *teach students to think*. Curricula are designed to *promote students' thinking*. And one of the major goals of all education is to *develop thinking students*. But alas, the press, parents, educators, builders of curricula, and the developers of goals generally fail to define what they mean by *thinking*. Therefore, the instances in which students receive the teacher's help in learning to *think* critically are more infrequent than frequent.

"Thinking" is a term used by almost everyone but one that few can define because it is a difficult task. Many of those who use the term "thinking" use it loosely. Thinking is confused often with recalling, remembering, and daydreaming. This does not mean that recalling, remembering, and daydreaming may not lead to serious thinking or become a part of serious thinking, but these perfunctory acts should not be mistaken as examples of thinking.

Philosophers, psychologists, and others have discussed and defined thinking in numerous ways. Although most of the theories and hypotheses about thinking are not in sharp disagreement, neither are they in complete accord. We have, therefore, selected three definitions of thinking propounded by recognized experts that will serve as guides for our use of *thinking.* For a more thorough discussion of thinking, the reader is referred to the bibliography at the end of this chapter.

Russell says, "Thinking is a process rather than a fixed state. It involves a sequence of ideas moving from some beginning, through some sort of pattern of relationships, to some goal or conclusion" (16, p. 27). Burton, Kimball, and Wing define thinking as ". . . the critical, reflective search for valid conclusions which solve our problems, resolve our doubts, and enable us to choose between conflicting statements of doctrine or policy" (6, p. 18). Dewey says, "Active, persistent, and careful consideration of any belief or supposed form of knowledge in the light of the grounds that support it and the further conclusions to which it tends *constitutes reflective thought*" (9, p. 9).

In this book we shall associate the following meaning with thinking: *thinking is a process initiated by some kind of unsolved or perplexing problem, belief, or idea that leads to a solution.*

Whenever thinking is discussed in any kind of gathering, people are interested. Someone inevitably asks, "Can students be taught to think?" As far as man now understands and defines thinking, no one can teach another to think. Thinking is an individual matter and is determined by a number of factors. But we do know that individuals can be helped to improve their thinking.

What Factors Contribute to Critical Thinking?

Intelligence definitely influences a person's thinking ability. The greater one's intelligence, the greater his potential for thinking, but a high degree of native intelligence is no guarantee that effective thinking will follow naturally. Interestingly, the experiments conducted in teaching critical thinking indicate that, relatively speaking, the students who profit most from instruction in thinking are those of lower intelligence rather than those of high intelligence. In addition to intelligence, numerous other factors help to determine the efficacy of thinking. Most of the factors are the same ones that influence a student's achievement in reading. Some of the specific factors that are relevant to a student's efficiency in learning vocabulary, concepts, and critical reading are: (1) background of experience, (2) attitude, (3) physical and mental health, (4) social adjustment, (5) language ability, and (6) general reading skills.

What Is Language?

Inasmuch as language is one of the components of critical reading, we should have some idea how language is defined, and how it fits into the total reading process.

Language has a broad general meaning that is commonly accepted by most people, but when one searches for a definition of language, he finds varying views. Although many of the definitions overlap, each has a uniqueness that sets it apart from the others. The linguistic scientist, the philologist, the psychologist, the philosopher, the sociologist, the communication engineer are all interested in language, but each one's viewpoint is somewhat different from the other's because each user's purpose is different from the other's.

For our purposes we shall verge on oversimplification to provide a working definition of language. In this book we shall consider that *language is a system of spoken and written symbols that enables humans to communicate and interact with each other.*

Our definition will not be fully accepted by some linguists because of the inclusion of two words—*written symbols.* Most linguists stoutly maintain that *language* refers only to the *vocal and audible* aspect of words. This means that written words are considered to be *records* of spoken language rather than a part of the total language of man.

Nevertheless, written words are an important part of man's communicative system. They cannot be overlooked or discredited when we consider language and its contribution to learning. Without writing there could be no recorded history of man's vast accumulation of knowledge. Progress of a society would be limited by the amount of learning that could be passed vocally from one generation to another. Writing makes it possible for man to acquire and profit from the knowledge of others without direct contact and without each generation having to start anew.

Written records, however, are utterly worthless unless they can be read by someone. Therefore, language must be considered in the manner in which it is used. A literate society has a basic or spoken language, but it also has a written language. And the reader must be able to associate the written symbol with the spoken word. The efficient reader, however, does not have to sound out and associate speech sounds with all the words he reads. How much actual vocalization or subvocalization of words takes place during the act of reading is not known at this time. Some authorities argue that all words that are read, no matter how efficient the reader, are subject to some degree of vocalization. Other authorities believe that much of what the efficient reader reads is never vocalized in any manner. The answer to whether efficient readers vocalize all or only certain words they read must await further research.

Yes, *written words* have a place in the scheme of language. The inclusion of written words in our definition does not negate the importance and role of the spoken word; it does point out that written language has an autonomy of its own. We shall so consider it.

Historical Aspects of Language

Linguistic science, a comparative youngster among the sciences, has contributed much to our understanding of language, including the history of language. No one knows how, when, or where language was first used. For many years scholars have speculated about the beginning of language and have proposed a number of theories of how man invented language. Although there may be apparent elements of truth in some of the theories, most have been rejected by present-day scholars and linguists.

Even though the origin and development of language probably will remain forever a mystery, there is much that we do know about it. Few disagree that language was invented by man because he had a need to communicate with others. Whether language developed from a single source or a number of sources is not known.

The use of language is distinctly a human characteristic. Granted that other animals do possess and use a number of warning cries and other sounds, such utterances are not systematized for communicative purposes as is human language.

Language follows certain patterns that allow historical linguists to compare existing languages and thereby group different languages into related families and subfamilies. But even the comparison of languages is circumscribed in time by the absence of written records. In all but a few instances written records are available only as far back as about two thousand years. In several cases available data permit linguists to study language as it was in about 6000 B.C. How much earlier than this that man had a written system of language is pure conjecture.

Language is a living, growing phenomenon. Changes are regular, automatic, and inevitable. Though the average person may seldom realize that he exerts an influence on language, the linguist knows that each person who speaks a language influences it in some manner and degree. Each individual injects a bit of his personality into the total language because he pronounces words in a slightly different way from other people; he attaches finely shaded differences to the meanings of words he uses. All who communicate with him or who hear his speech are subject to its influence.

Even though the changes in language at any given time may be subtle and ever so slight, the changes are evident when the speech of youth is compared with that of their elders. However, it should not be overlooked that in some instances a language may be subject to abrupt and radical changes. Words are forever moving in and out of a language. As the culture of a society changes, new words are needed to express many of the changes. Wars, scientific and technological advances, inventions, new and changing vocations, and improved transportation and communication systems among nations contribute to the growth and change in languages.

Some of the new words that push older words of a language into disuse are replaced oftentimes by other new words. Sometimes words that lose favor temporarily nudge their way back into popular speech while other words become almost obsolete in spoken language but remain active in written language.

Because some words lose favor in the spoken language but remain in the written materials, some youth are confused by words that were common to their teachers and parents. For example, experienced teachers sometimes fail to realize that few of today's youth, including young teachers, have ever had an occasion to use words such as "coal scuttle," "flivver," "gallusses," "macadamized," "macintosh," "mackinaw," "commode," "celluloid," and "Morris chair." Although most of today's youth recognize "icebox," "spectacles," "davenport," "chair car," and "streetcar," tomorrow's youth may be almost unaware of these words except through reading.

What Is Vocabulary?

"Vocabulary" is usually defined as *the total number of words an individual knows.* Such a laconic definition appears to be an ambiguous one to many students and some teachers. Actually, everyone has several vocabularies. Most writers agree that it is less confusing to teachers and students to discuss specific vocabularies rather than vocabulary per se. Therefore, we shall consider briefly the specific vocabularies of English. They are known as an individual's (1) listening, (2) speaking, (3) reading, and (4) writing vocabularies. Sometimes a person's *understanding vocabulary* is listed with the *listening vocabulary,* that is, *listening and understanding vocabulary.* It should be kept in mind that even though we discuss *specific vocabularies,* each contributes to the others and there is much overlapping among vocabularies.

Listening Vocabulary

Everyone understands more words than he uses in his writing and speaking. Students learn many of these words through listening and reading.

That children learn to use and understand many words before they enter school may appear to be a simple statement, but the implications behind the statement are not so naive. Understanding how children acquire their vocabularies should lead to a change in certain absurd practices used by some teachers in a vain effort to help students learn new words.

How do children learn words prior to entering school? In order to present a lucid picture of vocabulary learning by children, let us start at the beginning.

A baby usually begins life with vocal sounds called crying. He comes equipped with one of the necessities of speech—the ability to cause a disturbance by producing sounds that can be heard when he opens his mouth. Although he is unable to produce systematic, intelligible sounds immediately, he is preparing to do so at a later date.

Before a child learns to speak, he learns by listening. He has many listening experiences that prepare him for speaking. He hears words used in numerous and various situations. Some are repeated over and over. After a child has had many experiences in listening to words, he somehow begins to discriminate or isolate particular words or sound patterns that he later associates with specific objects, things, and people.

His parents, for example, may give him a cuddly toy they call a "puppy" or "doggie." Long before he learns to speak he knows that the sounds "puppy" and "doggie" refer to the toy. He responds to simple requests. When mother says, "Give me the nice doggie" or "Hug the good doggie," he shows that he understands mother by doing these little exercises for her.

While the child is acquiring experiences through listening and seeing, he experiments and tries to mimic speech by making vocal sounds commonly known as babbling. After much experience in listening and babbling, the day finally arrives when he produces a sound pattern that is interpreted by his parents as "daddy" or "mommy." Joy reigns when he repeatedly produces the sound pattern. If his first word is "daddy," the father's ecstasy may be dampened slightly but only temporarily when his offspring indiscriminately calls the cat, chair, refrigerator, and floor "daddy."

From this wobbly beginning, the child's vocabulary is launched. The moment he first associates a specific object, person, or thing with a particular word, he starts his vocabulary. By the time he is about six years old he has a speaking vocabulary of about 2,500 words (19, pp. 1–92). His listening or understanding vocabulary is thought to be from two to four times larger than his speaking vocabulary.

For years it has been accepted generally that the average American child has a speaking vocabulary of about 2,500 words upon entrance to the first grade. These figures are based upon a study conducted by Madorah Smith (19, pp. 1–92) in the mid-1920's. More recent investigations of children's speaking and understanding vocabularies have raised some questions and much discussion about the actual size of children's and youths' vocabularies. A study by Mary K. Smith (20, pp. 311–45) suggests that an average first-grader understands about 24,000 words and the average twelfth-grader has command of about 80,000 words. Seashore and Eckerson (17, pp. 14–38), using the same test as Mary K. Smith, estimated that the average college undergraduate has a vocabulary of about 155,000 words. Hartman (11, pp. 436–39) arrived at even greater figures. He estimated that university students in Alabama had an average understanding vocabulary of 215,040 words.

A number of investigators, however, say that the above figures appear to be in excess of the number of words that children actually know. Bryan (5, pp. 210–16), using an exact copy of the Seashore-Eckerson Test used by Mary K. Smith, obtained median vocabulary scores for children in grades 2 through 6 that are lower than those of Mary K. Smith (20, pp. 311–45) but higher than those of Madorah E. Smith (19, pp. 1–92). Bryan (5, pp. 210–16) found a median number of words known by children in grade 2 to be 4,080 and in grade 6 to be 25,573.

That the total number of words known by children and youth is greater than previously believed is beyond doubt. That elementary pupils, high school, and college students know the large number of words that some studies have estimated that they do is questionable. Years of experience in teaching and working with students of all age levels cause the writer to question seriously that students have a knowledge of words as great as the recent studies estimate.

On the other hand, students demonstrate that with proper teacher guidance they can improve their vocabularies greatly. And students' ability to improve their vocabularies, not only in quantity but in *quality*, appears to be the lesson to be learned from these studies. According to Mary K. Smith (20, pp. 311–45), it seems that we have overestimated the ability of the poorer students and underestimated the ability of the better students.

Factors That Influence Vocabulary Development

Factors that influence the amount, kind, and quality of words that a student learns and uses are the same general ones that contribute to all school learning. *Intelligence* definitely is a factor in vocabulary development. It has long been recognized that there is a close relationship between intelligence and vocabulary. Most tests of intelligence are heavily weighted with vocabulary items. Students who have meager vocabularies and are generally weak in oral language may be retarded in intelligence. However, adequate evaluation of a student's intelligence should be made by qualified examiners and not arrived at by choice or guess simply because there is a high relationship between intelligence and because a student demonstrates a low level of language development. Prejudging, guessing, and categorizing a student as mentally retarded because he has a limited vocabulary cannot be tolerated. Many factors other than intelligence both contribute to and restrict a child's vocabulary.

Experience. The kinds and amounts of experiences that a child brings with him increase or limit his understanding of vocabulary. The high school student who has attended a miserable, restricted kind of elementary school and who has been reared in an environment devoid of books and other reading materials, good conversation, and a reasonably stable home life, will certainly lack in adequate vocabulary.

Teachers at all levels should provide students with as many and as varied experiences as they can. It is not always possible for a teacher to provide as many direct experiences for students as he desires, but he can provide a number of vicarious or indirect experiences. Fortunately, even most of the poorer homes have a usable television. Teacher suggestions of programs that are worthwhile often will bear fruit. Other vicarious experiences that broaden student's backgrounds include: listening to records; viewing moving pictures, slides, photographs, and advertisements; listening to a teacher read; participating in discussions; watching a class or school dramatization; and reading widely.

Reading. A student's ability to read is one of his most powerful aids for improving his total vocabulary. Research shows that wide reading accounts for much of a student's growth in vocabulary. The inefficient reader, whatever the cause for his lack of reading skills, makes little headway in learning vocabulary through reading. But even the inefficient reader can improve simultaneously his vocabulary and reading skills if he is given help and reading materials at his *instructional* reading level.

The usual high school teacher seldom provides time for students to read materials of their own choice. We know from experience that most outside reading assigned by subject-matter teachers is difficult reading, even more difficult than the regularly assigned textbook. One reason for the difficulty is that most of the materials are written by recognized experts in a particular subject matter and are written primarily for use by people well versed in the specific content field. The vocabulary, therefore, is often highly technical or unusual, and the concepts and references are usually far beyond the experience of all but a few outstanding students. Such outside reading tends to defeat its purpose because it is frustrating and does little for developing students' vocabularies and understanding.

If students are to develop vocabulary through wide reading, they need time in class to read materials that *they choose* and that are at *their own levels of reading.* The teacher can promote vocabulary development and comprehension of subject matter by having a large assortment of materials at various levels of reading.

Although it is generally known that wide reading is one of the best means for learning new words, many pitfalls await the student who relies primarily upon context clues for learning the meanings of new words. Artley (2, pp. 122–30) and Deighton (8, pp. 247–50) have noted some of the weaknesses of using context for getting the meaning of an unknown word. Artley has suggested that writers should pay more attention to the needs of students (1) by using bold-face type or italics to call attention to difficult words, (2) by explaining the new word in a sentence, (3) by defining the word in a footnote or in parentheses, and (4) by substituting a phrase to indicate the meaning.

The four principles given by Deighton (8, p. 247) about the use of context clues for getting the meanings of words are: (1) context reveals the meaning of unfamiliar words only infrequently; (2) context generally reveals only one meaning of an unfamiliar word; (3) context seldom clarifies the whole of any meaning; and (4) vocabulary growth through context revelation is a gradual matter.

Additional techniques for improving vocabulary are discussed in Chapter 8, "Teaching Reading in Content Areas."

Summary

At this point, let us focus our attention on some of the important points we have discussed about helping students to develop vocabularies in keeping with their own potentials.

1. A student's native intelligence will determine greatly the extent of his ultimate vocabulary, but it is only one of numerous factors that contribute to vocabulary development.
2. A student's thinking is inborn, but the use of such an ability can be improved by competent teaching.
3. A student's ability to learn vocabulary is dependent upon his ability to understand and use language.
4. Language, as it is used in this book, includes both *spoken and written* words.
5. Language is ever changing and not static.
6. Vocabulary includes words used in listening, speaking, reading, and writing.
7. Reading extensively is one of the best-known ways of learning new words.
8. Vocabulary development is a gradual process.

CONCEPTS

What Is a Concept?

Students often find it difficult to understand a definition of a concept. Perhaps they are confused because defining a concept is not simple; it requires precise expression by the writer, adequate understanding by the reader, a purposeful intent by both author and reader, and unhindered communication of thought between them.

McDonald defines a concept as a *"classification or systematic organization of stimuli, characteristics, or events which have common characteristics"* (13, p. 183). Another view is that a concept is a "defined idea or meaning fixed by, and as extensive as the term that designates it" (6, p. 154). He also notes that a concept is the amount of meaning a person has for another person, thing, or process. Morse and Wingo (15, p. 201) define a concept as an abstraction, a generalization resulting from numerous experiences with specific things and events. Russell (16) and others define a concept as a generalized understanding of words or statements.

Concept Defined

In this book we use the term "concept" to mean the "systematic organization of the total meaning that one has for any idea, process, person, thing, place or word."

The Development of Concepts

Concepts are the systematic, organized meanings an individual acquires from his experiences. Children develop concepts before they understand language, and Serra (18, pp. 275–85) has aptly pointed out that a child may demonstrate the acquisition of a concept even though he is too young to express his understanding in words.

A young child makes no distinction between living things and inanimate objects. On leaving his home he may say, "Bye, bye, nice house. Don't go away. Bye, bye." In the same manner he will likewise consider the furniture of the house as animate. To him, everything has life. He will tell the chair to stand still so that his stuffed dog will not fall to the floor. At this stage he does not distinguish between the animate and inanimate.

As he matures, however, he ceases to talk to the house. Through some process, which as yet we do not understand, he realizes that the house is not living, that it does not move. But chairs, the table, and the doggy continue to be participants in his talk because they are different from the house. Thus, his concept of house, albeit a faulty one, is that the house is not alive because it cannot move. Later, he will understand that not all objects that cannot move are not lifeless. He will further alter his concept about whether or not stationary objects have life when he understands that, although trees, shrubs, and flowers do not move about like animals, they do have life.

The child's concepts are based upon concrete, direct experiences. The greater his background of direct experience, the greater his chances of developing a basic background of valid concepts upon which all succeeding concepts will be dependent.

A child learns much about such objects as a ball, a doll, or an apple by his close examination of them. Many objects will be tasted, bitten, smelled, patted, thumped, and tossed about by him. From such experiences, the games he plays, the little chores he does for mother, and the trips he makes with her to the market, from the persons, the places, and the things he notes from the window of the family car, he gradually develops conceptual understanding of the world around him. Meaningful experiences are necessary to enable the child to build new concepts or to alter old ones.

It is important that we realize that the child's concepts develop slowly and from many direct experiences. His concepts, the sum total of varied and numerous experiences, give him a foundation of understanding that he uses for solving problems, coping with his environment, developing present concepts, and acquiring new concepts. It is his ability to develop and use concepts that distinguishes the child from the lower animals. It is the human being's unique ability in using concepts that permits him to learn a language for communicating and thinking.

Until the child learns to use the language, he must learn from direct experience. For example, he may be curious about a steaming teakettle on the stove and tries to touch it. Mother rushes frantically to his aid, snatches him away from danger, cautioning, "No. No. Hot." He may or may not get some kind of message from the intonation of mother's words, but as yet, they may be without real meaning for him. Let mother turn her back and the curious little fellow, reaching and touching, gets a message that is loaded with meaning. In the future, he will not willingly venture near the offensive kettle. There is no need for words to warn him; he has made a definite association between pain and object. If he is sufficiently mature, the words "No. No. Hot." also have some meaning and association with a painful experience and can be transferred to other dangerous objects. Thus, he begins to make an association between mother's spoken words and direct experience. He is beginning to gain experiences indirectly through language, and as he builds his store of direct experiences he also begins to add additional experiences through language.

As the child learns language, he experiments with it. He asks questions and tests his conclusions. In a comparatively short time he realizes that humans who generally look like daddy, Uncle Don, and Uncle Charles are called *man.* At first they are specific men; there is the *mailman,* the *milkman* and the *garbage man.* There are also many people who are just plain *man.* While shopping with mother he sees many men of different sizes, shapes, and ages that have a certain commonalty. Not being certain, he checks his hunches of *man* by a ceaseless series of, "That's a man, Mommy?" Mother's reply of, "Yes, that's a man," verifies and strengthens his concept of *man.*

Thus we see that the child first develops his concepts from direct experiences and then as he learns the language, he has an additional aid for acquiring concepts. How do concepts and language development affect his reading? It is most important to understand that a child's success in learning to read and his growth in reading are determined to a large extent by his total background of experience, his meanings, concepts, and language. We must never forget that basic direct experiences are vital to the initial development of concepts; but once established, they need to be supplemented by a myriad of indirect experiences.

Reading will provide the child with innumerable experiences that can be gained in no other way. Without vicarious, or indirect, experiences man's concepts, language, and thinking would be irrevocably restricted to his immediate environment. Teachers, therefore, need to understand fully both the importance and limitations of such experiences that substitute for direct experiences.

The student who observes a demonstration of how to make a cake, to sharpen a chisel or to measure the velocity of wind is learning by *vicarious experience.* So also is one who views a film on conservation or hears a taped interview between doctor and patient or teacher and pupil. These vicarious experiences are of inestimable value in helping students to learn, but they should not substitute for direct experiences that are preferred when they are available. Students in the foregoing examples would have clearer, more meaningful concepts of baking, sharpening chisels, measuring wind velocity, and conserving natural resources if they could actually engage in those activities.

There are times, however, when vicarious experiences may be even more meaningful to the student than was his direct experience, *but in such instances he must have had the direct experience preceding the indirect one.* We may best illustrate this viewpoint by supposing that we are awakened in the middle of the night by the smell of smoke and the crackling of flames. We are in a house that has become an inferno. We must escape, save what valuables we can, and get the other occupants out of the house. Split-second decisions and automatic reactions blur into a series of dashes, shouts, snatches at objects, fleeting glances into bedrooms, and escape.

Because of the rapidity of our actions and our automatic responses, we may have only a vague or hazy idea of much that actually happened during our harrowing experience. We may recall only certain actions and, upon looking down at our hands, discover that we have brought with us a pair of discarded boots while the flames devour our best Sunday shoes that we left behind.

Later, we may read about a fire and relive the events pictured by the author even more vividly than the ones we experienced during our own escape. We may become so involved in the story that we breathe rapidly, perspire, twist, and recoil as we race through the burning building with the hero. We may actually get a greater emotional impact from the vicarious experience than we did from our own direct experience with the fire because the author has had time to record in a detailed and clear-cut manner those experiences that are so similar to our own. And because of our direct experience, we may react more meaningfully to the author's detailed description than someone who lacks similar direct experience.

The use of moving pictures, television, radio, recordings, guest speakers and books contribute to a student's learning when they are properly utilized. But teachers must continually be aware that because it is less troublesome to *talk* about events, processes, and meaning than it is to *develop* activities that require student participation, such practices may be poor substitutes for learning and may lead to faulty concepts of the learning process by both the teacher and the students. Some students may develop the attitude that learning is primarily verbalizing. Others may assume a passive role in learning and expect the teacher to provide them with understanding. In such instances, students fail to develop adequate and valid concepts for learning subject matter.

Every teacher has been plagued by students who actually believe that they understand subject matter because they can rattle off definitions, facts, and other information in almost the identical words used by their teachers or textbooks. Unfortunately, some teachers accept such verbalizations as evidence of learning. Inefficient readers often say that they can "read" but cannot remember what they read. In reality, most such inefficient readers have not read the material, have never actively engaged in the reading process, but have only gone through the motions of reading. They have pronounced and/or recognized words but have not associated meanings with the particular words, nor have they had the concepts necessary for understanding.

Our discussion to this point has stressed the role of both direct and vicarious experiences in developing concepts. We have given examples of some of the kinds of experiences which build concepts. Although scholars have provided us with some clues to understanding how concepts develop, none can present sufficient evidence to explain the exact sequence of that development. Russell has succinctly summarized the best of thinking about the sequential development of concepts in his statement that concepts "seem to move along a continuum from simple to complex, from concrete to abstract, from undifferentiated to differentiated, from discrete to organized, and from egocentric to more social" (16, p. 249).

Concepts Influence Thinking

What a person thinks and *how* he thinks is dependent upon the amount, kind, and extent of his concepts. Concepts may be totally false, inadequate, or only partially correct, but this does not alter the fact that they are concepts. Inaccurate concepts affect one's thinking and behavior just as much as do accurate, valid concepts.

If concepts are based upon opinions or information that is inaccurate and erroneously accepted as facts, concepts derived from them must also be inaccurate. Concepts are ever changing as new facts and new evidence are disclosed. What we consider to be valid concepts today may be invalid tomorrow. We must understand that one's concepts do change; they must change because such change is life. Had man's concepts not changed, he would still be burrowing into caves rather than shooting for the moon.

Concepts and Vocabulary

Concepts of subject matter are made up of facts, information, definitions, details, and generalizations that students must learn. Concepts are clarified, extended, and refined by teacher-student discussions that are based primarily upon knowledge acquired from reading textbooks and reference materials. And words, many of them specific to the particular subject matter, are the vehicles of thought to convey meaning. Teachers, therefore, must know how to teach students to learn and to use words for building and understanding concepts. Both teachers and students must realize that *a word is* NOT *a concept.*

A word may represent a concept, but the concept resides within the student, not within the word. No one can give a student a concept. One can teach him to pronounce a word, provide him with a definition of the word, and arrange activities in which the word is used but he, and he alone, must develop his concepts. The teacher's job is to arrange activities that involve the student in direct and vicarious experiences that lead him to develop concepts himself.

Words and Meaning

Students should be taught early that words have no inherent meaning. Many adults, including some teachers, have never learned that words do not have meaning, and they add to children's confusion about words and meaning by saying, "Look at the word. Tell me its meaning!" If words had meaning, one would only need to hear or pronounce a word and meaning would emerge. However, such magic exists only in fairyland and in the minds of crackpots.

Words are no more than agreed-upon symbols that represent certain concepts. The meaning that a particular word has for one individual may be quite different from the meaning that another associates with it. The meaning for words resides within each person and is derived from his experience with it. Because no two persons ever have exactly the same experiences, they never have exactly the same meaning for a word, nor do they necessarily attach the same connotations to its use. Human experiences, however, are sufficiently similar within a given culture to make communication with words a reality.

Students are often confused by being told to look up meaning of a word in the dictionary. Dictionaries do not give meanings, they provide definitions. Many times a student will find a word in a dictionary but he does not understand the definition because it is couched in terms that are also unknown to him. Sometimes by choice and sometimes by command, he memorizes the definition long enough to hand it back to the teacher, and then he promptly forgets such "nonsense."

A college student who was recently discussing her reading problems with the writer expressed a view current among high school students. She said, "I had only one decent teacher. He was my high school English teacher and during my senior year he really taught us vocabulary. We had to learn twenty-five definitions of words every single night for six weeks. We had a test every day. My mother helped me every night. She drilled me and drilled me."

When the student was asked if she actually learned the meanings of the words she said, "Oh yes! I got 90 or 100 words every day, but then after six weeks we had an exam on all the words and we had to learn them all over because we had forgotten them!"

"Do you remember any of the words?" she was asked. "I can remember one, *dogmatic,*" she replied. When asked what is meant by a "dogmatic statement" she confessed that she was not sure but thought that *dogmatic* might mean *sad.* And in this instance, the student's answer of *sad* adequately expresses the writer's view of such methods of "teaching" vocabulary.

Teaching and learning vocabulary is a fascinating and rewarding experience for both teacher and students. The English language with its rich heritage of boundless synonyms and colorful words should not be subjected to the shabby treatment it often receives in the classroom. When teachers provide opportunities for students to discover that the meanings for words are within them and not within a musty book or in the words themselves, learning new words becomes a stimulating activity. High school students are particularly interested in learning new words. They savor the tang of a well-chosen word in comparison to a thin, trite one. They need only to be shown how words may be made to serve them as they want to express subtle shades of meaning.

Following is an interest-catching approach that helps students to understand that words are merely symbols for meaning rather than the source of meaning. It will be necessary that you follow the directions exactly.

1. We shall write a sentence that contains an italicized word that few persons know or use.
2. When you read the sentence, try to remember the first impression that the strange italicized word evokes within you. Here is the sentence: "The girl was surprised to see a *cyprinoid* when she glanced at the pool." What did the girl see? What was your first impression of *cyprinoid?* Can you describe what you "saw"? What kind of a pool did you "see"?

If you are like other university students, you probably reacted in somewhat the following manner: You pronounced the word to yourself. You searched it for clues for meaning. You may have looked at the letters *oid* several times. But most of you do not know what the girl saw. If the word had meaning within it, would you know what she observed?

Let us work out a meaning for the word "cyprinoid" by using several words that you do know. Let us add *swimming* to the sentence so that it now reads: "The girl was surprised to see a *cyprinoid swimming* when she glanced at the pool."

Those who first saw a *tree, moss, statue,* or *lilies* will realize that they received an incorrect impression. Let us add *golden* to our sentence—"The girl was surprised to see a *golden cyprinoid swimming* when she glanced at the pool."

Those of you who have owned *goldfish* or who have observed them now recognize the meaning of cyprinoid because you associate the word with your concept of *goldfish.* A few students, however, fail to make the association without help because they have had little or no experience with this particular member of the carp family.

Meaning and Context Clues

The preceding example was used to acquaint you with the steps a student uses often in getting meaning for unknown words. Such a technique is known as using *context clues.* Most teachers in the elementary school teach pupils to use *context clues.* When their pupils cannot pronounce a strange word, they ask, "What word would make sense?" McKee (14, p. 73) says that the average fourth-grader uses context clues for getting the meaning of unknown words in about one out of three times. Experience indicates that some high school and college students rely almost entirely upon context clues. On the other hand, less-efficient readers in high school seldom use context clues. Spache and Berg (22, p. 109) suggest that high school graduates use context clues for getting meanings of unknown words about 50 or 60 per cent of the time.

Teachers of subject matter should realize that context clues have much value if they are not used excessively. Context clues help to make a student conscious on the meanings of words. They aid him in selecting and associating a particular word with a specific meaning according to the context in which it is used. But when a student uses *only* context clues in getting meaning for unknown words, he is often wrong. Teachers, therefore, may have to help the less-efficient readers to use other word-meaning clues. While many authorities stress the values of teaching *root words* as an aid in getting meaning for unknown words, the less-efficient reader should be taught *how* to use a dictionary when in doubt. Efficient readers have learned that there is no substitute for a dictionary in learning meanings for words.

The student's use of a dictionary, however, does not guarantee that he will associate the proper meaning with the unknown word. The particular word may have a number of definitions, and the student may be confused as to which meaning is associated with the puzzling word. In such a case, the student must carefully reread the context in which the word is used until he can determine which definition best fits the statement; only then will he get the meaning the writer intended.

When students use context clues for getting meanings of words and then refine and extend their knowledge of such words through reading and associating them with experience, they are also developing concepts. And such mental processes are essential to *critical reading.*

CRITICAL READING

In this chapter we previously discussed vocabulary and concepts. Now we consider *critical reading.* As teachers, we should understand *how* and *why* vocabulary, concepts, and critical reading are interrelated; *how* and *why* each of these areas must be taught to students. Some questions that need to be answered are: (1) What is critical reading? (2) How and where is critical reading developed? (3) When is a student ready to read critically? (4) What factors influence critical reading?

What Is Critical Reading?

At this time, there is some uncertainty and lack of agreement among authorities about a definition of "critical reading." Even the term "critical reading" is not fully accepted by all authorities; it is obvious that those who prefer to use another name for critical reading understand what is meant by the term. Some of the more commonly used names that are applied to the process we call *critical reading* are "creative reading," "inferential reading," "reading between the lines," and "interpretive reading."

No matter what the process is called, it involves comprehension of reading materials. Because slightly differing viewpoints about reading critically are expressed by different authors, teachers who teach children to *read critically* should understand some of the most commonly accepted concepts. Artley (2, pp. 122–30), for example, considers critical reading to be a process in which it is mandatory that *the reader severely judge the writer's ideas.* Williams (24, pp. 323–31) describes critical reading as a student's *intelligent, purposeful reading involving more complex thinking than does simple recall.*

Sochor (21, pp. 47–58) states that on the basis of thinking processes or language-experience relationships, *literal and critical reading cannot be differentiated.* Her thesis is that both literal and critical reading will vary according to (1) the reader's purpose for reading, and (2) the type of material he is reading. What may be literal reading, understanding what the author states, for one student, may be critical reading for another whose purpose may be entirely different from that of the first reader.

Strang (23) also stresses the point that reading tasks differ, that *not all reading needs to be critical reading.* The purpose for which the reading is being done will determine the kind of reading required. Betts (3, pp. 9–18; 4, pp. 146–51) expresses a similar viewpoint when he notes that assimilative and critical reading are not dichotomous *but vary in the degree of comprehension.* He notes that critical reading calls for the use of high-level thinking in selecting and rejecting ideas, noting relationships between ideas, and organizing ideas.

In this book, *critical reading means purposeful reading in which the higher-level thinking processes are used in making sound judgments on the basis of all available evidence.*

How and Where Is Critical Reading Developed?

According to our definition, a critical reader makes sound judgments. He must be an efficient, thoughtful reader, capable of withholding judgment until he has obtained all possible valid information about the topic under discussion. In order that he make such judgments, he must have a wide background of experience to aid him in evaluating the evidence presented. He must be capable of sensing the author's purposes and recognizing the validity of those purposes.

An efficient critical reader is not a "born reader," but is the product of a number of combined forces, processes, and time. He is an independent thinker and reader who has developed numerous skills, concepts, attitudes, and beliefs. He knows what he knows and why he knows. But as a constant seeker of truth, he knows that no one has *the* answer and is, therefore, willing to modify his beliefs when new evidence justifies such modification.

One who studies critical reading is impressed by several significant facts:

1. *Critical reading* and *critical thinking* are not synonymous terms although the two processes are almost identical. The only difference that the writer sees between the two processes is that *critical thinking* becomes *critical reading* when it is applied to written symbols. An individual uses written words when he is *reading critically* but when he *thinks critically* he may do so without using printed symbols.
2. Critical reading requires rigorous application of a student's total knowledge and skills.
3. Critical reading is learned only from adequate, systematic, continuous guidance. Teachers must not assume that a student will become a critical reader without competent instruction in critical reading.
4. Critical thinking, in its early stages of development, is not beyond the abilities of most five- and six-year-old children. Research has proved the first-graders are capable of using thinking processes. Children who have sufficient experiences, concepts, and vocabulary for beginning reading are ready to begin to learn to read critically.

Teaching Critical Reading Should Begin at the First-Grade Level

The question of *where* and *when* critical reading should be taught may be answered by using the preceding facts. It is evident that many first-graders are capable of profiting from planned guidance in critical reading when they receive instruction from a competent teacher at their own developmental level. Many teachers actually begin teaching critical reading at the first-grade level although most are unaware that they are doing so.

A first-grade teacher is teaching critical reading when she asks children questions about the reading that requires them to (1) distinguish between factual and make-believe stories, (2) make inferences from their reading, (3) anticipate how the story might end *before* they finish reading it, (4) reach tentative conclusions about what might happen next, (5) consider the validity of their conclusion, and (6) contrast or compare incidents or characters in one story with those in another story.

Each teacher, regardless of grade level, is contributing to his pupils' ability to read critically when he provides them with learning activities that are in keeping with their intelligence, backgrounds of experience, concepts, and general language development. Improving a student's skill in word recognition, for example, improves his comprehension of reading. Likewise, teaching vocabulary may improve a student's rate of reading and comprehension. Improved word recognition and vocabulary may also be reflected in improved concept development. Consequently, critical reading development needs to be taught by teachers who themselves are critical readers.

Teaching Critical Reading in Content Areas

English, history, social studies, science, home economics, and industrial and vocational education are examples of some subject-matter areas that are rich in opportunities for developing critical reading. Teachers of subject matter, therefore, are the key people responsible for developing a student's critical reading skills. In reading subject matter, the student continually meets problems that must be solved. Johnson (12, pp. 391–96) notes that before a student can read critically to solve a problem, he must have a definite need for solving a problem. We may conclude, therefore, that critical reading actually begins *before* the student reads a particular selection. The vocational student, for example, may need to know the maximum distance at which to adjust the points in a distributor. There can be no guesswork in such an instance. The distance must be measured to one-thousandth of an inch if the engine is to function properly. He, therefore, has a specific purpose for reading. He must read accurately and apply what he has read. Otherwise, he has not solved his problem; he has not read critically.

A student in an American history class discussing the causes for the war between the Northern and Southern states might argue that Lincoln's Proclamation freed the slaves thereby precipitating the war, or he might state that the Proclamation freed all slaves. When he is asked to present evidence to verify his statements instead of being told that he is incorrect, or being given the actual facts by the teacher, he has a valid purpose for reading critically.

In every content field, there are many problems that cannot be answered with certainty. Recognized experts in all areas regularly express opposing points of view. Students need to be taught that people do not always think alike even when presented with the same facts. They need to learn that all problems cannot be solved at present and that tentative conclusions are acceptable even if they are not agreeable to all. Students need to learn *how* and *why* an author may present his material in such a way that the uncritical reader is led into making fake conclusions.

The responsibility of the teacher for teaching students to read critically is without question. In order that the teacher may fulfill his obligation, he must be aware of some of the factors that influence critical reading. Let us, therefore, look at some of the pertinent factors.

Factors That Influence Critical Reading

At present, it is impossible to specify exactly which skills and abilities determine a student's ability to read critically. The present state of uncertainty is due to: (1) the extreme complexity of the reading process, (2) the lack of sufficient research in certain areas, and (3) the need for more refined instruments for evaluating critical reading development. Obviously, there are additional factors, but these three appear to be the major reasons for our inability to state precisely what critical reading is, how it is best taught, and which skills and abilities are most influential in determining a student's proficiency in critical reading.

Research and experience, however, provide us with certain evidence upon which we can base our teaching of critical reading. Such evidence has proved to be beneficial in teaching students to read critically. No doubt future research will provide teachers with additional information that will assist them in teaching students to read even more critically.

Authorities generally agree that *thinking, language,* and *concepts* play an important role in critical reading and that these processes must operate together when an individual reads critically. Because students' *thinking, language, vocabulary,* and *concepts* develop gradually and simultaneously in all disciplines, each teacher must understand his role in providing learning activities that will insure such growth.

Intelligence

It is evident that a student's inherent qualities will influence his ability to read, which is basic to critical reading. Intelligence is one of the determiners of the degree to which he can learn to read critically. A child with a valid I.Q. of 90, for example, is not capable of becoming a critical reader to the degree of proficiency as is a child with an I.Q. of 139, providing other things are equal. Nevertheless, high intelligence does not guarantee that a student will be a critical reader. Teachers cannot assume that a student will be a critical reader simply because he is highly intelligent. Such a student has the potential for critical reading but other factors may prevent him from reaching his potential. He may, for example, lack the desire, curiosity, or objectiveness for developing critical reading skills.

Experience

Students must have a wide and varied background of experiences before they can develop the understandings and knowledge necessary for critical reading. High school students must be taught how to use their experiences in judging whether an author's statements are based upon verifiable information or whether they are purely his opinions disguised as facts. Students must call upon all their previous learning, concepts, and knowledge in order that they have some criteria with which to judge whether the material being read is relevant to the solution of the problem at hand.

In order that a student develop additional experience for learning to read critically, teachers should assign controversial materials that will provide them with a need for seeking answers to such problems. Students need to learn that there are various points of view in almost any area of study and that such variance of views may be due to a variety of reasons. Simply because people disagree does not mean that one group is correct and another group incorrect.

In every classroom, there are students who have different experiential backgrounds and attitudes, and beliefs in part derived from those backgrounds. Therefore, they will have various and often conflicting viewpoints about a common problem. A teacher who allows each student to present evidence and discuss his ideas on controversial issues, in order that all viewpoints may be expressed and evaluated, may tread on some toes; but he is providing students with experiences that are vital to critical thinking and critical reading.

National and international problems cannot be solved by pretending that they do not exist, or by limiting their discussion to adults. Too few adults are critical readers because many of them were denied an opportunity to read and to discuss controversial issues under the guidance of a competent teacher. To avoid teaching students how to think and to read critically about controversial issues is a fallacious practice.

High school and college students must be challenged to read about and discuss controversial national and international problems. As much material as possible with differing viewpoints about a particular problem should be collected by the teacher and made available to students. Those who would restrict students' reading to only those materials that they as adults feel are proper are depriving them of their rights to learn to read and think critically. Critical reading cannot be learned when materials are limited to a single viewpoint.

It is most important that students not only read, examine, discuss, and reread controversial materials, but that they be taught to arrive at some tentative conclusions after considering carefully all the evidence gleaned from reading. The teacher's role is to help students learn to look at and to evaluate all the evidence in an objective, critical manner. DeBoer (7, pp. 251–54) discussed the school's responsibility for providing students with controversial reading materials, and his article is recommended reading for teachers.

Preconceived Ideas and Biases

By the time students reach high school and and college they have many ideas and biases that may interfere with or prohibit their learning to read critically. There is no question that a student's attitudes, biases, and prejudices determine what he reads and how he reacts to the reading. A student who has definite preconceived ideas about a particular controversial subject usually rejects all arguments, facts, and other evidence that disagree with his views. Teachers need to understand that the student's views are generally deep-rooted, often emotionally charged, and highly inflexible. And it is at this point that teachers need more evidence from research in order that they can better guide their students in the highest of all reading processes.

One of the most successful but not infallible techniques that the writer uses is to encourage students to present facts, evidence, and conclusions of experts to justify their statements. One of the most difficult problems a teacher faces is that of getting students to recognize the difference between facts and opinions. Students generally have been *told* to think but have not been shown *how* to think critically. Consequently they usually believe that when they say, "I think," this is sufficient evidence for the truth of any statement that they may make thereafter.

A student's attitudes, beliefs, and concepts are products of years of experience and living. It is not a simple thing to ask and to expect him to cast out or alter erroneous concepts, ideas, and biases. Concepts, attitudes, and beliefs are personal and are in various stages of development before the child enters school. It is, therefore, most important that all teachers, beginning at the first-grade level, help each student to develop accurate, unbiased concepts. At every grade level, students should be taught to support their statements with facts. When a student wishes to present an opinion, he should be allowed to do so as long as he recognizes and warns his listeners that he is presenting his own opinion.

When students are taught to recognize that there is a vast difference between a conclusion based upon facts and one based solely upon opinion, they are quick to detect such errors in another's arguments and thereby become more critical of their own statements. Such recognition is basic to critical reading.

Purposes

One theme that has been stressed in this book has been that of *purposeful reading*. A student's purposes for reading reflect the quality of education to which he has been exposed. His purposes, provided that he has learned the required skills for reading for understanding, also determine how critically he reads.

The student who is naturally curious, who wants to learn, who seeks to find answers to perplexing problems, has valid purposes for reading, and for reading critically. He is a student who has been taught how to set purposes and to know why purposes are a prerequisite to reading. He is therefore capable of interpreting what he has read, of organizing the meaning into usable units, and of applying the information for solving the problem at hand.

But before a high school or college student can read critically, he must have developed his basic reading skills. He must, for example, have gained a large sight vocabulary, mastered necessary word-recognition skills, acquired many direct and vicarious experiences, developed numerous concepts, and learned to use his language. Every teacher at each grade level, therefore, must help students to develop the basic reading skills that are prerequisite to critical reading.

Eller (10, pp. 30–34) has pointed out some reasons why Americans are not more critical in their reading. Most of the reasons can be traced to faulty practices by classroom teachers at all grade levels. Some of Eller's reasons are:

1. Overreliance on a single textbook
2. Acceptance of the halo effect of printed words
3. The avoidance of reading controversial subjects
4. Emphasis on conformity in thinking
5. Acceptance and use of stereotypes
6. Unawareness of the necessity for reading critically

SUMMARY

In this chapter, we have discussed the requirements that are fundamental to reading critically. It is evident that the teaching of critical reading is not an impossible task, but it is one that requires much preparation by the teacher and active participation by the student.

The teaching of critical reading should begin as soon as the child enters school. It should be reviewed, and retaught when necessary, and expanded at each succeeding grade level.

Students need much guided practice in using critical reading for making judgments that need to be tested for authenticity by their teachers and classmates. It is these kinds of opportunities that provide students with the experiences necessary for becoming critical readers.

Critical reading is the goal toward which all teaching of reading should be directed. It is the summit of the long, difficult, educational road that began in the elementary school. It is the culmination of the reading process.

SELECTED REFERENCES

1. Artley, A. S., "Teaching Word Meaning Through Context," *Elementary English Review*, Vol. 20 (February, 1943), pp. 68–74.
2. Artley, A. Sterl. "Critical Reading in the Content Areas," *Elementary English*, Vol. 36 (February, 1959), pp. 122–30.
3. Betts, Emmett A. "Guidances in the Critical Interpretation of Language," *Elementary English*, Vol. 27 (January, 1950), pp. 9–18, 22.
4. Betts, Emmett A. "Reading Is Thinking," *The Reading Teacher*, Vol. 12 (February, 1959), pp. 146–51.
5. Bryan, Fred E. "How Large Are Children's Vocabularies?" *Elementary School Journal*, Vol. 54 (December, 1953), pp. 210–16.
6. Burton, William H., Kimball, Roland B., and Wing, Richard L. *Education for Effective Thinking*. New York: Appleton-Century-Crofts, Inc., 1960.

7. DeBoer, John. "Teaching Critical Reading," *Elementary English*, Vol. 23 (October, 1946), pp. 251–54.
8. Deighton, Lee C. "Vocabulary Development in the Classroom," *Readings on Reading Instruction*, ed. Albert J. Harris. New York: David McKay Co., Inc., 1963.
9. Dewey, John. *How We Think* (rev. ed.). Boston: D. C. Heath & Co., 1933.
10. Eller, William. "Fundamentals of Critical Reading," *The Reading Teacher's Reader*, ed. Oscar S. Causey. New York: The Ronald Press Co., 1958.
11. Hartman, George W. "Further Evidence on the Unexpected Large Size of Recognition Vocabularies Among College Students," *Journal of Educational Psychology*, Vol. 37 (October, 1946), pp. 436–39.
12. Johnson, Marjorie S. "Readiness for Critical Reading," *Education*, Vol. 73 (February, 1953), pp. 391–96.
13. McDonald, Frederick J. *Educational Psychology*. Belmont, Calif.: Wadsworth Publishing Co., Inc., 1959.
14. McKee, Paul. *The Teaching of Reading*. Boston: Houghton Mifflin Co., 1948.
15. Morse, William C., and Wingo, G. Max. *Psychology and Teaching* (2d ed.). Chicago: Scott, Foresman & Co., 1962.
16. Russell, David H. *Children's Thinking*. Boston: Ginn & Co., 1956.
17. Seashore, R. H., and Eckerson, L. D. "The Measurement of Individual Differences in General English Vocabularies," *Journal of Educational Psychology*, Vol. 31 (January, 1940), pp. 14–38.
18. Serra, Mary C. "How To Develop Concepts and Their Verbal Representations," *Elementary School Journal*, Vol. 53 (January, 1953), pp. 275–85.
19. Smith, Madorah E. "An Investigation of the Development of the Sentence and the Extent of Vocabulary in Young Children," *University of Iowa Studies in Child Welfare*, No. 5, Vol. 3. Ames: University of Iowa, 1926. Pp. 1–92.
20. Smith, Mary Katherine. "Measurement of the Size of the General English Vocabulary Through the Elementary Grades and High School," *Genetic Psychology Monographs*. Provincetown, Mass.: The Journal Press, 1941. Vol. 24, pp. 311–45.
21. Sochor, Emma Elona. "The Nature of Critical Reading," *Elementary English*, Vol. 31 (January, 1959), pp. 47–58.
22. Spache, George D., and Berg, Paul C. *The Art of Efficient Reading*. New York: The Macmillan Co., 1955.
23. Strang, Ruth. "Secondary School Reading Is Thinking," *The Reading Teacher*, Vol. 13 (February, 1960), pp. 194–200.
24. Williams, Gertrude. "Provisions for Critical Reading in Basic Readers," *Elementary English*, Vol. 36 (May, 1959), pp. 323–31.

SUGGESTED ADDITIONAL READING

ALTICK, RICHARD D. *Preface to Critical Reading* (3d ed.). New York: Holt, Rinehart & Winston, Inc., 1956.

BAMMAN, HENRY. "Developing Reading Competencies Through Mathematics and Science," *Reading as an Intellectual Activity,* ed. J. Allen Figurel, International Reading Association Conference Proceedings, Vol. 8, pp. 110–12, 1963.

BLAIR, GLENN MYERS. "An Experiment in Vocabulary Building," *Journal of Higher Education,* Vol. 12 (February, 1941), pp. 99–101.

BOND, G. L., and WAGNER, EVA B. *Teaching the Child To Read* (3d ed.). New York: The Macmillan Co., 1960.

BRUNER, JEROME A. "Learning and Thinking," *Harvard Educational Review,* Vol. 29 (Summer, 1959), pp. 184–92.

CARROLL, JOHN B. *The Study of Language.* Cambridge: Harvard University Press, 1963.

Critical Reading. Bulletin of the National Conference on Research in English. Champaign, Ill.: National Council of Teachers of English, 1959.

CUROE, PHILIP R. V., and WIXTED, WILLIAM G. "A Continuing Experiment in Enriching the Active Vocabularies of College Seniors," *School and Society,* Vol. 52 (October, 1940), pp. 373–76.

DALE, EDGAR. "The Problem of Vocabulary in Reading," *Educational Research Bulletin,* Vol. 35 (May 9, 1956), pp. 113–23.

DALE, EDGAR. "Teaching Critical Thinking," *The Newsletter.* Columbus, Ohio: The Ohio State University, Vol. 24 (January, 1959), pp. 1–4.

DALE, EDGAR. "The Critical Reader," *The Newsletter.* Columbus, Ohio: The Ohio State University, Vol. 30, No. 4 (January, 1965).

DECHANT, EMERALD V. *Improving the Teaching of Reading.* Englewood Cliffs, N.J.: Prentice-Hall, Inc., 1964.

DOLCH, E. W. "Implications of the Seashore Vocabulary Report," *Elementary English,* Vol. 26 (November, 1949), pp. 407–13.

EDWARDS, THOMAS J. "The Language-Experience Attack on Cultural Deprivation," *The Reading Teacher,* Vol. 18 (April, 1965), pp. 546–551, 556.

GAINSBURG, JOSEPH C. "Critical Reading Is Creative Reading and Needs Creative Teaching," *The Reading Teacher,* Vol. 6 (March, 1953), pp. 19–26.

GLASER, EDWARD M. *An Experiment in the Development of Critical Thinking.* New York: Bureau of Publications, Teachers College, Columbia University, 1941.

GRAY, WILLIAM S., and HOLMES, ELEANOR. *The Development of Meaning Vocabularies in Reading.* Publications of the Laboratory Schools of the University of Chicago, No. 6. Chicago: The University of Chicago Press, 1938.

HEAVY, REGINA. "Vocabulary Development for the College Bound," *Journal of Developmental Reading,* Vol. 6 (Summer, 1963), pp. 281–83.

HEILMAN, ARTHUR W. *Principles and Practices of Teaching Reading.* Columbus, Ohio: Charles E. Merrill Books, Inc., 1961.

HENRY, NELSON B. (ed). *Reading in the High School and College.* The Forty-seventh Yearbook, Part II, National Society for the Study of Education. Chicago: The University of Chicago Press, 1948.

LORGE, IRVING. "The Teacher's Task in the Development of Thinking," *The Reading Teacher,* Vol. 13 (February, 1960), pp. 170–75.

MCCULLOUGH, CONSTANCE M. "Creative Reading," *Readings on Reading*

Instruction, ed. ALBERT J. HARRIS. New York: David McKay Co., Inc., 1963.

MANEY, ETHEL S. "Literal and Critical Reading in Science," *Journal of Experimental Education,* Vol. 27 (September, 1958), pp. 57–64.

PINGRY, R. E. "Critical Thinking: What Is It?" *Mathematics Teacher,* Vol. 44 (November, 1951), pp. 466–70.

ROBERTSON, STUART. *The Development of Modern English,* rev. FREDERIC G. CASSIDY. Englewood Cliffs, N.J.: Prentice-Hall, Inc., 1962.

RUSSELL, DAVID H. *Children Learn To Read* (2d ed.). Boston: Ginn & Co., 1961.

RUSSELL, DAVID H., and FEA, HENRY R. "Research on Teaching Reading," *Handbook of Research on Teaching,* ed. N. L. GAGE. A project of The American Educational Research Association, a Department of the National Educational Association. Chicago: Rand McNally & Co., 1963.

SEASHORE, ROBERT H. "How Many Words Do Children Know?" *The Packet.* Service bulletin for elementary teachers. Boston: D. C. Heath & Co., 2:3–17, November, 1947.

SHANKER, SIDNEY. "Is Your Vocabulary Teaching Obsolete?" *The English Journal,* Vol. 53 (September, 1964), pp. 422–27.

SHIBLES, BURLEIGH. "How Many Words Does a First Grade Child Know?" *Elementary English,* Vol. 41 (January, 1959), pp. 42–47.

SHICK, GEORGE. "Developing Vocabulary and Comprehension Skills at the Secondary Level with Particular Attention to Motivational Factors," *Reading as an Intellectual Activity.* International Reading Association Conference Proceedings, Vol. 8. New York: Scholastic Magazine, 1963.

SMITH, HENRY P., and DECHANT, EMERALD V. *Psychology in Teaching Reading.* Englewood Cliffs, N.J.: Prentice-Hall, Inc., 1961.

SMITH, NILA BANTON. "The Good Reader Thinks Critically," *The Reading Teacher,* Vol. 7 (February, 1954), pp. 160–68.

SMITH, NILA BANTON. "Levels of Discussion in Reading," *Education,* Vol. 80 (May, 1960), pp. 518–21.

SMITH, NILA BANTON. *Reading Instruction for Today's Children.* Englewood Cliffs, N.J.: Prentice-Hall, Inc., 1963.

SOCHOR, EMMA ELONA. "Literal and Critical Reading in the Social Studies," *Journal of Experimental Education,* Vol. 27 (September, 1958), pp. 49–56.

SPACHE, GEORGE D. *Toward Better Reading.* Champaign, Ill.: Garrard Publishing Co., 1963.

STAUFFER, RUSSELL G. "A Directed Reading-Thinking Plan," *Education,* Vol. 79 (May, 1959), pp. 527–32.

STAUFFER, RUSSELL G. "Productive Reading-Thinking at the First Grade Level," *The Reading Teacher,* Vol. 13 (February, 1960), pp. 183–87.

STAUFFER, RUSSELL G. "Children Can Read and Think Critically," *Education,* Vol. 80 (May, 1960), pp. 522–25.

STRANG, RUTH, McCULLOUGH, CONSTANCE M., and TRAXLER, ARTHUR E. *The Improvement of Reading.* New York: McGraw-Hill Book Co., Inc., 1961.

STRICKLAND, RUTH G. *The Language Arts in the Elementary School.* Boston: D. C. Heath & Co., 1951.

TABA, HILDA. "The Problems in Developing Critical Thinking," *Progressive Education,* Vol. 28 (November, 1950), pp. 45–48.

Traxler, Arthur E. "Improvement of Vocabulary Through Drill," *English Journal,* Vol. 27 (June, 1938), pp. 491–94.

Traxler, Arthur E. "What Does Research Suggest About Ways To Improve Reading Instruction?" *Improving Reading in the Junior High School,* ed. Arno Jewett. U.S. Department of Health, Education, and Welfare, Bulletin No. 10. Washington, D.C.: Government Printing Office, 1957. Pp. 5–15.

Triggs, Frances Oralind. "Promoting Growth in Critical Reading," *The Reading Teacher.* Vol. 12 (February, 1959), pp. 158–64.

Wiersema, Mildred Z. "Ceiling Unlimited!" *Education,* Vol. 80 (October, 1959), pp. 76–79.

APPENDIX

STANDARDIZED READING TESTS

Standardized reading tests are of value for identifying the more efficient and least efficient readers. They, however, need to be supplemented by other evaluative methods that are discussed in Chapter 5, "Evaluation of Reading in Subject Matter." Following are some reading tests that have proved their value and that may be used for measuring certain facets of reading. A more detailed and complete listing of reading tests may be found in Oscar Krisen Buros' *Mental Measurement Yearbook*, published by The Gryphon Press, Highland Park, N.J. *The Sixth Mental Measurements Yearbook* was published in 1965.

California Reading Test, 1957 Edition. Grades 1–2, 3–4.5, 4–6, 7–9, and 9–14. There are three scores: vocabulary, comprehension, and a total reading score. Published by the California Test Bureau, Los Angeles.

Cooperative English Test, 1960 revision, Reading Comprehension. Level 1 for grades 13–14; Level 2 for grades 9–12. Cooperative Test Division, Educational Testing Service, Princeton, N.J.

Diagnostic Reading Tests. Grades 4–8, and 7–13. Committee on Diagnostic Reading Tests, Inc., New York (also published by Science Research Associates, Inc., Chicago).

Gates Reading Survey, 1939–1958. Grades 3.5–10, 4–10. Bureau of Publications, Teachers College, Columbia University, New York.

Gilmore Oral Reading Test. Grades 1–8. Harcourt, Brace and World, Inc., New York.

High School Reading Test. Grades 7–12. Acorn Publishing Co., Inc., Rockville Centre, Long Island, New York.

Iowa Silent Reading Tests: New Edition. Grades 4–8, 9–14. Harcourt, Brace, and World, Inc., New York.

Kelley-Greene Reading Comprehension Test. Grades 9–13. Harcourt, Brace, and World, Inc., New York.

Metropolitan Achievement Tests: (Reading, 1960 Edition). Grades 3–4, 5–6, 7–9. Harcourt, Brace and World, Inc.

Minnesota Reading Examination for College Students. Grades 9–16. University of Minnesota Press, Minneapolis.

Sangren-Woody Reading Test. Grades 4–8. Harcourt, Brace and World, Inc., New York.

Scholastic Diagnostic Reading Tests. Grades 1–9. Scholastic Testing Service, Inc., Chicago.

Schrammel-Gray High School and College Reading Test. Grades 7–13. Public School Publishing Co., Cincinnati.

SRA Achievement Series: Reading. Grades 1–9. Science Research Associates, Inc., Chicago.

SRA Reading Record. Grades 7–12. Science Research Associates, Inc., Chicago.

Sequential Tests of Educational Progress: Reading. Grades 4–6, 7–9, 10–12, 13–14. Cooperative Test Division, Educational Testing Service, Princeton, N.J.

Standardized Oral Reading Paragraphs. Grades 1–8. Public School Publishing Co., Cincinnati.

Stanford Achievement Tests: Reading. Grades 3–9. Harcourt, Brace and World, Inc., New York.

Traxler High School Reading Test. Grades 10–12. Public School Publishing Co., Cincinnati.

Traxler Silent Reading Test. Grades 7–9. Public School Publishing Co., Cincinnati.

INDEX